Economics and Sustainability of Rail Systems

Steven Boldeman

© Dolans Publishing

Copyright Notice
All rights reserved. This work is copyright. No part of this work may be reproduced, stored in a retrieval system, or transmitted in any form or by any means with the prior written permission of the publisher. Except as permitted under the Copyright Act 1968, for example, any fair dealing for the purposes of private study, research, criticism, or review, subject to certain limitations. These limitations include restricting the copying to a maximum of one chapter or 10% of this book, whichever is greater.

National Library of Australia Cataloguing-in-Publication Data
Creator: Boldeman, Steven Author
Title: Economics and Sustainability of Rail Systems

ISBN: 978-0-9944340-9-8

Subjects – Railroads – Planning
Transportation – Planning
Transportation - Australia

Dolans Publishing

For David...

Table of Contents

Chapter 1 Introduction 1

Chapter 2 Describing a Rail System 2
    Number of passengers per day 2
    Route Length 3
    Number of Stations 5
    Traffic Type 5
    Power Supply 6
    Gauge 8
    Number of Lines 8

Chapter 3 Types of Passenger Rail Systems 11
    Light Rail Systems 14
    Heavy Rail 31
    Other Rail Systems 48

Chapter 4 Overview of Rail Infrastructure 60
    Track 60
    Signalling 70
    Electrical (Traction systems) 80
    Tunnels 86
    Bridges 92
    Road and Pedestrian Level Crossings 94
    Control Systems 97

Chapter 5 Supply and Demand 102
    Introduction 102
    The Supply Demand Curve/Model 104
    Elasticity of Demand 111
    Fixed/Variable Cost, and Marginal Costs 113
    Financial Comparison of Train Travel to Automobiles 116

Chapter 6 Externalities 119
    Introduction 119
    Changes in Asset Values from Building Rail Lines 121
    The Pricing of Road Congestion 123
    The Economics of Safety Benefits 128
    The Relationship between Property Values and Freight Systems 131

Chapter 7 Freight 133
    Introduction 133
    Overview of Freight Systems 135
    Different Types of Freight 145
    Rail Freight Terminals 154

Chapter 8 Economics of Rail Freight 161

Introduction 161
The Supply Demand Model Applied to Externalities 161
Price Elasticity for Rail Freight Used for Forecasting............... 163
Economic/financial Performance of Rail Freight....................... 166
Valuing Capacity of a Freight System 168
Construction of New Rail Freight Lines 169

Chapter 9 Emissions and Rail Systems 176

Introduction 176
Formulas and Calculations for Energy Consumption 179
CO_2 Emissions per Kilowatt hour per Country............................ 182
Power Consumption and the Population Density of Cities......... 183

Chapter 10 Power Consumption.................................. 191

Introduction 191
Typical Values for Power Consumption 191
Diesel Vs Electric... 203
Driving Trains Efficiency.. 205
Power Consumed in Stations and other Facilities..................... 208
Being more efficient with Power Consumption........................ 210

Chapter 11 Frequencies of Trains and Service Hours 219

Choosing a train frequency (and headway)............................... 221
Choosing Service Hours 229

Chapter 12 Demand Estimation.................................. 233

Introduction 233
Different Techniques... 234
Demand Elasticises... 238

Chapter 13 Financing Large Projects 243

Introduction 243
Public Private Partnerships... 247
Gifts and Aid.. 249
Success and Failure... 250

Chapter 14 Tourism and Rail Systems 253

Introduction 253
Economic Benefits of Tourist Railways 258

Chapter 15 Government Regulation 267

Introduction 267
Pricing Rail Tickets 267
Rail Freight Curfews 275

Setting Access Charges.. 276
Standardising the Regulation of Rail Freight............................ 277
Rail Freight and Government Policy.. 279

Chapter 1 Introduction

Rail systems have seen a tremendous upsurge in interest and construction in the last 10 to 20 years. Across the world many counties are in the process of building many new rail lines. It is considered to be something that industrialised nations need, and modern railways are seen as a strong indicator of the health and well being of the economy in a country.

Rail systems are constructed for their economic benefit. Any infrastructure, when constructed correctly, can bring tremendous benefits to the economy in which it is constructed. Rail systems are challenging to build, but there is no doubt that the benefits are there.

Public economics forms the basis for this analysis contained within this book. Rail systems are mostly constructed for public benefit, and so it is appropriate to consider their economics in those terms. Public economics involves considered the wants and needs of the public, and then attempting to meet those needs. This can be an involved problem, as it is not always possible to know what the public needs or wants.

This book also discusses sustainability, which is mostly concerned with carbon emissions. Rail transport itself is a solution to carbon emissions, and rail systems are very energy efficient, which is part of their attraction. This is partly because rail systems are designed to allow trains to stop and start only infrequently, so relatively little energy is wasted. It is important to understand the nature of energy efficiency offered by rail, and what it means. This is not difficult as rail systems typically consume about 1/3 of the energy that an equivalent transport mode would consume.

Economic analysis of rail systems often involves attempting to predict the future. Projects to build or modify rail systems mostly need to be approved by economists, so there needs to be some kind of prediction of how a freshly new rail system will perform. Any attempt to predict the future is difficult, and notwithstanding what any expert might say, it's hard, and challenging. There are standard and structured approaches to managing this problem, and these are presented in this book.

Chapter 2 Describing a Rail System

The type of rail infrastructure used for any rail system depends on the nature of the rail system. Rail systems come in a variety of different forms, and the rail mode determines the type of infrastructure installed, and how much of it is installed. We cannot sensibly discuss rail transport without first identifying, broadly, the different types of rail systems and how they are described. This is the purpose of this chapter.

There are several commonly used parameters that can be used to almost completely describe a rail system and many of these are described below. Some of them are related to the size of the network, the number of people that use the system, how the system is used by its passengers, and some other useful information.

Number of passengers per day

The size of any rail system is often judged in terms of the number of trips per day. A rail system that moves 10,000 per day is dramatically different to one that moves 1 million per day. Small rail systems can have a lot less infrastructure, compared to a large system that might move 3 million per day.

An alternative name for trips is boardings.

Below is a general guide as to the size of a rail system, and whether it is large or small.

Sizes of rail systems – Number of Passengers		
Trips per day	Description	Comments
<10,000	Very small	Tourist trains, some tram systems, a small light rail system, an APM in an airport
10,000 to 100,000	Small	High speed rail, most commuter rail systems, small to medium light rail systems

Sizes of rail systems – Number of Passengers		
Trips per day	**Description**	**Comments**
100,000 to 1,000,000	Medium sized	Metros with 2 or 3 lines, large light rail systems, large commuter systems
> 1,000,000	Large	Very large commuter systems, some metros in big cities. No light rail or high speed rail systems move this number of people, nor monorails

Rail as a transport system is capable of moving very large numbers of people. Buses may only move small numbers in comparison, as a reasonable sized bus may move 60 to 100 people, and a commuter train may move a thousand. One of the great advantages or rail systems is the ability to move large numbers of people. A BRT (Bus Rapid Transit) system that has 20 buses per hour, will only move between 1200 to 2000 people per hour for one line in any one direction, and for rail transport this would be considered a very low number. Even the largest BRT systems are small in comparison to a moderately sized rail system.

Route Length

The route length of a rail system is an important metric. Rail systems can be very small, but can also be very effective. A short length system can move very large numbers of people, especially if it is a metro, even it is quite small. Tram and light rail systems often have a very low number of kilometres of route length, whereas a regional rail system can be extremely large.

Route length is normally measured in kilometres, unless it's in North America or the UK. Care needs to be taken in not confusing route length with track length. The route is the rail corridor where the tracks pass through, and there can be more than one track in any rail corridor. Some rail corridors have many tracks, and up to six is quite common, and some places there are more. There are also some places where trains are stored, and this is called stabling. When counting track length, stabling and marshalling yards can add a lot of kilometres, but for route length add very little.

The table below shows how many route kilometres constitute a large or small system. Again, these numbers are just a guide, and are included to give the reader some sense of what a large or small system looks like.

Route kilometres		
Length	**Size**	**Comments**
< 10 kms	Tiny	One metro line, tourist railway, monorail, airport system
10 – 30 kms	Very small	One or two metro lines, mostly removed legacy tram systems
30 – 100 kms	Small	Many metro systems, many light rail systems, small commuter rail systems, no high speed rail
100 – 500 kms	Medium	Very large tram or light rail systems, commuter rail systems, smaller high speed rail systems
500 – 5000 kms	Large	Large commuter or high speed rail systems, no metros, light rail, monorails nor trams in this category
> 5000 kms	Extremely large	National rail systems, extensive regional train system

What is large for one system can be small for another. High speed rail systems tend to be large, hundreds of kilometres at least, whereas metros are far smaller.

Number of Stations

The number of stations is a key measure for any rail system. The number can vary enormously, as high speed rail systems may have only a tiny number of stations, for example the high speed rail system in Taiwan only has 8 stations. On the other hand, even small tram or light rail systems can have very large numbers of stations, as every street corner can serve as a station. Tram stops are often only 500 metres apart, and a stop on one side in one direction does not mean that there is a matching tram stop on the other side/direction. A tram system of 10 kilometres may have 20 stations. In a tram system there can be large number of stops.

Even for heavy rail, it is not always clear what constitutes a station for counting purposes. Some stations are only opened at certain times of the year, or for special events. Others, especially ones for horse racing or stadia, are only opened when an event is on. There are also small stations where trains do not ordinarily stop, and sometimes these are called halts. A halt is a stop where passengers need to ask rail staff for the train to stop, otherwise the train does not stop. Passengers who need to board a train from a halt need to signal to the driver to stop, and with some luck, this will happen.

Despite the problems with counting the number of stations in a rail system, most of the time it is a very good measure of the size of a system. In most situations a station can be clearly identified from the surrounding track.

Traffic Type

Many, or maybe most, rail systems move only one type of rail traffic. For example, a tram system moves only trams, and does not move commuter or high speed rail traffic. There are always exceptions to this, and some tram systems used to move freight, and there are still a very small number that still do. The different categories of rail traffic types are:

- Light rail

- Trams
- Freight
- Metros (heavy rail)
- Commuter (heavy rail)
- High speed rail
- Others

It should be noted that a rail system that has both passenger and freight traffic is often described as a "mixed" system.

Power Supply

The source of power for any rail system is a very important parameter for any railway. The choice of power source has a large influence on the type of infrastructure that needs to be built to support rail operations. As a rough guide, electricity is provided for rail services where there are large numbers of train movements per day, or for high speed rail. Freight, regional, overnight and commuter systems often use diesel power.

Many rail systems are powered through electricity. Steam power was once extremely common as a source of power, but has fallen out of favour with its high maintenance and running costs. The trend away from steam and to diesel and electric power took decades, and by the mid 70s most of the steam locomotives had been removed, although in some parts of the world continued to be used for another 10 years or so. Steam locomotives now are only used on tourist lines.

There are other methods of propulsion other than steam, electricity and diesel power. An extremely small number of rail systems still use cables, where the rail vehicle grabs onto the cable and is pulled along. This type of system was once common, and cables run underneath city streets, pulled from a central point called a powerhouse. One of the last remaining cable car systems is in San Francisco, and this system is still manual, so a tram employee (called the gripman) needs to apply a clamp to the cable to get the street car to move.

Most trains are diesel or electric, although there are some tourist trains that are steam powered. Diesel systems use diesel fuel to move trains, and electric systems use power generated far away at a power generator to move. Electric systems can be divided into a number of smaller categories, and these are based on the type of electrical power provided. Each rail system can be identified as using one or more power systems that are typically used in a rail system. Power systems are either AC (alternating current) or DC (direct current). AC is now the standard for new rail systems, although the voltages need to be higher, and in some cases this can present a safety risk, so for light rail and trams DC is still preferred. DC is the older power system that previously was commonly used, but now is being slowly replaced with more cost efficient AC power.

Also with the power system almost always a voltage is specified. Common voltages are:
- 750 volts
- 1500 volts
- 3000 volts
- 25,000 volts

The first three voltages are used for DC, and the last one for AC. There are other more unusual ones, but these are the more commonly used voltages. Specifying the power supply for an electric railway requires stating the voltage, followed by whether the power is AC or DC. So specifying a power system would be something like; 1500 Volts DC, or 25,000 Volts AC. The type of power system in use will further influence the choice of trains that are used on the system, and also may increase or decrease the costs and structure of any tunnels constructed.

Where a system has no electricity supply for traction, and there are many of these, then often the system is described as unwired. Power is needed for stations and lighting, but this may be unconnected to traction power.

Many rail systems deliver power through wires suspended over the train, and power is delivered through to the train through a structure on top of the train called a pantograph. However, another structure is also possible called a "third rail", and for this system power is delivered near the ground. This information is also included in any description of a rail system.

Gauge

The gauge of a railway is the distance between the insides of each rail. Most railways have only one gauge, although there are exceptions, such the Tokyo metro. The most common gauge, the one used in the

US and for almost all high speed rail, is standard gauge, which is 1435 mm. This corresponds to 4 foot 8.5 inches. Gauges wider than this are normally described as broad gauge, and narrower than this are described as narrow gauge. Common sizes are 1067 mm (cape gauge), and 1520 mm (Russian gauge).

Gauge Distance

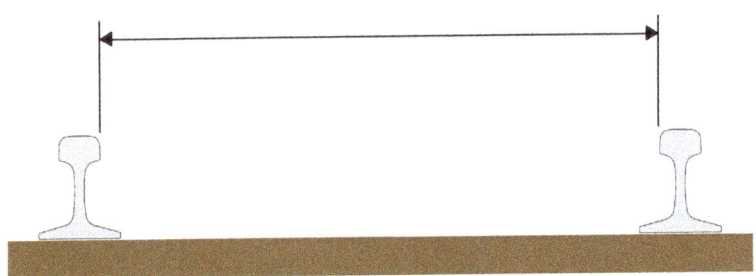

The gauge distance is measured from the inside of each rail to the other. This measure can change a little when the rail is worn, but for reference purposes the gauge is set for one railway (or line as the case may be).

Almost all high speed rail systems use standard gauge. Most modern installations, except where interoperability with older systems is needed, use standard gauge. Standard gauge is the most commonly used gauge, and more than 50 % of the world's railways, in terms of track length, use standard gauge. The use of non-standard gauges will impact upon rollingstock purchases and decisions.

Number of Lines

The number of lines is a useful measure for any railway. A line is a continuous length of track along which passengers can travel without alighting from a train or breaking their journey. In a metro system or a light rail system it mostly very clear how many lines exist, and where lines start and end.

Typically a system with over 6 lines would be considered large, and one with 1 or 2 lines is a small system. Some systems have over a dozen lines.

A commuter system may or may not be described in terms of the number of lines. Commuter lines can converge to a single large station, and there is often shared track where trains from different destinations share the one track. In this situation it can be very difficult to determine how many unique lines there are. In Sydney it is almost impossible to determine how many lines there are as many of the lines meet each other a large distance from the city. Alternatively, in the Go Transit system in Toronto Canada it is very clear how many lines there are because each is mostly separate from each other, and can be easily counted. Again, for a commuter system, more than 6 or 7 lines would be considered a large system.

REFERENCES

1. Zhang, Y & Yan, X & Comtois, C *Some Measures of Increasing Rail Transit Riderships: Case Studies*, Chinese Geographical Science, Volume 10, Number 1, pp 80 – 88, 2000

2. CFL, *Rapport Annuel*, 2011 (In French)

3. Metro de Porto, *Annual Report*, 2009

4. Jernbaneverket, *On Track 2010*

5. State of Florida Department of Transportation, *Central Florida Commuter Rail Transit Design Criteria*, October 2008

6. DB Netze *AG Network Statement 2014,* April 2013

7. Cheng, HY. *High Speed Rail in Taiwan: New experience and issues for future development*, Transport Policy 17 (2010) 51-63, Nov 2009

8. Chun-Hwan, K. *Transportation Revolution: The Korean High-speed Railway*, Japan Railway & Transport Review 40, March 2005

9. Texas Department of Transportation *Austin San Antonio Commuter Rail Study*, 1999

10. Metro de Porto *Annual Report 2011*, http://www.metrodoporto.pt/en/

11. Burge, P. et al Modelling Demand for Long-Distance Travel in Great Britain, www.rand.org, 2011

12. Cataldi, O. & Alexander, R. *Train control for light rail systems on shared tracks*, Railroad Conference 2001

13. Transport for London *Rail and Underground Annual Benchmarking Report* June 2012

14. Prescott, T. *A Practical Scheme for Light Rail Extensions in Inner Sydney*, Transit Australia, vol 63 no 11, 323 – 330 Nov 2008

Chapter 3 Types of Passenger Rail Systems

There are many different types of rail systems, and each has advantages and disadvantages. When one thinks of rail images come to mind maybe of high speed trains or of metros running underneath major cities. The range of different types of rail systems is actually quite large, and the reader might be surprised as to the variety and large differences between them all.

The distinctions between the different types of rail systems is not always clear. Whilst it is easy to distinguish between a freight system, and a commuter one, things are not always so easy. For example, the distinction between a light rail system and a tram system is particularly difficult, as the different types of systems in many cases are quite different, but in others extremely similar. Whilst some tram systems, especially historical ones, appear different to light rail, more modern trams are almost indistinguishable. As such separating out the different types is not an easy task, and an attempt is made here to classify the different rail systems, and it is not possible to consider all the different variations, but nonetheless an attempt must be made.

Rail systems fall under larger headings, and one of those is light rail. This is particularly problematic, as light rail is both a heading and a rail type. This makes things extremely confusing, as the term can refer to either a whole group of different systems, or one particular type of system. The convention that has been adopted to manage this crazy and almost impossible situation in this book is to describe the group of rail systems that fall under the heading of light rail as "light rail systems" and the specific system referred to as light rail as just "light rail".

The choice has been made in this book to separate all the smaller rail systems into the heading of "light rail system". There is no real definition of what this means, especially as a heading, but it is a term commonly used in Australia. It seems clear when looking at the different systems which is a light one, and which heavy, but it is difficult to provide a clear definition. Some of the characteristics of a light rail system include:
- Trains are narrower
- Trains are shorter

- Trains move at slower speeds
- The capacity of any rail lines is lower
- They are physically lighter, and the maximum axle loads can be quite low
- Stations are smaller
- They tend not to have large complex junctions
- They are often much cheaper to construct
- Each individual rail line is quite short, and a maximum line length would be about 30 to 40 kilometres. In contrast high speed rail lines can be hundreds or even thousands of kilometres long.

Alternatively, some light rail systems can be quite expensive to build, especially where the frequency of trains is very high, and the system is driverless. Light rail systems with high capacities can resemble much larger rail systems, and the number of people moved can be reasonably large, ie, one hundred or two hundred thousand per day. The platform heights for light rail systems can also be very low, but in some systems platform height is the same as a heavy rail system.

It is also possible to operate two separate rail systems over the same tracks. Freight trains often share their tracks with regional or commuter trains, and more rarely light rail. Light rail trains can share tracks with heavy rail, so that the infrastructure supports two or potentially more rail systems at the same time. This situation would typically be described as a "mixed system", with at least two different rail systems.

Freight systems can be described as either light rail system or heavy rail classification, and particularly serious rail freight systems, with high axle loads are called "heavy haul".

To the casual observer the type of rollingstock is often the best way to determine which type of rail system is which. Rollingstock has been designed for each different system, and they look different, so this is quite a good way to start. There are however lots of other system parameters that are also relevant, and the top speed is one, and the number of passengers moved is another.

One of the key distinctions between railways is whether they are "at grade" or "grade separated". Grade separation refers to putting different types of transport modes, or even the same ones, at different heights so that traffic on each can pass one another easily, without having to wait for the traffic to clear an intersection before proceeding. The development of light rail, where trains are often at the same grade as road traffic, has changed the perception that grade separation is always necessary for a rail system.

The photo below shows two grade separated metro lines. This design allows one train to pass over another. For high frequency rail services grade separation is the key to ensuring that trains move smoothly. Where one of the lines crosses another at a junction, the junction may be described as a "flying junction" (as it is in this case in Singapore).

Elevated Metros

Another important distinction between rail systems is the ability of some rail vehicles to have articulation. Articulation is the presence of a joint in a vehicle, so that the vehicle can "bend" around corners and curves. Trucks and buses can be articulated, and rail vehicles also. Light rail vehicles may be articulated, to allow them to turn around very sharp curves. Whilst in the past the lack of articulation in trams was an easy way to separate these vehicles from light rail vehicles, some modern trams are articulated as well.

It is sometimes possible to blend two different types of system together. There is no rule that dictates that a rail system must have characteristics from only one type of system, and hybrid systems have been created. Possibly the best known hybrid is the tram-train system that was pioneered in Karlsruhe city in Germany, where trams were re-designed to operate with higher speeds on main line tracks.

Light Rail Systems

Trams

Trams are a very old form of rail transportation. They evolved from the horse drawn carriages that were common in large cities in the mid nineteenth centuries, and were initially steam powered (or pulled by cables). Almost all remaining tram systems in the world are now powered through overhead power lines, where power is supplied from a remote generator to the tram.

Trams are called streetcars in the US and Canada. They are still used in parts of North America, including San Francisco, and Toronto. Trams can be used as simple tourist railways, as they are slow, but a good way of seeing different parts of the centre of a city. Trams may be free in some parts of the centre of large cities, and can be a very pleasing experience to travel on.

Trams were an extremely common system in the Western world until the 1950's, when governments started to remove them. Before their removal they were a central part of the transport for the public for many cities, and some of the tram systems removed were extremely large. The tram system in London was particularly large, and was dismantled with surprising haste in the late 40's and early 50's. Now tram systems are something of a rarity, and very few cities have any kind of remaining tram system. This was particularly the case in the US and Canada, where almost all the old tram systems were removed. Only Toronto and New Orleans operate trams systems that resemble what they were 70 years ago.

In Australia, and the Asia Pacific, the only significant remaining tram system is the one in Melbourne, although there is a much smaller system in Hong Kong that continues to operate for over 100 years. By route kilometres it is the largest remaining tram system in the world, although in the past there were systems that were much larger. The now dismantled system in Sydney was much larger than the one in Melbourne, but has been entirely removed.

Tram systems are rarely double decker (or bi-level) Trams are usually quite narrow, and it is challenging to construct a double decker tram that is both stable and comfortable to use. The trams in Hong Kong are a very rare example of bi-level tram, and offer a quite rough ride.

It is important to distinguish between light rail and tram systems. This distinction is often very difficult to make, but there are significant differences. Light rail is often seen as the logical evolution of tram systems, as light rail is capable of moving more people faster than tram systems. In this book light rail and tram systems are treated as being quite different. Light rail is often contained in separate rights-of way from road traffic, but can have grade separation as well. Light rail vehicles are also longer than trams, wider, and capable of higher speeds and carrying more passengers. Perhaps the most significant difference between trams and light rail vehicles is that trams are have hard chassis with no articulation, and light rail vehicles are longer and can have many articulated sections. Having said that, many trams are now also articulated.

Trams owe their popularity, and demise, to where they operate. They operate down the centre of streets in the middle of major cities, in what in Australia we would call the CBD, but in the US would be described as downtown. They are very slow, but are often filled to capacity. This should be contrasted to the situation with light rail, where trains often run on grade separated tracks, or in the middle or roads where road traffic cannot intrude with their separate right of way.

Loading and unloading times on trams can be very long. As there are only a small number of entrances and exists, overcrowded trams can be very slow in moving off from one stop to the next. Trams are not a very effective mass transit system, for moving large numbers of passengers. They are really too small to move millions of people per day, and are better suited for applications where the number of people moved is modest.

Trams are at the same grade as road traffic, and so collisions between trams and cars are possible, and even common. In one year in Melbourne there were over 1000 collisions between trams and road vehicles. Trams need to be strong enough to withstand a collision with a road vehicle from almost any direction. Whilst the collision between any train and road vehicle is serious, the collision of a heavy rail train and a road vehicle can be catastrophic.

The main differences between light rail and trams are:
- Trams are much shorter than light rail vehicles
- Trams travel down the middle of roads in the centre of cities, something that is often described as being "at-grade", and do not have a separate right of way
- Trams are not connected together
- Trams make a large number of very frequent stops
- Trams are often 2.45 metres wide, whereas light rail is often 2.65 metres wide

Very old trams often look like this one below. This is a W class heritage tram from Melbourne. Note the shape and structure, and that passengers need to step up from the ground to get into the tram. It is also very short, and is only 14 metres in length. It is also rigid, so that there is no articulated section where the tram can bend around corners.

Melbourne W Class tram

Notice that the tram stop has protection for passengers. Passengers wait alongside the fencing, protecting them from road traffic. The gap between the tram and the fence is quite narrow, but this situation is far preferable than having people wait on the side of the road and cross in front of traffic to reach the tram.

The tram shown below is also in Melbourne and was built in the 80's and 90's. It is not single body like the W class, and is articulated to allow it to pass through tight curves. This tram still has high floors, but looks more like a conventional light rail vehicle than older trams. In Melbourne this type of tram is known as a B class tram.

Melbourne B Class Tram

This is a tram stopped on Brunswick St in Melbourne. Notice that there is no dedicated tram stop in the middle of the road, and passengers must cross the road from the kerb to reach the tram. Cars are expected to stop before the end of the tram to allow people to board the tram. This situation, very common in a large legacy tram system like Melbourne, is probably mostly unacceptable in any modern tram system.

It was a common feature of trams that passengers had to step up into the tram and this was a major problem for people with disabilities. There has been a major design effort since the 90's to reduce the height of the floor on trams to make them more accessible for wheelchair bound passengers and others who might struggle to climb the stairs.

Trams, and light rail, can be classified as ultra low floor, low floor, or high floor. Whilst the low floor design is popular with passengers, maintenance costs are higher. Ultra-low floor trams and light rail vehicles have been plagued with numerous engineering problems, cracked structures and shells, although things do seem to be getting better for this technology.

High Floor Tram

Passengers boarding this tram will need to climb from the lowest step to the highest. The tram above is considered to be high floor, as for the purposes of determining if this vehicle is low or high floor, it's high floor because this calculation is made from the ground to the floor of the tram where people are sitting, not to the first step.

Low floor trams and light rail vehicles are typically 300 to 350 mm from the ground to the floor of the tram. Ultra low floor trams that distance can be even lower, even as low as 180 mm. High floor trams the distance is often 550 mm or even more. This distance can be reduced by elevating the surface of the road or sidewalk.

It should be noted that many trams and light rail vehicles which are low floor are not consistent height throughout the entire vehicle. The floor above the bogies may be raised, so that passengers moving through the tram will need to walk up and down steps to get from one end to another. This is undesirable from the perspective of passengers with disabilities, but better than having a high floor where disabled passengers can't get on at all. Where the tram is only partly low floor, passengers with limited mobility will need to stay near the doors, as they can't move up and down throughout the steps that are in the vehicle.

The percentage of floor area that is low floor is an important percentage for any tram or light rail vehicle. A typical number seems to be about 70%, although the number can be lower than 50% or up to 100%. This figure is important in purchasing any tram or light rail vehicle.

Given the obvious convenience of low floor trams, why was anything built with a higher floor? Surely it made more sense to design all the trams and light rail vehicles with a low floor? The answer to this is that it was only recently that the technology was available to build a successful a low floor tram. High floor rail vehicles structurally stronger, and trains with higher floors are stronger than those with lower floors. So very long trains, and definitely those over 100 metres in length, will need to have high floors. Even comparatively short trains, such as the DLR or the Bangkok Skytrain, which are only 60 to 80 metres in length have quite high platforms, as it is easier to design trains with higher floors. Rollingstock manufacturers are designing stronger and stronger vehicles, which can combine low floors with longer trains, but there are still limits on the length of these trains.

Note the significant differences between this tram, and the ones above, it has a much lower floor, is articulated in several places, and looks a bit "space age". This particular tram had very few seats, and most of the space inside was for standing passengers. It is also 100% low floor, and there were no steps other than the one into the tram.

Low Floor Tram

The vehicle in the photo above is a good example of rail vehicles that can lie between light rail and trams. Given where the vehicle operates, and its width, and the average speed, its probably best to consider this vehicle operating as a tram, even though there are signs and advertisements throughout Melbourne describing this vehicle as light rail.

The photo below shows tram tracks running down Bridge St in Melbourne. Notice that the street is very wide and that trams and road vehicles have a separated right of way. Trams are free of interference from road traffic, and most of the system in Melbourne is like this. This good design is a key reason why the tram system in Melbourne was able to survive, and it's crucially important for any new tram system to be separated from road traffic as much as possible.

Separate Right of Way for Trams

Most trams are only one level, but there are a small number of systems with double decker trams. Trams in Hong Kong are double deckers. This system is a very old system, and operates wooden double decker trams with two sets of stairs at either end of the tram. There is not much suspension, and it's a very bumpy ride. The cost of a ride is very low, somewhere around 40 US cents (as of 2012), and it's extremely heavily used. These trams operate at amazingly frequent intervals, and there are hundreds of trams in use at any one time.

Double Decker Tram in Hong Kong

The tram system in Hong Kong seems a bit neglected, and there were and still are a lot of ways to improve it. One very significant problem was that tram stops were often not located at traffic lights, but 10 to 30 metres before an intersection. One result of this is that trams stop to let people out, then travel a short distance to the traffic lights, and then stop again. Tram stops should be located at traffic lights, so that when stopped at the lights people can still board the tram, and the tram does not need to accelerate and then stop at the traffic lights.

A modern trend has been to install computer control over traffic lights so that trams get priority. Infrastructure is installed to detect the presence of any tram, and then change the lights to allow the tram to proceed sooner than the normal sequencing of the lights would allow. This situation is particularly common for light rail, where the number of road crossings is much lower than for trams, and the intention is to get the train moving as fast as possible. So doing can substantially increase the average speed of trams, and this is a good way to improve the quality of the system.

An interesting feature of tram systems, and this is especially true for Melbourne, is that often tram stops are marked only with sign, and nothing more. Tram stops are not really stations, and are very low key, and those new to an area with trams may not even notice that the tram stop is there. Stations for other types of rail systems, even light rail, are much larger and more expensive to build.

As a guide for the design of new tram systems, it's best if:
- Trams operate on separate right of ways from road traffic
- Critical intersections are identified and equipment installed to give the tram priority over other road traffic
- Tram stops are located at traffic lights, where there are traffic lights along the tram route
- Passengers are provided with a place to stand next to where the tram will stop
- Trams should be located in central areas of cities or in places where the population density is very high.

(Classic) Light rail

Light rail is seen by many as the next evolutionary step in the development of tram systems. Light rail vehicles are usually larger and longer than trams, and several vehicles can be combined into one longer train, something that is unusual for trams. Whilst there does not seem to be any formal definition anywhere that supports this rule, it seems that light rail vehicles are normally 2.65 metres in width, which is larger than the 2.4 metres common for trams.

Light rail vehicles are designed to travel along city streets. They can climb steep grades, and turn through very tight curves, much like trams. They are a very versatile train type, and can go almost anywhere. Light rail vehicles can climb grades of 10%, and almost unthinkable grade, and far more than any other rail system other than a ratchet and pinion rail line. Light rail vehicles can also negotiate around very tight curves, and curve radii of as low as 20 or 30 metres is possible. Heavy rail is often limited in the size of the curve, and a typical lower value for the tighest curve is 200 metres.

The picture below shows the light rail vehicle moving through central Sydney. Notice that it is a larger and wider vehicle than the trams pictured above. Whilst trams are often only 25 to 40 metres in length, light rail vehicles can be much longer than that, up to 60 metres, and can be coupled together to form even longer trains. This particular light rail vehicle is not designed to be coupled with other light rail vehicles.

Light Rail in Sydney

Once again we note that light rail vehicles can operate on city streets, and building a rail line with a shared right of way with road traffic can be a very effective way to save money on construction costs. As always it is better if the rail line is separated from road traffic as this allows average speeds to be higher, as there is no need for light rail trains to stop for road traffic, although achieving this is sometimes very expensive and not economic.

It is important to distinguish between classic light rail, and an intermediate capacity metro. The DLR (Docklands Light Rail) is often classified as light rail, and it is a light rail system, but it is much more like an intermediate capacity metro, and has many of the features of one. It is not considered to be classic light rail within this book. The DLR is fully automated and there are no drivers, and it does not operate down city streets, but is fully grade separated. The DLR is a very good system, re-classifying it as an intermediate capacity metro is no insult. This type of system will be discussed further below, under the correct heading.

Light rail vehicles traditionally have drivers, important because light rail vehicles need to avoid street traffic, and collisions. At the time of writing it is not possible to design a light rail system that is able to avoid street traffic and pedestrians in all situations, so drivers are needed. Light rail vehicles are designed to be able to withstand an impact from a road vehicle, and are toughened up to resist collisions and not allow any injury to the passengers inside. This toughening can add a lot of weight to the vehicle.

Light Rail in Hong Kong

Light rail has become very popular in the US, and in Germany, although it exists in many different countries. The pictures above and below show a light rail system in Hong Kong. Note that the system used there has high platforms and vehicles are not joined (amalgamated) together to make longer trains.

One of the main attractions of light rail systems is the relatively low construction cost. Costs are lower because the light rail trains travel along city streets, and expensive tunnelling can be avoided. Light rail is also a solution where the number of passengers is not that high, and there is a need or desire to install a rail system. Heavy rail systems are excessive in many situations, and a light rail system can be a more appropriate solution. Aside from the lower construction cost, light rail is seen as a sexy and attractive looking system, and this type of rail system has proved very popular with passengers throughout the world.

An added advantage of the light rail system is its simplicity. Unlike heavy rail, which is technically very complicated, light rail is a lot simpler and easier to install and manage. Lower speeds, and the lower loads associated with smaller trains, means that the system is relatively simple to install, and the complexity associated with speed calculations and vertical curves for example is avoided.

Automated People Mover

Automated people movers (APMs) are automatic trains that are driverless, and operate on separate right of way with grade separation. They are often very small and often installed in airports, theme parks, and other large facilities. These vehicles fall within the family of light rail systems, and are common in airports in Asia. Also sometimes included in this category are larger automatic trains such as the Docklands Light Rail (DLR), which is driverless, and technically speaking an automated people mover. Larger APMs are very similar to light metros, or intermediate capacity systems, and are also discussed under that category.

The picture below shows an APM in Singapore. The vehicle is very short, and it runs on rubber tyres. It is also driverless, and moves around the small network by itself picking up and dropping off passengers. This particular system is a contained within an airport. The capacity of this system is not large, and the distances travelled are short.

An APM Vehicle in Singapore Airport (Changi)

Airports often have trains that move travellers from one terminal to another. A particular large airport may need such a system, as the distances between terminals are so large that transport is needed. These rail systems can be quite significant, and the system in Hong Kong Airport contains two short lines. The APM in Changi airport has several lines, all of them quite short. APM systems in airports are provided as a convenience for passengers, and add to the value of the airport. APMs also exist in theme parks, particular large ones such as the different Disneyland parks.

Intermediate Capacity Metros

Intermediate capacity metros are a system that is designed much like a metro system, with few seats, low headways, and many doors to allow fast and easy boarding and alighting, but much lower capacity and smaller trains. Some intermediate capacity metros are also Automated People Movers, some are not. As a group these rail lines are sometimes described as a "light metro".

What distinguishes an intermediate capacity system from a full metro is:
- Trains are less than 60-70 metres in length
- The trains narrower than full metros
- Stations are much shorter in length, therefore cheaper to build

- In some cases built with rubber tyres rather than metal wheels, although there are some full sized metros with this technology too

Intermediate capacity metros seem to be increasing in popularity, and their numbers are slowly increasing. There are a few rail systems of this type of system in Asia, and the Bangkok Skytrain is probably the best example. The picture below shows a train in the Bangkok Skytrain.

Bangkok Skytrain

There is much to recommend these systems. They are often extremely cheap to build, and well below the cost of a metro system. The Bangkok Skytrain was constructed at a cost of only $20 million per route kilometre, and amazingly low price, and this cost was achieved 2009 to 2011, relatively recently. Trains in an intermediate capacity metro are also very short, 50 to 60 metres is common, and costs are kept down so purchasing rollingstock is very cheap. Stations in an intermediate capacity metro are also short, and an 80 metre station would be considered large. As such it is easy to place stations in convenient places, as they are so short. Stations are also cheap to build.

Intermediate capacity metros would normally be classified as light rail systems. Recall with light rail systems, the lower capacity of this type of system means that the total capacity in people per hour is lower than a metro. A medium capacity system will usually have less than half the capacity of a metro, maybe even a third, and so there is a significant risk of severe overcrowding. Intermediate capacity metros often operate full, even late at night and on weekends. This type of system is attractive to use because of its cost and versatility, but is frequently overcrowded, a trade-off that is sometimes worth making.

Intermediate capacity metros are commonly installed on concrete viaducts, which makes them cheaper than tunnelled full size metros or at least in South East Asia that seems to be the case. It seems common to install this type of system in elevated viaducts, and this also reduces the cost compared to tunnelling. Intermediate capacity systems can operate at very low headways, similar to metros.

Freight Systems (Light Rail)

Freight trains are rarely small enough to be considered light rail, but in a small number of cases they do exist. Sugarcane railways are where sugarcane is transported from the farm to a sugar mill, and these freight systems are often, but not always, operated on 2 foot gauge (61 cm). This is the smallest gauge in operation in a rail system in any significant way at the time of writing of this book. The locomotives and freight wagons are much smaller than traditional freight trains, and their signalling systems are very simple indeed.

The photo below shows some wagons transporting sugar cane in Northern Queensland. Notice that the wagons are very small, and maybe only 3 to 4 metres in length. The ones in the photo below are fully loaded and on their way to the mill.

Sugar Cane Wagons

Small rail freight trains in some mines were also common, but the author is not aware of any that have continued in operation, although they were once common in Australia.

Heavy Rail

Heavy rail systems have much longer trains, move more people faster, and longer distances. It would be very surprising for a light rail system to move passengers one hundred kilometres from one large city to another. Heavy rail systems are more expensive to build, and ordinarily require a larger space (structure and loading gauge).

Metros

Metros are the mainstay of many transport systems. There are hundreds of metro systems installed around the world, and they have been installed in places such as Algiers and San Juan in Puerto Rico. Many more systems are currently being built.

The metro has become the standard for transport around large cities. The metro system forms the backbone of any transport system in many large cities, and bus lines and other forms of public transportation integrate into the rail system. The key to the success of the metro is its ability to move large numbers of people quickly and efficiently from one place to another, as well as its engineering simplicity, and relatively low cost of operation.

Metros almost always have very few seats. People need to stand most of the trip, and consequently many people can be packed into a metro. More people stand than sit, as seating takes up a lot of space. The number of people that can be moved by a large metro is extremely large, over 70 thousand pph (people per hour) in one direction, and this can be done at relatively low cost. The ability of a metro system to move such large numbers of people quickly is one of the key reasons why this system has become so successful. The cost of operating a metro system can also be low when compared to the number of people moved, and in very busy cities it may be possible to operate a passenger service at a profit, without any kind of government subsidy.

Metro trains also have a large number of doors. Metro rail carriages are never double decker (bi-level) and so can have large numbers of doors. Dwell time is an important parameter for many rail systems, and it is defined as the time a train spends at any one station waiting for passengers to alight and board. The minimisation of dwell time is critical to getting trains through a rail system quickly, and on many different types of system, especially commuter systems, the dwell time can be very long. Metros have very low dwell times because doors are numerous and people can move into the train quickly as most people stand. The low dwell time of metros is another contributor to their success.

Inside a Metro

The picture above shows a metro train in Hong Kong. As with many metro trains, there are seats along the side of the train, and none in the middle. This allows a very high concentration of people in the train.

Metro trains mostly move along a single line, starting at one end, finishing at another, and then returning along the same path. More unusually, the metro line may bifurcate, and split into two, with maybe half the trains going to one terminus, and the other half to the other. This is different from a commuter system, or a light rail system, which often has a main station where many of the services converge, and passengers can make their way from one service to another quickly and easily. Metro lines do not converge to a central terminus, and so passengers that need to use more than one line must change trains at a large interchange station. These interchange stations usually have the metro lines passing over and under one another, so that passengers need to use stairs or escalators to move up and down to get to the right platform. This is one of the main disadvantages of metro systems, but can be managed quite effectively with good station design.

Metros have high service reliabilities. Metro trains are almost always on time, mostly due to the simplicity of the system, and that metros operate grade separated from other road and rail traffic. As metros run backwards and forwards all day, from point A to B and then back again, there is very little track infrastructure needed and so there are very few engineering failures. A metro can be compared extremely favourably with commuter rail systems which are often plagued with problems and are frequently late. An on-time-running (OTR) figure of over 99% is the minimum for a properly maintained and operated metro.

Metro trains are not physically very high. Commonly 3.5 metres in height from the bottom of the wheels to the top of the roof would be considered normal for a metro train. This allows tunnelling costs to be significantly reduced, as the size of the tunnel that needs to be excavated is smaller than for commuter trains, especially double decker commuter trains.

Metros can move immense numbers of people. Most rail systems can only move 10 to 15 thousand people per hour (pph) in one direction, but metros can move 60 to 80 thousand in an hour. Some metro lines in Asia and other countries can move over 1 million passengers per day, a truly enormous figure.

Metro systems can have a powerful effect on transport within a city. A good quality metro can clear the roads and allow cars to move through cities very effectively. Even a small number of metro lines can have this effect, and 3 or 4 metro lines is usually enough for cities with even 5 to 6 million people. Hong Kong, which has 4 metro lines (as of 2017) and some other lines that are basically commuter lines, is well served. The same can be said for Taipei, where the city has effectively 3 metro lines and one medium capacity line (although they claim there are many more lines than that, essentially there are three main ones). The utility of metro lines is often very high, and even a small number can transform transport within a city.

Metros are not as suited for long distance travel. As most passengers stand, a journey that takes hours would require passengers to stand for hours, and many people can't or won't do this. High speed and regional trains are never metro trains. So the question arises as to how far passengers will be able to stand when travelling on a metro line, and whilst no one seems to have written or researched this topic, perhaps the answer should be about 1 hour.

Metro lines seem to be getting longer and longer. Traditionally metro lines where quite short in length, and lengths of 10 to 15 kilometres were common. For example, the longest line in the Paris metro is only 24 kilometres long. The author used to believe that one of the lines in

Shenzhen was far too long, at 41 kilometres in length, and then another line was constructed in New Delhi that was 49 kilometres long, and another line is under construction in Malaysia that is 51 kilometres long. There is even a line being extended in Shanghai, which was completed in 2010, which is over 61 kilometres long.

The reader should remember at this point that metros typically average 35 kms/hr as an average travel speed, which can be higher or lower depending on the spacing of stations. A metro line that is 60 kilometres in length may require someone to stand for 2 hours to get from one end of the other, and even more if they need to change trains and use another rail line. Older people and those with disabilities will have difficulty in completing this type of journey, as standing for hours may be difficult or even impossible.

The picture below is of a metro station in Taipei. This type of open layout for a metro station is a little unusual. Note the platform screen doors.

A Busy Metro Station in Taiwan

Metro systems may or may not have drivers. Older systems will have drivers, but a more modern approach has been to build systems that are entirely automatic and require no drivers. As metro trains are usually captive along one line, and underground, it is relatively easy to program a computer to drive the train. Often rail staff are on board the train, and may control some aspects of the train operation such as opening and closing doors and making announcements. In this case rail staff are described as "operators" rather than drivers.

The design of stations in a metro system is very important. The large number of people present in the system, and on each train, means that it is very important to get people on and off trains quickly. The key to designing a good metro station is to allow people to move freely in both direction, and this often involves separating passengers walking through the station in different directions. The correct design of stations is very important for metro systems, as most stations are underground, and so there is a rick of fire. Also the large number of people using the system means that dwell times can be very large is the station is not designed with care.

Metros can operate at very short headways, 2 ½ minutes is common. Another common headway between successive trains is 5 minutes. This extremely high frequency of trains contributes much to the popularity and convenience of metro systems.

Commuter/Suburban rail

Commuter rail is a rail system where passengers are moved from an outlying area into the centre of a city, and then back out again. Commuter rail is often considered a rail system for working people, as most trips occur on weekdays. Commuter trips are often from suburban stations far from the centre of the city, to the business centre, and then back out again at the end of the working business day.

Commuter trips are often 1 hour or more in length. Commuter trains have lots of seats, and are not metros, so most people are not expected to stand. It is often the case that people stand on a commuter train, but often this is only for the last few stops before the train reaches the centre of the city.

Commuter trains differ significantly from metros. Commuter trains often travel at higher speeds than metros, a common maximum speed for a metro is 90 kms/hr, whereas commuter trains often reach speeds of 130 kms/hr or even faster. Commuter trains are larger, heavier, and longer and often longer than metro trains. The additional speed requires a heavier and more powerful train. Commuter trains also have extensive seating.

The train below is a commuter train in Brisbane (in Australia). This one is on an elevated concrete viaduct, and at Brisbane airport.

Commuter Train on a Viaduct in Brisbane

Commuter trains can be either single or double deck. Double deck trains are common for commuter trains, especially in Europe, and also the US and Canada. Double deck trains can be an effective way of increasing the capacity of a rail line, as more passengers can be seated for one carriage. Double deck trains are used extensively in the Sydney rail system as well.

The photo below is of a double decker train in Paris.

Parisian Double Decker Train

Commuter trains may operate on a large number of different stopping patterns. The stations that a service stops at is called the stopping pattern, and there are many different possible combinations of stopping patterns even on quite simple lines. A metro system, and light rail, trains almost always stop at every station. With any commuter line there are sometimes stations where very few people board and alight from, and so not every train needs to stop there. Commuter trains, because of the large distances they travel, will need to travel as quickly as possible, and not stopping at smaller stations can reduce the travel time. This is common with commuter systems.

The need for up to date information on a commuter line is very important. Again, as commuter services may not stop at every station, passenger information systems need to display where the train will stop, and when it will arrive at the station. As commuter systems can be very complex, and therefore difficult to understand for passenger, and trains can move in many different directions, providing prompt and accurate passenger information is very important in a commuter system, as it is in any rail system.

The photo below shows the inside of a commuter train in Brisbane. This configuration is 2 x 2, and most of the space inside the train is taken up by seating.

Inside a Single Deck Commuter Train

Commuter systems often have a large central station where all the commuter rail services converge. Easily the most famous of these is Grand Central Station in New York, which has the largest number of platforms of any station in the world (but not the largest number of passengers). Metro systems do not converge to a single station, and this is a good way of distinguishing the difference between the two different types of rail system.

Commuter rail systems often have much more rail infrastructure than metros and light rail. At the commuter main station there are many tracks that carry trains to the station, and many points to move trains to the right platforms. The infrastructure at a main station can often be very expensive to install and costly to maintain.

In a small number of commuter systems, trains carriages are split between 1st and 2nd class. Different fares are charged for each, and more comfortable seating is provided in 1st class. Hong Kong has such a commuter rail line (it's not really a commuter line, as it goes to the border with mainland China, but close enough) with two classes. Passengers in 2nd class get metro style seating, which is very limited and not comfortable at all, and in 1st there are quite "standard" fabric seating in a 2 x 2 arrangement. The fare for 1st class is double that for 2nd class.

Again, comparing commuter systems to metros, most commuter rail systems operate above ground. In the centre of the city, there are sometimes some commuter stations below ground, but most stations away from the centre of town are above ground. Commuter systems are longer and larger compared to metros, and can be over 500 routes kilometres in length. The commuter system in Sydney is over 800 route kilometres in length.

Commuter systems almost always have drivers. The long distances commuter trains travel makes automation difficult, and drivers are almost always used. There may be other staff on the train as well, for example a guard who opens and closes doors, or a ticket conductor that goes through the train and sells tickets of checks passengers have paid for tickets. Commuter trains are more difficult to drive than metros, within the rail corridor many things can happen that require intervention by a driver. There can be landslips, or animals on the track, or trespassers. Trees may fall over onto the track when winds are high.

Commuter systems may share rail tracks with freight, commuter trains operate at low frequencies and over long distances, and so it is often not economical to separate commuter lines from freight ones. Commuter lines that share tracks with freight trains as well typically have a lower capacity.

Commuter trains mostly do not have toilets, unlike regional services. Commuter trips are typically about 1 to 1.5 hours and this is considered short enough that toilets do not need to be provided.

Commuter systems can have a very low service frequency, and one train every 20 or 30 minutes or is quite common. In some systems one train every hour is considered acceptable. Passenger information becomes very important in this environment, as passengers need to plan to meet the train they need.

Regional rail

Regional rail services are those that move from a large city or town to remote or rural towns or villages. They can be, but often are not, commuter services, and regional services can have travel time of up to 3 or 4 hours. Regional services can be very infrequent, from one every half an hour to one per day. Regional services always have a driver, and maybe other staff on the train. Some regional services may have toilets, or even a buffet car where light refreshments can be ordered.

In Australia regional services often pass through areas of national park and wilderness, where there are large numbers of animals and very few people. Collisions with animals are frequent. There is often no mobile phone reception for large parts of the trip for regional services.

Sydney Regional Train

The photo above is a regional train. Note the clear differences with the other doubler decker trains displayed earlier, the much smaller doors, and the greater overall length of the carriage. Loading and unloading of passengers can be very slow for a regional train, but that doesn't necessarily matter because regional services move only moderate numbers of passengers, and the trip length is commonly 3 to 4 hours. It is preferable to design small doors because this increases the structural strength of the train. Carriages in a train designed for regional services can be very long because this reduces the overall cost of procuring the train.

Regional services can be powered by either electric power, or propelled by diesel motors. Many regional services are diesel powered, as there is relatively little rail traffic on many regional lines, and the cost of installing overhead power cannot be justified. Where trains are powered by diesel, then a refuelling depot is needed to top up trains when they run low on fuel.

The photo below was taken at Southern Cross station in Melbourne. This regional train was destined for Albury. Non-driven carriages, drawn behind a locomotive, are referred to as coaches. This configuration is often used for regional services as it is cheaper then electric multiple units (EMUs), or diesel multiple units (DMUs)

Melbourne Diesel Hauled Regional Train

Regional services may operate with very few passengers, and as such don't generate a lot of revenue. Many regional services are provided as a community service, and so are not profitable, and need government subsidies to continue to operate. The regional services that the author has seen in Asia, such as in Thailand, Taiwan China and Malaysia, and in Australia are often dirty and not really very pleasant at all, but provide a basic service to those living in remote places with small numbers of people.

High Speed rail

High speed rail (HSR) is a flashy, sleek and sexy system that is the glamorous side of rail transport. High speed rail is often defined as being any rail system where the train reaches 200 kms/hr, or 125 miles per hour.

High speed rail can be divided into two broad categories; trains/systems where trains travel at less than 250 kms/hr but over 200 kms/hr, and those that travel above that. Below 250 kms/hr, HSR trains are sometimes diesel powered, and do not have the extreme aerodynamic streamlining that gives high speed trains their futuristic look. The more sophisticated high speed rail systems all have top speeds in excess of 250 kms/hr, alternatively HSR rail vehicles that use existing lines have top speeds mostly below 250 kms/hr. Some high speed trains are designed to tilt, although most are not. At high speeds tilting as a strategy is not effective for high speed trains.

Below is a high speed train in Taiwan. High speed trains in Taiwan are based upon a Japanese design (as of 2012) and based on the 700 series Shinkansen.

Taiwan High Speed Train

High speed rail is offer a very high level of service. Its speed and convenience often contribute to this perception. The installation of high speed rail often refreshes and renews the rail system in a country or region. High speed rail sometimes codeshares with airlines, so that passengers can buy a ticket that combined flights and rail trips.

While most high speed trains are single deck, there are a small number of double deck high speed trains. The Japanese have the E4 Shinkansen, and the French have the TGV duplex, but other than those specific trains, all other high speed trains are single deck. Double deck trains have higher capacity, which can be important where route capacity is limited.

High speed trains are almost always powered through overhead power, at 25 kV AC. DC power cannot propel trains at high speeds, as high voltages are needed, and diesel trains can only reach about 250 kms/hr, with difficulty. The higher voltages are needed to drive trains to higher speeds.

High speed trains can be very comfortable. The rail infrastructure that supports the train, such as the track, sleepers and ballast, needs to be very strong and in very good condition so that trains can operate smoothly. This results in a very smooth ride quality that provides very little sensation of movement to passengers. Walking around the train is easy, because the ride is so smooth, and some high speed trains have buffet or dining cars where passengers can get meals.

It is a great achievement for a country to install a high speed rail system. Despite the volume of discussion in Australia and other countries concerning high speed rail, very few systems have been installed. There is only one small high speed line in the US, and it operates at around the 200 kms/hr mark, and so does not have the glamour of the French or Japanese systems. Even in the UK there is only one dedicated high speed rail line, which links the Chunnel to London.

Countries where there are significant high speed rail systems, in 2012, include:
- France
- Germany
- Spain
- China
- Japan
- South Korea
- Taiwan

Other countries have smaller parts of a high speed rail system, one such country is Sweden, where a lot of research has been conducted into high speed rail, despite the small size of their high speed system. The line between Moscow and St Petersburg also has some high speed trains, but the line is shared with freight, and this reduces the average speed and the route capacity.

High speed rail systems face many technical challenges. High speed trains are moving too quickly to move through curves quickly, and can only move through very high radius curves. This often means that high speed rail systems cannot move around mountains and other obstacles, so the rail line often passes through mountains and over other natural obstructions. The alignment of a high speed rail line is very inflexible, and the line can only be designed around any kind of natural barrier with great difficulty.

Tunnels present all sorts of problems for high speed trains. Tunnel design requires the consideration of air movement caused by the train as it moves through the tunnel. The pressure of the air in front of the train is higher than behind the train, and the faster the train moves the worse this problem gets. The pressure drop can cause discomfort to passengers, as the pressure inside the train will equalise with the pressure alongside the train. Rapid changes in air pressures will cause passengers to experience pain in their ears. What is commonly done is to seal the train as much as possible, but even so the seals are not perfect, so the pressure will drop in the train as it passes through a tunnel. Sealing the train can reduce the impact of pressure changes to passengers, but in particularly long tunnels the pressure drop will be significant, even in a well designed train.

High speed trains moving through tunnels can cause an effect often described as similar to sonic boom, and the boom is generated at the exit of the rail tunnel. A high speed train entering the tunnel will generate a pressure wave, which creates the sonic boom. A number of design features can be installed into tunnels to attempt to mitigate this problem, but the most effective strategy is to reduce the speed or the increase the cross-sectional area of the tunnel through which the train is moving. In many cases neither of the strategies will be available.

High speed trains in Taiwan and Japan have very interesting ticketing systems. One feature of these systems is that passengers can buy either first or second class tickets, and first class is more comfortable than second class. But the major difference with "normal" ticketing is the difference between a reserved seat and a non-reserved seat. Reserved seats are those where a seat number is allocated, and these are more expensive that non-reserved. The risk with a non-reserved ticket is that a seat is not available, and it is possible that a passenger may have to stand for part or all of their trip.

High speed rail systems may have services with different stopping patterns. All stops trains alternate with express services, and passengers will want to take the service that takes the minimum time to get to their destination. Prices can be different between HSR services with different stopping patterns, those trains with more stops are cheaper.

Given the appeal and popularity of high speed rail, it is surprising that more of these systems have not been installed. High speed rail competes effectively where the total travel time between one major city and another is 3 hours or less. High speed rail is particularly effective where the travel time is 2 hours or less. When this is so, high speed rail can be so dominant that air services between the two cities is discontinued, for example, Paris and Brussels. Where the travel time is less than 3 hours but more than 2 between cities, then air services will continue but will have a small percentage of the overall market.

Where the travel time is over 4 hours, high speed rail is no longer competitive with air travel. The trip time is simply too long. Many (or most, depending on the type of engine) planes travel at approx 850 kms/hr, less for turboprop planes, and at that speed a trip of 1000 kms is slightly over an hour. For a high speed train, for a top speed of 300 kms/hr, longer journey distances can. High speed rail will only have a small percentage of the market for trips of this length.

Long Distance Rail

One type of rail system that is often forgotten is the long distance rail system. This book uses this title for this type of rail system, but in truth there is no universally accepted definition for this type of system. This category applies for trains that travel over 5 or 6 hours to get to their destination, or even longer. In Australia the train trip from Sydney to Perth takes 3.5 days.

Long distance services are often overnight, and passengers sleep on them. More expensive tickets offer passengers a sleeper berth, and they may sleep in comfort on the train. In some cases a full bed is provided. The experience in Australia has been that sleeper berths are easily the most popular option for long distance rail, despite their additional cost, and are always booked out before other ticket classes.

Below is a photo of a travel compartment in a sleeper carriage in the long distance train that travels from Kuala Lumpur to Singapore. Long distance travel is still somewhat common in Malaysia, and sleepers are available on many night time trains. In a private room there are two bunk beds, as well as a toilet and shower.

Sleeper Compartment in Malaysia

Long distance services are common in Australia, as the distances are so large. There are a number of train services where travel takes well over a day, and these trips can get very boring. The author's experience of this trips is that many of them are rather dull.

Where a rail line has not been upgraded to HSR, or even to a reasonable speed, then overnight distance trains are common. For passengers sleeping on the train makes the trip appear to pass faster, even though it is still a long trip. To justify having sleeper berths on trains, the travel time needs to be at least 7 hours, but preferably 9. Otherwise passengers will have an interrupted sleep, and arrive at their destination at an early time in the morning. For example, a train that leaves at 9pm, and takes 6 hours to reach its destination, will arrive at 3am in the morning. Unless passengers are allowed to stay and sleep in their beds then many will be unwilling to wake at this time in the morning.

Where the train trip is especially long, and the rail operator has made an attempt to upgrade the service, then sometimes the long distance trip is referred to as a rail cruise. A rail cruise can be extremely expensive, thousands of US dollars, and can be over 10 thousand US dollars for 2 people. A rail cruise is often slower than a normal long distance service, and may stop for a time in different cities, and provide tours to places of interest in the city. This kind of service is rare in Australia, but the small number of services provided are profitable, and it's a rare example of a rail company operator generating a healthy profit. In Australia a company called Great Southern Railways provides rail cruises that are very long, in some cases 21 days, and their trains travel all over Australia. These cruises are very expensive, and are more similar to ocean cruises than rail a service.

Long distance overnight trains that offer sleeper berths seem to be disappearing, especially from Europe. Only a very small number of people can be moved in a sleeper carriage, in one sleeper carriage in Malaysia, the capacity of the carriage was 12 people, a very small number. Sleeper carriages are rarely economical to operate, and the cost to passengers to have a separate cabin with beds can be very high. The role and significance of overnight travel seems to be shrinking.

Other Rail Systems

Monorails

Monorails are normally classified as a type of rail system even though monorails systems are significantly different to almost all other rail systems. Monorails were a popular transport system in the 80's but have since fallen out of favour. There are many monorail systems installed in the world, and possibly the most significant is the commuter monorail system in Tokyo, which connects Haneda airport with the rest of Tokyo city. This monorail moves more people than any other monorail in the world per day. Kuala Lumpur also has a monorail line, which is very heavily used.

Maglev systems are a type of monorail, but are discussed separately below. Maglevs differ from monorails in the way the rail vehicle is propelled.

Mumbai in India has constructed a new monorail line, although their enthusiasm for monorails seems to have waned.. Whilst monorail systems are still being built, they are mostly installed in airports, theme parks and other entertainment related venues, such as casinos and hotels. Serious commuter monorails are rare, and there may be only 20 in the entire world. Overall the experience with monorails has not been a happy one, and several monorails have been installed, only to be removed later. Bankruptcies and failed companies are common with monorail systems.

Monorails can perform very similarly to any other rail system. Rubber tyred monorails can climb grades of up to 6% and top speeds of 80 to 90 kms/hr seem common. Monorails are most comparable to intermediate capacity metros, as they travel at about the same speeds, and carry similar number of people. They also cost about the same amount of money per route kilometre. The system under construction in Mumbai has an estimated cost of only US $22 million per kilometre (2012 dollars), which is a good price, but similar to what was paid for the Skytrain in Bangkok.

The picture below is of the Kuala Lumpur monorail. The vehicle length is rather low, but it is a very effective rail system and moves large numbers of people, despite its short length.

A Monorail in Kuala Lumpur

One criticism of monorails is that the monorail itself, what the monorail vehicle runs on, is unsightly. Another way of saying the same thing is to describe the monorail as visually intrusive. This is true, although not as visually intrusive as an intermediate capacity metro, built on an elevated system.

Monorails are for all practical purposes intermediate capacity systems. The capacity of a single monorail is unlikely to be more than 500 people, which is about the limit for light rail and intermediate capacity metros. A small number of monorails are able to carry thousands of people in one train, as a full metro can.

The high frequency of failure of monorails as a system is somewhat baffling. As a transport system they are safe, and cheap to build, and operate at reasonable speeds. It is surprisingly that monorails have been so unsuccessful in so many cases. Perhaps some reasons for the many failures of monorails are:
- Monorails compete with light rail and intermediate capacity metros, such as the DLR, or the Bangkok Skytrain, and do not quite perform as well
- Monorails cannot be expanded to have the same capacity as full metros

- Monorails cannot travel large distances, as most passengers stand when travelling on a monorail
- The ride quality in a monorail is not quite as good as light rail or metros
- Many monorail systems suffered from excessive political interference, especially during the planning stage
- Many monorails had a very low design capacity, and so were unlikely to ever generate a profit
- Transport orientated development is more difficult with elevated monorail stations, as they are smaller, reducing revenue
- Monorails have no real cost advantage compared to intermediate capacity metros
- Most importantly, a power failure for a monorail can have terrible consequences, as cranes need to be employed to remove trapped passengers, unlike intermediate capacity metros, where passengers can walk to the next station

On the other hand, some of the advantages of monorails are:
- Quick to build
- Cheap
- Monorails can accept sharp curves, down to as low as 50 metres (that said, light rail vehicles can accept 15 to 25 metre curves)
- The airspace needed for monorails is smaller than for light metros

Overall, one could easily say that monorails offer no real advantages over a light metro system, and have only disadvantages, the most important of which is the inability to get passengers off a train that breaks down. It would seem reasonable to recommend that monorail systems should only be used where light rail or an intermediate capacity metro is impossible, and this would generally be rare.

Maglevs

Perhaps one of the most interesting rail systems is a technology called the "Maglev". This has been in existence since the 80's and there is constant talk of the installation of new maglev systems. At the time of writing of this book only one commercial Maglev system is in operation, and this connects Pudong airport to the Shanghai metro system. A picture of this system is below:

Shanghai Maglev

Maglev is a contraction for magnetic levitation, and the train itself does not have any wheels and does not even contact the monorail. The train floats above the monorail and, as it has no contact with any surface, can reach speeds of over 400 kms/hr.

Despite the promise of Maglev technology, in practise only one commercial system has ever been installed. There also exists a low speed Maglev system in Japan, but its top speed is very low, so the full potential of the technology has not been achieved.

The author is not convinced by the arguments for a maglev train. The major problem to be overcome is economics, and central to this is the cost of accelerating trains to speeds over 400 kms/hr. A number of high speed trains have been developed, using conventional tracks, where speeds of over 350 kms/hr have been achieved. These trains rarely operate over 300 kms/hr as the power consumption required to drive trains at any speed faster than that is very high. Power consumption seems to increase exponentially with speed, and at 400 kms/hr power consumption must be very large indeed. This problem cannot really be resolved, other than constructing a vacuum tunnel for the maglev, something that seems rather improbable.

Tilt Trains

Tilt trains are an interesting type of technology used on intercity and regional services. The train tilts so that it can go around sharp curves at a higher speed. The speed increase can be considerable, and this technology, and the equations to calculate maximum speeds.

The greater the degree of tilt, the better the train can accept sharp curves. Tilt trains have revolutionised rail travel between many different centres, and can dramatically increase higher average speeds on existing rail lines, especially where those lines contain a lot of curves.

Tilt trains are normally only single deck, and passengers must be seated. The tilting action makes standing on a tilt train a little difficult.

The photo below is of a tilt train in Taiwan and from the outside it does not really appear any different to any other trains, although the outer shape is slightly different from other trains.

A Tilt Train in Taiwan

Tilting trains are usually regional or intercity trains, that travel from one city to another. It would be strange to use a tilt train within one large city, as a substitute for a metro or commuter system.

Tourist Trains

A tourist train is a train which provides an enjoyable experience to passengers, and may or may not connect important destinations that passengers may want to go. Most tourist railways go nowhere important, and the experience is the reason why the service is popular. Alternatively, a tourist railway may connect tourist destinations to the main rail system.

Tourist railways often use old rollingstock, which is custom made for that particular application. The structure of the rollingstock may be very unusual, and may not even afford protection from rain or wind. Some tourist railways connect hard to reach places, and the rollingstock required to achieve this can be very distinctive.

The picture below shows two different types of tourist tram in the town of Christchurch in New Zealand. On the left is the tourist tram that runs around the city, which is an old style tram that is rigid and very short. On the right is a tram that has been converted to be used as a restaurant.

Tourist Trams in Christchurch

Tourist railways can be divided into several categories:
- Railways through parklands, mountains, and other areas which are very scenic and the entire trip might last 1 to 2 hours. The Kuranda railway form Cairns in Australia up into the nearby mountains is probably the best known example of this type of train in Australia, but there are several others.
- Rail cruises, where the rail trip might take weeks, or in some cases, months. The cost of the ticket is extremely high, potentially thousands or tens of thousands of US dollars, for one ticket. Food is provided, and the quality can be very high. Passengers will sleep on the train. The Indian Pacific in Australia is an example of this type of rail service.
- Trains that are mostly "normal", but are richly decorated, and connect the rail system to an area which tourists commonly visit. The commuter train in Paris to the palace at Versailles is a good example of this kind of train, other examples include the Disneyland train in Hong Kong, or the Xinbeitou train in Taipei to the hots springs resorts. These trains are often visually impressive and richly appointed. There are no trains like this in Australia
- Old heritage trams that move throughout cities. These trams are often 100 years old, and have a lot of charm. The distance moved might be quite small. The best known example of this type of tram is the San Francisco heritage tram.
- Trains, that are more like trolleys, that climb steep inclines, and connect major destinations to carparks or other access points to a high value destination. This type of tourist railway is relatively common, and Perhaps the best known of these is the Peak Tram in Hong Kong, which connects the Peak on Hong Kong Island with the rest of the island. This type of tourist railway is sometimes used to connect mountains and ski fields to access points.
- Small railways, sometimes monorails, contained entirely in amusement parks, and are paid for an operated by the amusement park owner.

As can be seen from the list above, tourist railways are actually quite common and varied.

Tourist trains have high ticket prices, and so can operate at a profit. Passengers rarely would use a tourist railway for daily transportation.

REFERENCES

1. Zhang, Y & Yan, X & Comtois, C *Some Measures of Increasing Rail Transit Riderships: Case Studies*, Chinese Geographical Science, Volume 10, Number 1, pp 80 – 88, 2000

2. Smith K. *Alstom puts weight behind Citadis Dualis*, International Railway Journal, Feb 2010

3. ALSTOM, *AGV Full Speed Ahead into the 21st Century*, 2009, www.transport.alstom.com

4. BTS Group, *Annual Report 2009/2010* (the Bangkok Skytrain)

5. Kemp, R. *T618 – Traction Energy Metrics*, Rail Safety and Standards Board, Interfleet Technology, Dec 2007

6. Taipei Rapid Transit Corporation *2013 Annual Report*, http://english.metro.taipei/ct.asp?xItem=1056448&ctNode=70219&mp=122036

7. Dearien, J. *Ultralight Rail and Energy Use*, Encyclopaedia of Energy, Elsevier Publishing, March 2004

8. Siemens, *Siemens Velaro datasheet*, www.siemens.com/mobility

9. Fabian, J. *The Exceptional Service of Driverless Metros*, Journal of Advanced Transportation, Vol 33, No 1, pp 5-16

10. Kimijima, N. et al *New Urban Transport for Middle East Monorail System for Dubai Palm Jumeirah Transit System*, Hitachi Review Vol 59, (2010), No 1

11. IBI Group, E&N Railway Corridor Study: Analysis of Tourist Train Potential, (Date Unknown)

12. Hassan A The Role of Light Railway in Sugarcane Transport in Egypt, Infrastructure Design, Signalling and Security in Railway, Chapter 1

13. Parsons Brinkerhoff *High Speed Rail*, Network, Issue No 73, Sept 2011, http://www.pbworld.com/news/publications.aspx

14. Chun-Hwan, K. Transportation Revolution: The Korean High-speed Railway, Japan Railway & Transport Review 40, March 2005

15. Alstom Metropolis 21 st Century Metro Train Technology, http://www.alstom.com/turkey/products-and-services/-alstom-transport-turkey/rolling-stock/

16. Scomi Rail, *Monorail The Revolution of Urban Transit*, http://www.scomirail.com.my/

17. Duncan, B *The Hunter Rail Car: A versatile design solution for regional rail transport*, Australian Journal of Multi-disciplinary Engineering, Vol 7, No 2

18. Burge, P. et al Modelling Demand for Long-Distance Travel in Great Britain, www.rand.org, 2011

19. Railway Gazette *Commissioning the world's heaviest automated metro*, Metro Report 2003

20. Stadler *Electric Double-Deck train KISS*, www.stadlerrail.com

21. Transportation Research Board *Integration of Light Rail Transit into City Streets*, 1996

22. Turnbull, G. *The development and retention of Melbourne's trams and the influence of Sir Robert Risson*, ISSN 1038-7448, Working Paper No. 01/2002, Aug 2002

23. Transportation Research Board *Track Design Handbook for Light Rail Transit*, Second Edition, TCRP Report 155, 2012

24. Mora, J. *A Streetcar named Light Rail*, IEEE Spectrum Feb 1991

25. Sarunac, R. & Zeolla, N. *Structural and Crashworthiness Requirements of Light Rail Vehicles with Low-Floor Extension*, Transportation Research Circular E-C058: 9th National Light Rail Conference

26. Schroeder, M. *Developing CEM Design Standards to Improve Light Rail Vehicle Crashworthiness*, Proceedings of JRC2006 Joint Rail Conference April 2006 Atlanta

27. Daniel, L. *Light Rail Systems – Assessing Technical Feasibility*, Conference on Railway Engineering Melbourne May 2006

28. Swanson, J. & Thomes, C. *Light-Rail Transit Systems*, IEEE Vehicular Technology Magazine, June 2010

29. Transportation Research Board National Research Council *TCRP Report 2 Applicability of Low-Floor Light Rail Vehicles in North America*, 1995

30. Coifman, B. *IVHS protection at light rail grade crossings*, Proceedings of the 1995 IEEE/ASME Joint Railroad Conference, 1995

31. Swanson, J. *Light Rail Systems Without Wires*, Proceedings of the 2003 IEEE/ASME Joint Rail Conference April 2003

32. Maunsell Australia Pty Ltd, *Perth Light Rail Study*, 0284/05, August 2007

Chapter 4 Overview of Rail Infrastructure

Track

Track is the system that provides a running surface for rail wheels, and supports the rail vehicle. Track is easily one of the most important engineering systems for a railway, and is a central part of the design of any new rail system. Track is mostly standard in its design and configuration from many different railways, although there are some different types used for light rail systems.

Most rail systems use a fairly standard track system, with the exception of trams, monorails, and some light rail. For trams the rails are often embedded into the road, so as to allow road vehicles to pass over the rails as well as trams. Rails for trams have a separate and quite different design to normal rail. The shape of the rail, as well as the system by which the rail is held in place, is quite different.

Rails are made of steel. Some smaller rail systems run on concrete viaducts, but the vast majority of rail systems use steel rails. Train wheels are also often made of steel, and the behaviour of this steel to steel physical interface is very important. Surprisingly, the steel wheels of the train can often slide over the steel top surface, and when this happens the top of the rail and the wheel can be badly damaged. Care must be taken in ensuring that the wheel never slides over the rail, but rolls instead, and this requirement is central to the design of any rail system. One way to avoid this problem is to use rubber tyred trains, and this is occasionally done, such as the Montreal metro, but so doing adds a lot of cost as rubber tyres need to be constantly replaced as they wear.

Much of the track around the world is ballasted, which means the sleepers and rails sit on ballast. Ballast is made up of crushed rock, and major railways use substantial quantities of it. Sleepers sit within the ballast, and the ballast holds them in place. The major alternative to ballasted track is slab track, where the sleepers and rail sit directly on concrete. The track structure for ballasted track is shown below.

Figure 4.1 Track System

[Diagram showing a cross-section of a track system with labels: Rail, Ballast shoulder, Capping layer, Sleepers/ties, Ballast, Formation/subgrade]

The function of each of the components of the track system is:
- The rail; supports the train, provides a running surface for the wheels of each train.
- Sleepers; which support the rails, hold the rails at a fixed distance from each other, and transfer the weight and load of the train into the ballast. Sleepers are often made of wood or concrete, although other materials such as steel or polymer are also used
- Ballast, which sits under the rails, and is made of hard crushed rock. Ballast distributes the load from trains, reducing wear, so that many trains can pass without causing serious damage to the track system. Ballast is a sacrificial item, which means it is designed to degrade over time. The degradation of ballast, and managing its replacement, is one of the key maintenance activities of any railway.
- The capping layer; which provides separation between the ballast and the subgrade. The capping layer maintains the separation between the ballast and the formation. The capping layer is sometimes replaced with geosynthetics, which is a type of textile matting, keeping the formation and ballast separate.
- Formation: which is usually the compacted ground underneath the track structure. The formation supports the track, and the condition of the formation is one of the key parameters for determining the maintenance of track.

Tracks are normally in pairs. Away from the track the ground normally has a fall to it, this is to allow for the water to run away from the track.

Figure 4.2 The Double Track System

Drainage is very important for any track system. Drains need to be provided so that water can be removed when the track is rained on. Drainage, or the lack of it, can cause substantial problems in any rail system.

The rails are fastened to the sleepers with specially designed fasteners. The picture below shows the clips holding the rails to the sleepers.

Rail Track

If the reader looks carefully, notice that most of the rail is rusty, but on top of the rail there is part of it where train wheels sit when travelling over the rail. This patch of worn shiny rail is called the wear band, or the contact band, and it's important for a rail system to maintain this clear band of clean steel for signalling equipment to operate. The picture below shows it better.

Rail Fastenings

Rails are quite standard, and come in a number of sizes. Rail sizes are usually expressed in weight per unit of length, and in metric countries this is often 53 or 60 kgs per metre. Other sizes are also possible, with 40 and 50 also being common. In the large heavy haul freight networks in northern Australia, 74 kg/metre is now being used (as of 2012), which is a very large size and suitable for very heavily loaded trains with a high frequency. The imperial unit of measurement is pounds per yard, and 40 to 100 pounds per yard is common.

Increasing the size of the rail increases the size of train that can pass over the rails. For a light rail system, only a small rail is needed, and where small trains operate only small rails are needed. For larger trains, and especially freight lines, the rails need to be large to accommodate the higher weight.

Figure 4.3 The Rail Profile

Above is a very standard profile for rails. The top is called the head of the rail. Different sizes of rail have slightly different shapes, but overall they mostly look similar to the rail shape above. Tram rails look significantly different, and monorails do not have rails, but just the one beam. The image below shows the profile of a tram rail, and it is designed to allow trains to run on it and allow road vehicles to drive over it as well.

Figure 4.4 Tram Rail Profile

The ballast underneath the track plays an important role. The main purpose of ballast is to maintain and support the track, which is generally does well, but also to suppress vibration. Trains moving over tracks generate a lot of noise and vibration, and the ballast, surprisingly enough, suppresses this. Ballast is even used in tunnels, to suppress noise, again which is does quite well. It seems strange that ballast does this, but it does.

Ballast is made up of many small hard rocks. The amount of ballast placed under the track is not fixed, and more is usually better. Putting more ballast is expensive, as the stuff is unexpectedly expensive, and actually quite heavy. The best ballast if tough and rough, and locks together to form a tight bed for the sleepers and rails. Generally the harder the better, and quartz and granite are often considered the best materials, but many different types of rock are used. Railways often use materials that are found locally, to reduce costs and ensure the ballast does not need to be shipped very far.

Achieving the great noise reduction that ballast achieves is done through breaking down the ballast. Each time a train passes over the ballast, a small amount of it breaks into smaller pieces. Over a long period of time, such as decades, the ballast breaks down into such small pieces that most of it becomes powder. The powder intermixed with the rocky ballast is often described as fines. Once the ballast is full of fines it needs to be either cleaned, or entirely replaced, and both of these options are not cheap. Also, the track will be unable to hold track geometry, and this can be a real problem for high speed track where maintaining good track geometry is quite important.

So in summary ballast is a sacrificial item. This means that it is designed to be destroyed, which on most tracks it will be sooner or later. As ballast degrades, it gets smaller, and so the track starts to sink. Over a period of time the track can sink up to 200 mm, and if this occurs at a platform, train floors will be lower than the platform. For maintenance, railways often top up ballast as it degrades.

Ballast maintenance drives a very large part of the maintenance for a rail system. There is much to be said about what type of ballast to install, when to clean it, and when to replace it. These decisions are important for the maintenance of a rail system, and a good rail maintenance organisation will carefully consider how to make these decisions. For the purposes of rail transport planning, the choice of ballast, or even if it is to be used, can influence the way services are provided to customers. This very detailed and interesting topic is unfortunately a bit too long to be fully explained here; one of the many compromises needed to complete this book and not let it get too long. But to provide a very quick summary:

- Better quality ballast costs more, and degrades more slowly. Reducing the maintenance can sometimes mean spending more on the ballast when it is purchased
- Better quality ballast provides more track stability and the geometry degrades more slowly
- Providing more ballast when the track is installed, or deeper ballast, allows the load from trains to be spread more evenly and the ballast will degrade more slowly. An alternative is to use lighter trains, or a lower frequency of service
- The geometry requirements for high speed rail are very high, and so using ballast means that track geometry will need to be constantly checked

Below is a very simple illustration of how ballast degrades and its effect on track geometry. The diagram below looks at track side on, so we can see what happens when ballast degrades.

Figure 4.5 Track in Good Condition

The track above is nice and flat and will provide a lovely smooth running surface for trains. Once the track has been used for a few years, and depending on a few things like the type of traffic, how much of it there is, and the amount of rainfall and the quality of the drainage, then the track will start to sink. When it sinks then it will start to look something like what is drawn below:

Figure 4.6 Degraded Track

Again, the overall mechanics of track degradation have been heavily simplified here. There are a number of other track geometry parameters, and these also degrade, and need to be checked and measured by qualified maintenance personnel. Despite this, what is shown above is the most common cause of track geometry problems, and the one that usually determines much of the maintenance spending.

The degradation of ballast is a real problem for station design. It needs to be accounted for, and the track and rail position "moves around". This presents many problems, the most important of which, is that the platform gap needs to be increased in size. In some cases the platform gap is enormous, and this can be a real problem for people with disabilities.

The photo below is of tram tracks in Hong Kong that have been uncovered during maintenance work. Rarely is there any ballast for tram tracks, and as can be seen from the photo below the tracks are embedded into the road, and surrounded in bitumen. This type of systems does not allow the noise suppression that normally comes with using ballast, especially at joins, ie, where two rails are joined together.

Uncovered Tram Tracks in Hong Kong

So why is more slab track not used? Slab track, or putting the rails and sleepers onto concrete, seems to eliminate many of the problems associated with ballast. Ballast is expensive, and needs to be replaced after it has degraded. When it sinks it creates all sorts of track geometry problems, which can only be fixed with expensive track maintenance vehicles.

Slab track in Bangkok is shown below, on the Bangkok Skytrain. Note that on this track a third rail is also used, and it is located in between both running tracks.

Slab Track in Bangkok

Slab track is technically more complex to install. Problems with vibration usually mean that the concrete base can be damaged, and so vibration damping is needed. Whilst this function is normally provided by ballast, this is not possible with slab track, so some complicated vibration dampening scheme is needed. Different types of these have been designed and are in use, and quality control when they are installed is very important.

In some cases track may be designed for two gauges. Dual gauge track is sometimes needed in boundaries between areas with different gauges. Below is dual gauge track, this one is located in Brisbane, the inside rails are narrow gauge, and the outside are standard gauge. As Queensland uses narrow gauge, the inside rails are used more often than the outside ones.

Double Gauge Track

Signalling

The signalling system plays a critical role in any railway. Train movements are constrained by the signalling system. Trains are not like cars where they can travel along, and then stop when reaching an intersection. Almost all railways (excluding trams and light rail) operate on the principle that all rail tracks are divided up into sections, or blocks, and to enter each section trains need authorisation. For the most part trains are authorised to enter track sections using signals.

The signalling system is more than just signals, although this is the most obvious part of the signalling system. The purpose of the signalling system is to authorise the movement of trains, communicate this to drivers, and to keep trains separate so that one does not collide with another. The signalling system is composed of many different parts, including:
- Signals
- Track circuits and axle counters (train detection)
- Points installed over turnouts
- Signal boxes, and the control panel that display where trains are
- Interlockings

Signalling, like track design and the design of electrical power systems, is a huge area that has specialist people working in for decades, and there are courses and textbooks written on this asset system. Again, it is not possible here to provide anything but the simplest explanation of how this system operates.

Signals provide information to drivers of trains; the driver sees the signal, and then knows what to do. The driver has control over the motor of the train, and the brakes, and can instruct the motor to drive harder, or slower, or brake the train. He/she does this in response to what the signal displays. The driver almost always cannot determine the direction of the train, and so his control of the train is limited to setting the speed.

Some signalling systems do not have signals by the side of the track, but instead replicate signals in the driver's cabin. The driver can see the relevant indications on his control panel, and this is called "in-cab signalling". This style of signalling system is becoming more and more common, as it eliminates the need for lineside signalling, which is expensive to install and maintain. For the purposes of explaining how the signalling system works, it is helpful to examine how lineside signals work, as this can effectively explain how signals control the movement of trains.

The purpose of the signalling system is to prevent trains colliding with each other, as well as managing the passage of trains through the rail system. Trains stop by braking, and this means that the wheels use the rail to stop the train. As trains have steel wheels, and the rails are made of steel, then trains need to stop by braking through their wheels onto the rail. Steel normally slides quite well over steel, so trains need to stop slowly, and a typical trains moving at 70 kms/hr might need 500 metres to stop. Trains moving at higher speeds may need greater distances to stop, and the signalling system needs to inform the driver well ahead of time that there is a stop signal ahead, and then the train needs to be slowed so that it can stop.

Many rail systems require the signalling system to provide something called a "movement authority". This is the permission to move through a rail system, and to perform any movement. Many signalling systems grant movement authority for trains to move, often through the use of signals. More advanced signalling systems also use movement authorities.

Light rail and trams often use road signals for movement authorities. Trams may use traffic signals like road vehicles, although sometimes they have rail like signals that direct their movements. Signals on light rail and trams systems, where they exist, tend to be very simple. Light rail and trams also run on steel rails, and have steel wheels, so their ability to stop will be similar to that of any other rail vehicle. The steel on steel sliding problem, mentioned above, applies equally to trams and light rail vehicles but trams do not move very fast, and so can slow down in time to stop at red traffic lights. Modern light rail vehicles are equipped with magnets that latch onto the rail and provide additional deceleration. It's this new braking system that allows light rail vehicles to brake hard, and so use traffic lights as signals.

What colours are used on the signals, and how the lights are arranged, varies substantially from railway to railway, and from country to country. There is very little standardisation between countries, even within the same country. Even in Australia, which has only a rail system moderate in size, the style and structure of signals varies from railway to railway. This makes explaining signalling in a book of this type extremely difficult, as it's impossible to explain all the different scenarios, the US is different to French signalling, and so on. The method used here is to use NSW signalling, as the author is familiar with it, and it looks like traffic lights, so it's a bit easier to explain. Again, this situation is a difficult one, and there is no real best answer as to how to explain signalling systems in general.

The picture below is of a signal is the Sydney rail system. This one has two red lights illuminated, with a black background. This signal is described as a double light signal, as there are basically two signals, one of top of the other. The use of two heads for a signal allows the provision of additional information.

A Double Light Signal

The signalling system was designed to give drivers the warning time they need to stop the train, otherwise a collision could result. The most common way to do this is to put "signals" alongside the track to tell the driver what to do. As the driver drives his train he sees the signals, and based on what colours are displayed he knows what to do. It is the signalling system that determines the number of trains that can pass through a section per hour, and this is called the train frequency. The minimum time between trains is another important measure, and this is called the headway.

So who controls the signals? Signals can display many different meanings, and there needs to be some sort of decision making process to determine what is displayed. For road traffic lights many of these are controlled by computer, or sometimes by controllers at a control centre somewhere. Rail signals can be computer controlled, and many are, but many are also controlled by a person with a job description of "signaller", or in the USA and Canada a "dispatcher". The signaller sets the signals, and so controls the movements of trains. Signallers are physically located in signal boxes.

Signalling systems around the world can be divided into two broad categories; speed signalling, where the driver of the train is told the maximum permitted speed, and route signalling, where the driver is told the direction he will go, and not the actual speed. It might seem strange that the driver may not know where he is going, but in complex junction there might be many points lying in many different directions, and it may not be clear to him which track is the one that he will take. In a complex junction there may be ten or even more different possible directions, and the driver will need to know which one his train will take. Of course almost always the driver is not free to choose the path his train will take, but will need to follow the path chosen for him by the signaller.

Below are some lights and signals for the trams system in Hong Kong. At this turnout trams can go either to the left or the right, and the traffic light shows either a white line perpendicular up, or sloping to the left. This traffic light is operating as a route indicator. Trams can possible go two ways, to the left and right, to the tram stop ahead. The traffic light gives the tram permission to proceed, and in the middle of the picture is the route indicator, that displays how the points are set, so the tram driver knows where the tram will go. Route indicators such as the one below are more common in rail systems in commonwealth countries.

Hong Kong Route Indicator

There is absolutely no standard for signalling systems around the world. There are a very large number of different ways of constructing signalling systems, and signals can vary even within the same country. The enormous variety of different ways of building signalling systems makes it difficult in a book like this one to explain how this kind of system works, and it is necessary to find a common thread between the many different signalling systems. An attempt has been made below to do this, but the reader must remember that is impossible to explain anything more than the very basics of a signalling system.

What is described below is the British method of signalling. It is used in most of Australia, and places like Hong Kong and Singapore. It is obviously also used in the UK. The structure of the signalling is common to many countries, and has the basic rule of red/yellow/green, also used for traffic lights. This basic structure is also used in France and the US, but this is really the only commonality. For this reason these basic signals are described, and nothing more complex than this is explained.

The driver of a train needs to know the speed he should drive the train at. In speed signalling the driver is told the speed, but for route signalling a speed is not explicitly displayed. For route signalling the driver needs to have extensive route knowledge, and need to know the speed for different areas and different signal indications. This, for a large system, can be a lot of knowledge, and it may take years to train a driver to know all of the speeds in all of the different locations. Even in a route signalled railway (such as the rail system in Sydney) there is usually some information on speeds, and speed signs telling the driver his maximum speed are common. Information on speeds however is not complete, and for any speed other than a full proceed indication it may not be clear what speed the driver of a train should go, and experience will be his guide. To the casual reader this might seem pretty crazy, but in practice it is possible to successfully run a railway where the speeds in many situations are known only by experience.

The schematic below shows a very basic signal. The top part of the signal is called the signal head, and signals may have one or more of these. There are lights installed in the head of the signal, and there may be only one, or multiple of these. Remember that many railways do no structure their signal this way, but some do, and for the purposes of explaining how signalling works, this signal design is clear and easy to understand.

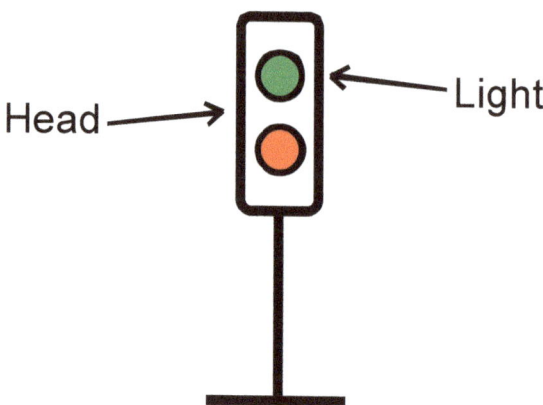

Notice that the green is on top, and the red is below the green. Whilst this is not always how signals are structured, this layout seems to be common. Normally only one signal light would be lit at any one time.

The "*aspect*" of a signal is its appearance, so if the green light is on we say that the signal is showing a green aspect. The "*indication*" of the signal is the meaning of the signal to the driver, and for a green aspect this will be a proceed indication.

So what do the colours mean? Well green means "Proceed", which is go at full line speed, at the place where the rail signal is located. The red means "Stop", which obviously means stop. These two colours are the minimum for any signal that can display different indications, but a signal can also be a single red light. Many more different meanings can be created, and some of these are discussed below.

Whilst in principle the signalling system is simple, in practice it is a bit more complicated than that. The interpretation of the signals can get quite complicated, especially in freight yards, and where there are many possible different routes. It can get even more complicated where there are level crossings and marshalling yards next to each other. A full discussion of what signals can display and what the meaning is far outside the scope of this book.

In practice the use of a two light signal has serious limitations, and so it is often not used, despite its simplicity. The table below shows a three light single headed signal, and the relevant indications. This type of signal is very common.

3 Aspect/Light Signals with Indications (Example)

Signal	Indication (meaning)
(green over yellow over red signal, green lit)	**Proceed**, travel at full line speed to at least until the next signal can be seen. This signal is called "**Clear**" in the US.
(green over yellow over red signal, yellow lit)	**Caution**, be prepared to stop at the signal in advance of this one. Drivers seeing this signal would reduce speed. This signal is called "**Approach**" in the US.
(green over yellow over red signal, red lit)	**STOP,** do not drive any further than this signal. This signal is also called "Stop" in the US.

There are many other possible indications that can be created, such as for shunting moves, but these are not discussed any further.

The use of the three colours, red, green and yellow is very common. Where signals need to display additional information, then some more lights of the same colour may be added, or one of the lights may flash to provide a different indication. In the US there was a fourth colour, lunar white, which is a blueish white.

Where four indications are required to control the speed, then sometimes a fourth indication is used. In the US this signal is called "*Advance Approach*", and in Australia the name "*medium*" is commonly used. This indication is used to tell drivers that, 2 signals in front the current signal, that this signal is at stop.

A Fourth Indication	
Signal	**Indication (meaning)**
(signal with flashing yellow light)	Medium, driver should be aware that the second signal after this signal is at stop, and to be prepared to stop at that signal. Called "Advance Approach" in the US. To provide this indication, sometimes, the yellow light will flash, with no other lamp lit.

With speed signalling, the signalling system tells the driver the speeds, and for the US, the table below provides a rough guide as to what speeds are common. These names are

US Speed Signalling Speeds and Names

Indication	Speed (approx)
Normal (full proceed)	Line speed (which depends on the location)
Limited	40 – 45 miles per hour (about 60 kms/hr)
Medium	30 miles per hour (about 45 kms/hr)
Low	15 miles per hour (about 20-25 kms/hr)
Restricted	15 miles per hour or less, and the driver should be prepared to stop quickly

The relationship between the signal indication and the most desirable speed the driver should drive at can be a bit complicated.

The signalling system includes more than just the signals that control the actions of train drivers. Another important component of the signalling system is the method of detecting the presence and location of trains, and this is commonly done with two pieces of engineering equipment; the track circuit and the axle counter. These items are able to sense when trains enter and exit fixed blocks of track, and provide this information back to the signalling system. The signalling system uses this information to make decisions about what signals should display, as well as provide this information to the signaller.

The heart of all signalling systems is the interlocking. An interlocking is the key device that prevents trains from running into another. In a junction, or a crossover, one trains passes in front of another, and it is possible for the two trains to collide. The interlocking checks that there are no trains in the way when a train is sent through a crossover or a junction. The interlocking takes information from the train detection system and makes some calculations, and then decides if trains can be allowed through junctions. Interlockings are very safety critical, and they must be designed with great care to ensure that there is no possibility that trains will collide with each other.

Signals are very important to calculating the capacity or headway of a rail system. This topic is extremely important for calculating how many people can be moved by a rail system.

Electrical (Traction systems)

Electrical power is often supplied to power them. Electricity is generated at a power station, or possibly locally and closer to the railway, and is then transmitted through transmission lines, to the railway. Once the power has reached the railway it is transformed down to the appropriate voltage, and then delivered to the trains.

Connecting an electricity network all this distance is expensive, and there needs to be a good reason to build the infrastructure that allows this to happen. Whilst it is true that the emissions from electrical power is mostly lower than from diesel locomotives, there are other reasons why electric power is preferred over diesel engines. These include:
- Electric trains are quieter than diesel trains
- Electric energy is much cheaper than diesel fuel
- Diesel engines produce a lot of smoke from combustion, and in tunnels the smoke is quite unpleasant for passengers
- Diesel engines require fuel, which in certain circumstances can ignite, and this is a fire risk which requires additional mitigations in tunnels
- And as mentioned previously, normally CO_2 emissions are higher from diesel fuel than from electrical energy supplied from a generator
- For high speed trains diesel trains are limited on the top speed to 250 kms/hr, which is too slow for many high speed rail services

Almost all rail services in major cities are electric, although there are some exceptions. Freight services are mostly diesel, although as with many things in rail, there are some more exceptions. In Australia the Mount Black railway line is entirely electrified, and very large amounts of coal are moved on that rail line, so it certainly is possible to electrify freight lines.

There are two main ways to supply power to a train, using overhead wiring, or a third rail. Overhead wiring is generally preferred, although it makes the rail line look messy. For overhead wiring the wires hang down from above the train, and then the train has a matching system that allows it to reach up and touch the wires. This part of the train is called the pantograph. As a general observation, overhead wiring is preferred as the live electrical wires are far above the track, so that track workers can walk along the track without the need to isolate power. Also trespassers are not in any danger when entering the rail corridor as the wires are too high.

The alternative to overhead wiring is a third rail system. Third rail systems are often used because they are cheap to install, and tunnels with third rail systems are smaller and so are cheaper. Many urban rail systems have third rails installed. One challenge with third rails is that anyone that touches them will be instantly killed, and they are at ground level and so easy to reach.

The schematic below shows how overhead wiring is often configured.

Figure 7.7 Overhead Wiring and Structure

Overhead wiring needs to be supported and usually strong beams are concreted into the ground to hold the entire structure up. These beams in Australia are called stanchions, and are visually unappealing. Rail lines with no electric power are definitely visually more appealing than those with electric power. Recently there have been attempts to smarten up the appearance of rail lines with overhead wiring, with colours that are similar to the colours of the surroundings, with some success.

Overhead wiring structures come in many different shapes and sizes. The one below is for 25 kV, and is bolted onto a tunnel wall.

Registration and Contact Wire Support

Below is a pantograph that conducts electricity from the contact wire into the traction systems in the train. The top of the pantograph has a strip of carbon, and this wears as it rubs along the contact wire. The pantograph is pushed up hard against the contact wire with springs, and so if the contact wire is removed then the pantograph will spring up high into the air.

A Pantograph

Below is a substation in Perth for converting power. A substation is a truly ugly thing, but it is needed to convert and use the power successfully. Substations also contain electrical power equipment, much of which is fatal to the touch. Preventing trespassers from coming into contact with any of the equipment in a substation is a key requirement.

A Substation

The photo below shows a number of third rails in and around a couple of crossovers. Trains need to maintain contact with the third rail, and if contact is lost then the train will come to a stop, not immediately, but relatively quickly. Notice how much cleaner and nicer the track looks, and the appearance of the tracks is really much better.

Ballasted Track in a Viaduct with Third Rails

Installing power onto railways comes with many problems. Electricity in a DC (Direct Current) system can leak away, and if the leak is large enough, passengers or the public can be injured or even killed. The leaking electricity can do damage through a chemical process called electrolysis, which can result in metals near to the track being reduced to a soup of unpleasant chemicals.

For AC powered systems, there are other different problems to a DC system. The power moving through the overhead can induce currents in nearby metal objects, which means that there is now electricity in something that should not have it. For example, pipes along a tunnel in a system with AC power can now have currents passing through them. Again, this problem needs to be managed, and specialist technical people are needed who understand the problem.

A problem often encountered in Australia is that providing power to rail lines requires high voltage power lines running from generators to the rail line. In Australia generators are often located in remote areas next to coal supplies, and transmission lines need to run through national parks. Providing maintenance to transmission lines is raises some issues, as trees may need to be cut down. This is especially difficult where the trees are protected or endangered. Running power lines through a national park is a real problem, as access roads will need to be cut, and no one wants to do that. Even for a very conscientious and diligent railway, managing transmission lines through environmentally sensitive areas is difficult and constant problems emerge.

Overall providing electrical power to trains can be quite technically complicated. Specialist technical people are needed, and their salaries are not low. From the perspective of rail system design, only when the case for electric power is clearly overwhelming should electric power be used. Electric power provides many benefits and is the correct solution in many cases.

Railways in the past often generated their own power, and owned power stations. In Sydney the railways owned White Bay power station, as well as the Ultimo Power Station, which was effectively the first power station in Sydney. Rail systems in Australia now rarely own any form of power generation, and this is not changing. There has been a trend in Australia in the past 10 years to move power generation back closer to cities, and this is sometimes referred to as distributed power. There is much to be said about the case for railways having some form of power generation, especially in countries where power is very expensive to purchase. The author is of the opinion that a railway possessing some form of power generation is not necessarily a bad thing.

Tunnels

Tunnels provide many benefits, the main one being the ability of a rail line to avoid obstructions and other immovable objects, and still provide a transport service. Tunnels require large amounts of specialised infrastructure, and so are costly to construct and maintain. No discussion of rail infrastructure would be complete without a discussion of tunnels.

Tunnelling is a challenging area of engineering. The soil conditions are important to the costs and challenges associated with tunnelling, and there is no real way to know what the soil conditions will be like without actually tunnelling. To get an appreciation of the ground conditions, a project may organise for test bores to be drilled to sample what the ground is like, and this will provide some information on what the ground conditions are like. Whilst test bores provide some information, the actual ground conditions won't be known until digging actually commences.

Tunnels, and the management of fire in a tunnel, will impact upon station design. A "standard" tunnel will have ventilation, although many do not. All the ventilation equipment will normally be located at a station. An underground station can have a large amount of equipment, located in several large rooms within the station, including ventilation. The need to ventilate a tunnel significantly adds to the cost of constructing an underground station.

The picture below shows a rail tunnel, with the photo taken from one end of an underground station. Rail tunnels are commonly black or very dark with not much lighting. In this case this tunnel is single bore, and the track is ballasted, rather that being slab track. Note that the lighting is very close to the floor of the tunnel, so that drivers won't experience flashing lights when passing them, something that in rare instances can cause epileptic seizures.

A Tunnel and Portal

Whilst underground stations are also strictly speaking tunnels, they are not referred to as such, and the tunnels connect two underground stations. The transition from station to tunnel is shown below, with the station being light coloured and well-lit, and the tunnel dark and black. The transition from station into a tunnel is called a portal.

Rail tunnels can be described in terms of the following:
- The length of the tunnel
- What type of traffic is permitted to move through the tunnel
- The diameter of the tunnel, or if not round, the cross-sectional area
- The type of ventilation
- If the tunnel is single bore or double bore, and the configuration.

So let's discuss each of these in turn.

The length of the tunnel is probably the most important parameter for any rail tunnel. Usually measured in metres, it is measured as a distance that a person following the rail track would walk, rather than a linear distance from one portal to another. A long tunnel would be over 1 km in length, although there are many tunnels over 10kms, these are a small percentage of the total number of tunnels worldwide. In the US tunnels less than 160 metres are not described as tunnels, and are not normally classified as tunnels (at least under NFPA 130).

Most rail tunnels have passenger traffic moving through them. The composition of the rail traffic is quite important for a rail tunnel, but a casual observer would probably not be able to tell from looking at the tunnel what type of traffic was using the tunnel. Putting either diesel freight or passenger trains through the tunnel may change the equipment installed into it, or maybe not. Most freight trains are diesel powered, and this fuel is carried on board the train, and fuel leaks and fires are possible. Diesel engines can also catch fire, and this is particularly the case with older or more poorly maintained locomotives. Diesel locomotives dramatically increase the risk in a tunnel, and typically are excluded from tunnels used by passenger trains.

The risk and challenge with rail tunnels is fires. As tunnels are confined spaces, any fires can quickly incapacitate any passengers in the train. The heat itself is not the danger, but the smoke produced from the fire. Small fires are often started through vandalism in trains, but large fires are rare. The hazard of a large fire has a very low probability of occurrence, but when they occur the number of deaths can be very large. Preventing fires, or providing some method of escape for a tunnel can greatly add to the cost of the construction of a rail.

The diameter of the tunnel is an important parameter. Most tunnels are roughly circular in shape, so it's possible to customary the cross-sectional area of the tunnel from the diameter, using the very simple formula $Area = \dfrac{\pi D^2}{4}$. A typical diameter for a rail tunnel is about 7 metres, and a typical cross-sectional area about 40 to 60 metres. Larger cross sectional areas make ventilation and management of the movement of air in the tunnel easier, and overall a larger tunnel is better than a smaller one. Trains need to push the air out of the way when moving through a tunnel, and where there is little room between the walls of the tunnel and the train then the power needed to move the train is significantly greater. Also very narrow tunnels will make the air hotter as trains pass through, and the heat can become very great.

The type of ventilation is also relevant, and there are a number of different types. Many tunnels have no ventilation at all, but for new tunnels ventilation is often installed. Ventilation is required based on the length of the tunnel, the frequency of traffic, and the cross-sectional area of the tunnel. Ventilation can be described as either transverse, or longitudinal. For transverse ventilation, air is pushed into the tunnel from the walls towards the middle of the tunnel, whereas longitudinal the air is pushed in from the end of the tunnel, from one end to another.

And the final part of describing a rail tunnel is its configuration, and it can be single or twin bore. The table below lists many of the different configurations possible for a rail tunnel.

Different Tunnel Configurations

Tunnel Type	Comment
	This is a single cut and cover tunnel. Cut and cover tunnels often have straight sides, unlike the curved sides of the other tunnels below. As cut and cover tunnels are often close to the surface, tunnels can be naturally ventilated.
	This is a tunnel with two

Different Tunnel Configurations

Tunnel Type	Comment
	tracks, in a single bore tunnel. There is no separate tunnel for escape or for service vehicles. The shape of the upper tunnel is often described as a horseshoe.
	A tunnel with two tracks, with a circular tunnel. There is no separate escape nor service tunnel. This type of tunnel is common for deep tunnels..
	A circular rail tunnel with a supporting rail passage. This configuration is helpful if the need arises for an escape from the tunnel, and getting maintenance staff to equipment in the tunnel. The additional tunnel is expensive to construct.
	A horseshoe shaped tunnel, with a large concrete wall down the middle. The tunnel is split into two sections, which allows passengers to escape should the need

Different Tunnel Configurations

Tunnel Type	Comment
	arise down one of the two tunnels. This tunnel construction is commonly used in Hong Kong, and is relatively cheap.
	A double bore tunnel with cross-passages between each of the tunnels. This kind of configuration is common for long tunnels and those that carry freight.
	A double bore tunnel with a service tunnel in the middle, with cross passages. This is the configuration used on the Chunnel between England and France. This configuration is a very good one, and convenient for maintenance and escape from fires. Unfortunately it's really expensive.

Below is the layout of a twin bore tunnel in plan view. The key features are shown.

Figure 4.7 Rail Track through Tunnels

The main components of this tunnel system are:
1/ the tunnels
2/ the tracks
3/ the walkway next to the tracks
4/ the cross-passages
5/ the doors in the cross-passages.

We note that rail tunnels are with the two tracks side by side are normally built with side platforms, and those with twin tunnels are island platforms. Will this rule does not need to always be followed, it often is.

Bridges

Everyone knows what bridges are and what they do. Any large rail system will have dozens, if not hundreds of bridges. Bridges are used to get the rail system across natural obstacles such as rivers, roads, valleys, and other natural obstacles.

Bridges are an attractive asset for any rail system. They are usually low maintenance, and they rarely contain any moving parts. In some cases rail lines pass over draw or swing bridge, but generally this is uncommon. The Skelton viaduct in Yorkshire is one rare example of a rail system using a swing bridge, and the El Ferdan bridge in Egypt over the Nile is another.

Bridges need to be very strong, but constructed properly they are can last hundreds of years. The one below is over the Cooks River in Sydney.

A Rail Bridge

Bridges that move, such as swing bridges and drawbridges, have some safety issues. There have been a number of fatal accidents in the US on swing bridges. Bridges that need to be opened and closed can be a problem, and these are usually situated over bodies of water, and are installed to allow large boats to pass underneath them. Care needs to be taken that the train does not enter over the bridge when it is open, otherwise the train can plunge into the water, and that's not good.

One problem with rail bridges, especially where the railway passes over a highway, is that occasionally trucks with high loads will strike the bridge. When this happens care must be taken that the bridge has not been damaged, and sometimes it is damaged, and trains need to slowly pass over the bridge just in case it has suffered some damage. Raising rail bridges is an important part of investing into rail infrastructure, as the higher the bridge over the highway, the smaller the chance that there will be a collision. Where a truck does hit a bridge, it can make a terrible mess and the damage to the truck can be considerable.

A more complicated version of a bridge is a viaduct. A viaduct is a long section of bridges that are all connected together. Viaducts are often used over marshy or swampy terrain, or for high speed rail.

The Viaduct connecting Italy with Venice

The picture above is of the viaduct that connects Venice to mainland Italy. This viaduct is needed because the ocean separates the historical city from Italy, and so the viaduct is quite long.

Road and Pedestrian Level Crossings

Level crossings are places where road vehicles are able to cross rail tracks. The picture below shows a level crossing outside of Paris, and it has lights and bells installed. Level crossings are sometimes described as being an "at-grade" crossing.

A Level Crossing in Paris

Level crossings can have a boom or booms installed, which descends when a train is approaching the level crossing. The boom provides an additional visual aid to drivers that the road level crossing is alarming, and that a train is coming.

Level crossings are installed in huge numbers around the world. The majority of level crossings in Australia do not have any form of protection or warning system installed over them, and they are just a place where road vehicles can cross the track. Many level crossings only have lights and bells and no boom.

Level crossings can pose some serious risks to trains and users. Every year there are fatal accidents at level crossings, and people are killed. In almost all cases the driver of the road vehicle has crossed the level crossing without looking, and there has been a collision. There have also been accidents involving buses and can result in the deaths of dozens of people.

Level crossings are places of high risk for any rail system. The construction of bridges is a viable alternative, and bridges pose almost no safety risk to trains. The cost of bridges is not small, and replacing hundreds of level crossings with bridges is simply not possible for many railways operating on limited budgets.

Tram systems operate at road level, and so effectively the entire system is one giant level crossing. There are rarely fatal accidents involving trams, as the operational speed is rather low, and the drivers know to look out for cars. Low speed collisions between road vehicles and trams are however very common, and in one year there were over one thousand collisions such as this in Melbourne. Fatal accidents with trains seem to occur when the train is moving fairly fast, and the impact to the road vehicle has the energy to cause substantial mechanical damage.

Level crossings can be a part of the signalling system, because if the level crossing has bells and lights then the signalling system needs to tell the level crossing when to activate. A level crossing with no protection other than a sign has no connection to the signalling system. Complex level crossings can be expensive to maintain.

Papers have been written in the US where the benefits of installing lights, bells and booms has been analysed. The US has an extraordinary high number of deaths at level crossings, typically over 300 per year, a figure that would not be accepted in almost any other country in the world. The US government has had a long term plan to close, remove, or install lights and booms over as many level crossings as possible, and this program has been very successful in reducing the number of deaths per year. It is clear that booms work quite well in reducing the number of deaths at level crossings.

Another significant problem with level crossings is making sure that the lights and bells don't ring for too long. Car drivers quickly get bored waiting at level crossings, and they are tempted to drive around the boom after waiting even a short period of time like 1 or 2 minutes. Many of the accidents have occurred this way in the world over level crossings. In practice signalling systems have difficulties in allowing for the different speeds of trains, and so for a slow moving train the lights and bells may flash and ring for a time period much longer than a couple of minutes.

Sometimes there are pedestrian level crossings attached to road crossings. A pedestrian crossing is designed purely for passengers, and it operates in a very similar way to a road crossing. Pedestrian crossings are much smaller than road crossings, and have lights and booms. Pedestrian crossings in Australia at least are less common than road crossings.

There are also other types of rail crossings, but they are fairly unusual. There are sometimes crossings provided for animals, and in Sydney there is a horse crossing next to Rosehill Racecourse. Crossings for animals needs to be designed differently than for people, and more space needs to be provided, depending on the size of the animal. Given the rarity of level crossings designed for animals, they won't be discussed any further.

Control Systems

A control system for a railway is an engineering system that displays the position of trains and the status of signals. Control systems normally have a computer screen where trains and their position are displayed. Large rail systems have particularly large control system displays, and these can cover the wall of a large room.

Control systems display tracks as divided up into sections, and each section is displayed as either empty or occupied. Trains are often identified with some sort of alphanumeric code, such as 111A, which identified which run it is. Alternatively, the set number (ie the train identifier) can be displayed.

Control systems also allow the signaller to set trains to routes. This means that the signaller can set the direction of turnouts, and can direct the movement of trains. Remember that drivers mostly cannot set turnout directions themselves (although there are exceptions to this rule, once again), and this function is performed either by the signaller, or in modern times, a computer program.

Tram systems and light rail systems can also have control systems, but they operate differently, partly because of the simpler network design. There is often no track detection system for trams, or almost never, so trams need to be detected and found using a different system. GPS, or some system that effectively operates the same as GPS, can be used to locate where the trams are. On the control system the screen will show the location of the trams, but unlike a control system the trams can't be directed with points and track infrastructure to different routes. The control system for a tram system is much more passive.

A control system links in closely with the signalling system, but is not the same thing. The purpose of the signalling system is to prevent the collision of trains, and the purpose of control systems is to manage the movement of trains. If the control system is directed to allow two trains to collide with one another, then the signalling system will prevent it and send an alarm to the control system.

It is also common to refer to other systems that manage rail infrastructure as control systems. For example, a system that displays information on lifts and escalators may be called a control system. It is important to distinguish between the train control system, and a system that manages other rail infrastructure.

REFERENCES

1. Zhang, C. & Li, L. Zhang, D. & Zhang, S. *Types and Characteristics of Safety Accidents Induced by Metro Construction*, 2009 International Conference on Information Management, Innovation Management and Industrial Engineering, 209

2. Kimijima, N. et al *New Urban Transport for Middle East Monorail System for Dubai Palm Jumeirah Transit System*, Hitachi Review Vol 59, (2010), No 1

3. Murphy, E. *The Application of ERTMS/ETCS Systems*, IRSE Technical Convention Melbourne, Oct 2007

4. State of Florida Department of Transportation, *Central Florida Commuter Rail Transit Design Criteria*, October 2008

5. DB Netze *AG Network Statement 2014,* April 2013

6. Parsons Brinkerhoff *High Speed Rail*, Network, Issue No 73, Sept 2011, http://www.pbworld.com/news/publications.aspx

7. Lindahl, M. *Track geometry for high-speed railways*, Department of Vehicle Engineering Royal Institute of Technology, Stockholm 2001

8. Oura, Y. *Railway Electric Power Feeding Systems*, Japan Railway & Transport Review 16, June 1998

9. BSL Management Consultants *The Cost of Railway Infrastructure Status-Quo and Ways Ahead*, Presentation to the ProMain Council of Decision Makers, Brussels Nov 2001

10. Tateishi, Y. *Broadband Radio Transmissions in Railways*, JR EAST Technical Review-No 20

11. Zhang, W. et al *Pantograph and catenary system with double pantographs for high-speed trains at 350 km/hr or higher*, Journal of Modern Transportation, Volume 19, Number 1, March 2011

12. Eyre, P. *Signalling of the Southern Suburbs Railway*, IRSE Technical Convention – Perth, July 2007

13. Rail Industry Safety and Standards Board, *ROA Manual Section 01 Civil*

14. Kohel, J. *Optimised catenary maintenance measures on Austrian Federal Railways, Rail Engineering International Edition*, 2002 Number 1

15. Huth, P. *Overview of QR Signalling Principles*, IRSE Technical Meeting, Brisbane, July 2008

16. Kerr, D. Rail Signal Aspects and Indications, http://dougkerr.net/Pumpkin/articles/Rail_signal_aspects.pdf

17. Broderick, E. & Lemon, S. *Case Study: Application of CBTC on DLR*, IRSE Australasia Technical Meeting, March 2011

18. Thales *SelTrac CBTC Communications-Based Train Control for Urban Rail*, www.thalesgroup.com/security-services

19. Siemens Transportation Systems *GSM-R Terminals Flexible GSM-R Dispatcher Systems, Terminals and Cab Radio Solutions*, http://www.siemens.com.au/files/Mobility/RI/Documents/mob_gsm-r_terminals.pdf

20. Railway Gazette *Commissioning the world's heaviest automated metro*, Metro Report 2003

21. Thales *Netrac 6613 Aramis*, www.thalesgroup.com

22. Victorian Rail Industry Operators Group Standards Track Circuit Types Characteristics and Applications, Nov 2009 http://ptv.vic.gov.au/assets/PTV/PTV%20docs/VRIOGS/VRIOGS-012.7.4-RevA.pdf

23. Davey, E. *Rail Traffic Management Systems, IET Railway Signalling and Control Systems Course*, May 2012

24. Ancarani, G. et al *Mobile radio for Railway Networks in Europe*, June 1999

25. Hillenbrand, W. *GSM-R The Railways Integrated Mobile Communications System*, Dec 1999, http://www.tsd.org/

26. Mok, S. & Savage, I. *Why Has Safety Improved at Rail-Highway Grade Crossings?*, Risk Analysis, Vol 25, No 4, 2005

27. Klinger, R. *Radio Coverage for Road and Rail Tunnels in Tunnels in the Frequency Range 75 to 1000 MHz*, Vehicular Technology Conference, 1991.

28. Ahren, T. & Parida, A. *Overall railway infrastructure effectiveness (ORIE)*, Journal of Quality in Maintenance Engineering Vol 15 No 1 2009, pp 17 – 30

Chapter 5 Supply and Demand

Introduction

In many cases rail systems and transport is provided for the public good. Governments collect taxes, and use these taxes and other resources to provide services for their taxpayers. This includes providing infrastructure and other services, that for whatever reason, cannot be paid for from a user pays basis. There are many such goods and services, and rail is one of these. Rail systems rarely recover their costs from their users, but the economic benefits from possessing a rail system far outweigh the cost of providing them. For this reason, many rail systems are build and provided that do require subsidies from government for their continued operation.

Given this, it is important for government to fully assess the economic benefits of rail systems before subsidizing them. Economics possesses the methods and tools to perform this assessment, and through economic analysis that a rail system can be assessed and its worth determined. These tools are common, and are based mostly on the supply and demand model that is taught throughout any economics course. Economic appraisal of almost any rail project is made through attempting to assess the demand and supply curves of a rail system, and then determine the overall economic benefit, which is made of consumer and producer surpluses. This basic principle is used extensively throughout transport economics, and indeed, economics for rail systems.

Projects are the way in which improvements are made to rail systems, and it is through the project approval phase that the economic benefits of projects are really examined in detail. Many countries have formalised systems and manuals on how to perform these appraisals, and they vary in quality from place to place. The appraisal of large projects is a well researched area, and there are numerous good quality references available to the reader to further explore this process. The process itself can generate a lot of meaningful insight rail projects, and a good appraisal is both logical and easy to read.

Large and small transport projects are approved based on the economic and financial case that is prepared to substantiate them. Large transport projects can cost billions of dollars, and it is important for governments and large corporations that the economic return that is often promised with large projects is genuine. Governments and corporations assess benefits differently, governments use an econometric evaluation, and corporations use a financial one. Financial appraisals are normally made on a purely financial basis, which does not include an assessment of economic benefits. Government cost benefit analysis includes (or should include) all economic costs and benefits.

Economic appraisals are often performed by economists in the private sector, or more commonly working in universities. These departments normally have databases of economic information relevant to the local area in which they operate, and have detailed reports on externalities, costs of congestions, pollution, etc. They also have information on the Willingness to Pay (WTP) of the local population for different transport services, and can predict what level of demand will be generated by different transport services. They can do quite a lot, and often in large rail projects their services can be quite helpful.

The underlying principle for assessing whether projects should proceed is cost benefit. Cost benefit is the ratio of the benefits to the cost, and the ratio for these two numbers should normally be greater than one for the project to be considered. There are a number of variants on this system, where the benefits are quoted as an absolute number in dollars, as a ratio of benefits to costs, or as a rate or return over the life of the project.

This book will not consider in depth how to evaluate the financials of large private sector projects. Costs for the buying of locomotives, wagons, and the construction of terminals change with time, and so any discussion of these costs would be out of date even as this book was being printed. Also the mechanics of evaluating this type of project is quite well known, costs are estimated and tallied, and then compared to the money saved through the project, or the additional capacity that can be created. Capacity calculations for freight are based on the number of trains that can be moved per day, and how much freight they can carry.

Economics plays a role in many different aspects of rail transport planning and this includes:
- The assessment of large capital projects
- Setting the prices for tickets throughout a rail system
- Setting the price for access to a rail network

- Estimating the demand for rail services when new rail lines are built
- Estimating the change in demand for rail services when critical parameters such as train frequency or punctuality are changed
- Estimating the change in land values when rail lines a built nearby
- Changes to industries such as tourism when new rail lines are built
- And for freight, increases or changes in the amount of freight moved on each different transport mode

The Supply Demand Curve/Model

A standard concept in economics is the demand supply curve. Supply and demand, often thought of as a graph and a curve, is actually a model that is used to estimate how price and quantity of any good is determined. This curve/model is extensively used to explain how free markets are able to determine the price of goods sold, and the quantity of goods sold. The supply demand model is applied to only one good at a time. The supply demand model is taught in economics at a very early stage, and is one of the key basic concepts upon which microeconomics is based.

The amount of a good demanded will change depending on the price, and the lower the price the more of the good that will be demanded. Alternatively the supply curve shows the prices at which suppliers of goods will be prepared to sell the good, and the higher the price the more of a specific good that suppliers are prepared to provide. Market equilibrium is the point where the number of goods sold is equal to the number of goods made, and the price and quantity at equilibrium is very important for economics.

There is almost no limit to the number of goods that the supply demand model can be applied to. Transport is one good to which this model can be applied, and commonly is applied. Not all goods have a market, for example the sale of air is in most countries not a good that is manufactured and sold, and so there is no supply and demand curve. This might potentially change in a country where the air quality is very poor, and clean air can be bought.

Economic Theory

The graph below shows the standard supply demand curve used in economics. This curve demonstrates the way markets find an equilibrium point which determines both the price paid and the quantity of a good supplied. The supply curve slopes up, as more and more of the good can be supplied where the price paid is higher. The demand curve slopes downwards, as when the price drops the quantity demanded increases. The two lines meet at the equilibrium point, which is where the market stabilises at. Note that the two lines do not need to be straight, curves of almost any shape are acceptable (with some conditions).

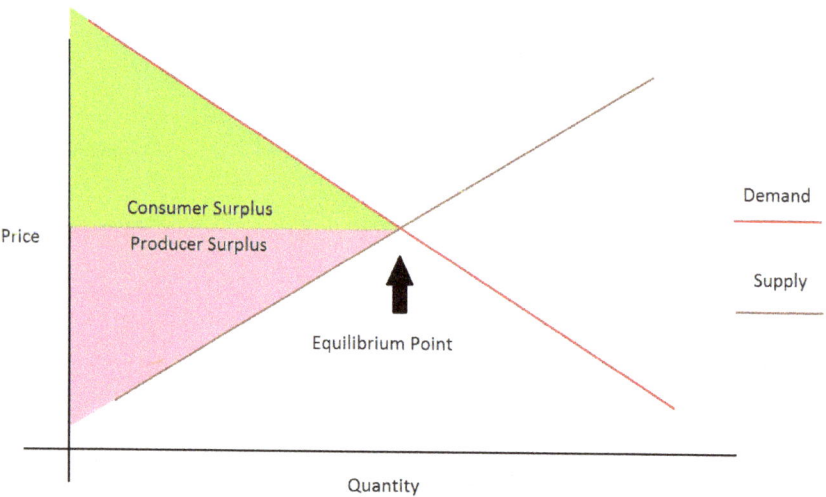

The supply and demand curve drawn above also shows the consumer and producer surplus. The consumer surplus represents the benefit to consumers from buying and consuming any good. As some consumers would be prepared to pay more for the good than the equilibrium price, their economic benefit for buying the good is the difference of the price they were prepared to pay, and the final equilibrium price. The consumer surplus can be calculated by estimating the area as shown on the graph, which can be calculated through an integral.

The same can be said for producer surplus, where the equilibrium price is far higher than the price some producers were prepared to provide goods at. The difference between the equilibrium price and the sale price the producer was prepared to accept is known as the producer surplus. In economics the producer and consumer and producer surplus are considered to be real money, and included in any estimate of the economic benefit of creating or changing a market. Combined the producer and consumer surplus are known as social surplus.

All this works well when the supply and demand curve includes all the costs and benefits to society. In many markets, the supply and demand curve as presented above is more than adequate to represent the social benefit of creating a market, and for rail systems such as a tourist railway this curve is perfectly adequate. Unfortunately, often, the full benefits of providing rail services are intangible, or there may be benefits to third parties other than the buyer and seller, and so may be a little difficult to include, as they cannot be directly measured. For rail, most of these other factors are benefits, and regardless of good or bad, these other factors are called "externalities". Externalities impact upon other parties, or members of society, other than the ones that partake in the transaction between the buyer and seller. Transport is one good where the externalities are very significant.

The existence of large positive externalities for rail transport is the reason why governments are so keen to fund railways, which are often loss making. In many cases the value of externalities to the community are greater than the benefit provided to passengers. The economic benefits from a rail system can be very substantial, and it is in the interests of governmental bodies to provide rail services where they need to be subsidised. Externalities, by definition, are not included in the graph above, and need to be considered by other means in making an economic appraisal of a project. Care needs to be exercised that the benefits to society are real, and the rail system is not just another cost placed upon tax payers.

The demand supply curve is used as the basic model for predicting changes to quantity demanded when changes are made to a good, which is how things are calculated for transport. Investment in infrastructure will often (or should) change the supply curve, or in some cases the demand curve. Infrastructure projects will allow more for less, which means that more can be done with the infrastructure for a lower cost. For example, redesigning a freight line so that it allows double stacking may increase the capacity of freight trains by 30%, reducing the cost of the freight movement because more of it is moved at one time. The reduction in cost allows the supply curve to move, and in economics it is said to "move to the right". A constriction in supply moves the supply curve to the left.

The graph below shows a common result of an infrastructure project. The supply curve has moved to the right, which normally means a successful infrastructure project. The equilibrium point has been moved, so that it is now lower in price and higher in quantity than the original equilibrium point. There has been a change in consumer surplus, which is clearly larger than before, and producer surplus may or may not be higher, but if the supply curve is straight as shown below then it will be higher. This situation, desirable, is the economic benefit of many infrastructure projects.

Change in Supply for Rail Transport

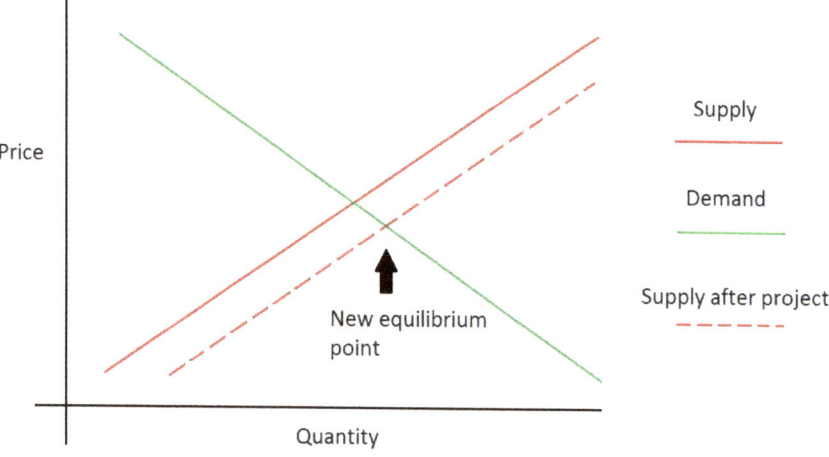

The rail industry is a very capital intensive industry, and requires substantial investments of money to make changes to it. In a modern economy, it is possible for the suppliers of goods to make changes to the supply curve, by upgrading their production equipment when they are too old and need to be replaced, or buying better equipment, so that their productive capacity is greater. In these cases the slow replacement of old equipment can increase the performance of any business, and this happens in the rail industry as well. Rail infrastructure can be upgraded to provide a better service, but the costs can be high. Changes to the supply curve ordinarily take time and effort.

In economics the situation is often discussed or considered where the demand curve is moved about, and this is a result of population changes, or change in income levels, or a change in technology. Demand shifts in economics are considered to be common, and with transport they are also common, but usually not as the result of the actions of government planning. Demand in transport may change, and this may be the result of changes to population centres, or freight and the type of freight moved on freight trains. It is often considered, especially in Australia, that demand for rail services is fixed, but this is not necessarily so. In unusual cases the government may be able to shift the demand for transport, and to increase it for great advantage. Some of these more unusual situations for increasing the demand for passenger services include:

- Feeder rail lines are built, such as a light rail that connects into a heavy rail system
- Building a network of overpasses, so that people can walk comfortably into train stations, increasing demand for rail services
- Transport orientated development (TOD), where apartments, shops and other facilities are installed around a station to increase demand.
- A very major facility such as a theme park, or a casino, is also built at the same time as the rail line

Changes to demand are also possible for freight. Some of these include:
- Changes to the regulatory environment, making transport modes that compete with rail less attractive (particularly license fees or increases in fuel taxes)
- Increases in terminal capacity, which allows more goods to be shipped at a cheaper price. Many terminals are not part of rail lines, and so there is a change in demand
- Approval given to a variety of mining leases, which increases demand in the area for rail transport
- Free trade agreements, or other diplomatic efforts to allow greater access to foreign markets

The supply demand curves drawn below show what happens where this is an increase in both supply and demand, at the same time. This highly desirable situation shows that there is a new equilibrium point, where the price may be maintained, and the quantity demanded increases. This has a wide variety of economic benefits, GDP increases, the size of the market increases, the taxation and revenues base increases, as potentially productivity increases as well. Managing demand for rail transport is a key way to successfully managing a rail system, and the Hong Kong rail system has used this strategy successfully for decades.

Movement of both Supply and Demand Curves

Supply side projects are far more common, and represent the majority of rail projects. Supply side rail transport projects, such as building a rail line, will provide a service where previously there was none. Other projects will improve the quality or cost of a service, and this will shift the supply curve to the right. When the supply curve shifts a new equilibrium will form, and there will normally be an increase in quantity demanded, with a drop in price. This is beneficial for the economy as a whole.

Changes in price do not represent changes in demand, but the level of use of the service will of course increase or decrease as the price is changed. In economics terms changes to the amount of a produce or service demanded is called the "quantity demanded", but changes in demand refer to movements in the demand curve. Railways and governments can set the price of their services, and for lower prices the quantity demanded will increase, and vice versa for price increases.

The reader may notice that moving around the supply curve will result in the equilibrium point moving from one place to another on the demand curve. As the demand curve infrequently shifts, at least as a result of rail projects, it is possible to use this knowledge to determine some forecasts for the change in demand based on changes to services. Particularly important is the slope of the demand curve, and a gently downward sloping demand curve will result in a large change to demand when the supply curve shifts, and a steeply sloping demand curve will result in very small changes to demand. This situation forms the basis for demand elasticity.

Demand Elasticity

The graph above describes changes to demand as a result of changes to the supply of a good, which can include rail transport. Notice that the price has fallen, but the quantity demanded has increased. This is common with infrastructure projects.

In economic assessments of rail projects, it is desirable to know the shape of both the supply and demand curve. In practice obtaining the precise shape of these curves is a time consuming and difficult process, and any econometric department that has succeeded in obtaining them should be commended. Detailed surveys of both providers and customers of a rail service would need to be surveyed, and analysis made of any potential new entrants into the market should a rail service be improved. Acquiring a complete picture of the supply and demand curves is not easy, and is an expensive exercise. In practice only two points are needed, the starting point and the final point where the market stabilises when any infrastructure changes are made. It is much easier to calculate two points rather than an entire curve.

Elasticity of Demand

An extremely useful concept is the elasticity of demand. This represents a change in the quantity demanded, and is the ratio of the change in quantity demanded to the change in price. The equation below is for "arc elasticity", and is a commonly used and useful formula.

The P's represent price, and the Q's represent quantity. P_1 is the price before the movement along the demand curve, and P_2 the price after the movement.

$$E = \frac{(Q_2 - Q_1)/Q_1}{(P_2 - P_1)/P_1}$$

This equation can be re-arranged as:

$$\frac{\Delta Q}{Q} = E \times \frac{\Delta P}{P}$$

Where $\frac{\Delta Q}{Q}$ is the change in quantity demanded. Note the format of this equation, a value of 0

.1 is a 10% increase in demand for a doubling in price, a value of -0.1 is a drop of 10%. A value of 1 is a 100% increase in the quantity demanded for an increase in price, and -1 a drop of 100%.

Demand elasticity is a very commonly used concept in attempting to predict what changes will result from an infrastructure project. Demand elasticity is also used to attempt to estimate the change in demand for rail transport for a wide variety of government policies, such as ticket prices, changes in the frequency of services, or the cost of alternatives or their components, such as the fuel price. Demand elasticity is commonly used as below:

Change in demand = E x Δ cost or parameter

The cost or parameter can be almost anything. Note that where the cost increases, then the demand will almost always decrease, so there should be a negative sign in front of the E (but is excluded because it seems a common practice to exclude it). Demand elasticises are mostly negative, so when cost increases demand will fall, but most reports into transport demand elasticises leave off the negative sign, which can be very confusing. The reader should remember that in most cases demand elasticises have a negative sign.

In practice the above equation seems to be applied to changes to a market for a good that can be either a supply side change or a demand one. For example, a change to the price of tickets for rail passengers is a supply side change, but an increase in the price for parking for road vehicles in city areas may increase the demand for rail, which is a competing market for road transport. Nonetheless, both of these changes can and are assessed through the same mechanism.

For an example, let's use a change in frequency of rail services to determine the change in demand. So for this example, we will use an increase in frequency of trains of 15 trains per hour to 20, and a demand elasticity of 0.1. What is the change in the demand for rail services?

This would be:

$$\frac{\Delta Q}{Q} = -0.1 \times \frac{(15-20)}{15} = +0.033$$

We interpret this as a 3.3% increase in the quantity of passengers using the rail service. Also note the addition of the negative sign, often left out of the equation, but very important.

Where the demand elasticity is equal to one, then this is referred to as unit elasticity. If the demand elasticity is less than 1, demand is inelastic, and greater than 1, elastic. A higher value (in absolute value terms), means a greater change to quantity demanded when prices and parameters change.

A large body of research exists that attempts to determine the demand elasticises for a variety of different parameters. The published research has produced many of these and the range over which the demand elasticity is possible for any one parameter is very large. In general demand elasticises are challenging to use successfully, as published elasticises vary so much it is difficult for economists to know which one to use. There is a very large difference between an elasticity of 0.1 and 1, and yet it is common for published elasticises to vary between these two numbers, or even more.

An important distinction needs to be made between short and long run. In economics many studies look at what happens when changes are made to a market, and many of these changes will result in the short run price and quantity changing only slightly, but in the long term the change is more pronounced. For example, where the government increases the prices of tickets, in the short term there will be a reduction in the number of passengers, but in the long term the effect of the price change will be much more pronounced. The long term effect is almost always far more pronounced than the short term effect, and it is common to use the long term impact in assessing projects and infrastructure changes. Studies attempting to estimate the demand elasticity of changes to government policy may calculate two elasticises for the same change, one long term and one short. Care must be taken in choosing which one to use.

For freight, as price is the most important variable in determining the quantity demanded, most of the published research concerns this. Even given the vast body of literature on freight elasticises, things are still rather difficult. Freight elasticises, even for the same product within the same country, can vary enormously, with some studies reporting low values, and others high.

Fixed/Variable Cost, and Marginal Costs

An important distinction needs to be made between fixed and variable cost as this can play an important role. In accounting it is very common to divide the costs of running a business into two separate categories, fixed and variable. Fixed costs, also sometimes called sunk costs, are those large costs that are incurred in setting up the business, and do not change if the business produces either a large or small amount of product, within a practical range. Variable costs are those that change with the number of products produced, or units sold, and are directly related to the volume of business that a business might have, in a short time period such as a week or a fortnight. The distinction between the two is an important concept in accounting, and also for rail transportation.

Rail transportation is an industry with extremely high fixed costs. Many large rail lines may take 10 years to build, and cost billions of dollars, so the fixed costs of almost any rail business is extremely high. Some rail operators, such as passenger service companies, may have much lower fixed costs, as they do not own much fixed infrastructure, and are not required to invest in rail lines that take 10 years to build. Nonetheless rail is often correctly considered to be an industry with extremely high sunk costs.

For any industry with high fixed costs it is important to maximise the utilisation of assets. Once constructed, infrastructure should be fully exploited, and not left unused. Whilst this might seem obvious, one potential trap for any railway, when allowing access to its network, is to charge the full cost of infrastructure and the network to any rail operator, as the full cost is, for most railways, dramatically different to the variable costs. The full cost is in many cases far too high for any operator to pay, such as a private passenger company, or a freight company, but the variable cost is much lower and these companies mostly can afford that.

The variable cost for a freight company might be the cost of fuel, access charges for the network, wages for train crew, and any other fees that might be incurred in performing a freight movement. For a private passenger rail company, variable costs will be similar. For an infrastructure company, variable costs might be the cost of preparing the train plan, creating a path in a timetable, or maintenance costs for equipment and facilities that are only needed for that rail operator. The costs of installation of the fixed infrastructure, such as the track, signals and electrical power system is often not included in any access charges for the network. This makes the distinction between fixed and variable costs very important.

Fixed costs may include depreciation. Fixed costs can also include interest charges for any money borrowed for construction of the rail line. Many of the costs associated with operating a railway are fixed, and very few are variable. Railways have such a large volume of equipment, and need so many people to oversee their safe operation, that the fixed costs of most railways are very large.

Economic Theory

The marginal cost is the cost for a business of providing any additional service or product. It also is the slope of the cost curve, and it is really the derivative of the cost curve. Marginal costs often drop as more and more trains are added to a rail system. The graph below shows the common situation where the total cost of operating the rail system increases as the number of rail services is added. Fixed costs must be paid, even where there are no rail services operating. Also note that the cost of adding more rail services is lower each time a service is added.

Fixed and Variable Costs

The graph above is typical for what a rail company would experience. The fixed costs are high, and with each additional trains added to the system the costs increase, but that increase reduces for each additional train.

Financial Comparison of Train Travel to Automobiles

One of the key benefits of installing rail lines, especially for passengers, is the reduction in cost to society for providing transportation. Rail systems are often much cheaper than road travel, and so the "derived demand" of transportation can be met with lower resources. Consider that the alterative to rail travel is often road vehicles, which are expensive to buy and maintain.

Some of the advantages of rail transportation over road is:
- A train carriage can take hundreds of people, whereas a private road vehicle can take only up to six or eight
- The fuel consumption of a train is mostly much lower than a car or a bus
- The separated right-of-way means that most rail systems are not delayed by heavy road traffic, and so are able to move into city centres without much difficulty
- Rail carriages typically last over 20 years, whereas road vehicles often last only 10

The costs of road vehicles varies substantially from country to country, and even city to city. Many highly densely populated cities have taxes, and levies that discourage people from buying cars, and these costs make the ownership of cars the exclusive domain of the wealthy. Alternatively, some countries have cheaper running costs for cars, especially where fuel is cheap.

In Australia a number of attempts have been made to estimate the cost of running and owning a road vehicle. It's a complicated calculation, as insurance, servicing, and taxes need to be paid regardless of the use of the vehicle. There are also some direct costs associated with operating the vehicle, that increase as the number of kilometres the vehicle is driven increases. Also bigger cars tend to be a lot more expensive to operate, and consume more fuel than smaller vehicles.

Perhaps the best way to estimate the cost of operating a road vehicle is to use the taxation deductions allowed for owning a road vehicle. In Australia, when used for work related purposes, the cost of operating a vehicle is deductible from the income of a business, and the Australian tax office provides a table which is to be used. The cost per kilometre ranges from 63c to 75c per kilometre (Australian currency), based on the size of the engine. These figures seem appropriate for comparing with rail.

Consider that in Hong Kong, where the metro system is not subsidised, that the cost for adults is about $9 to $12 Hong Kong dollars for a trip of about 15 kilometres, which is about $1.40 US. This translates to a cost of about US10¢ per kilometre. This is far less than the cost of operating a road vehicle, and remember that this is the cost for an adult, and in Hong Kong, as in many rail systems, there are discounts for the elderly, children and those with disabilities, so they pay even less.

Australia rail systems tend to be expensive to operate, as they have smaller numbers of passengers, and operate on long sections of track through wilderness where rail infrastructure is difficult to maintain. Even in this very difficult environment, the cost per kilometre for a rail passenger is no more than about 35¢ US per kilometre, which is substantially less than the cost of road vehicles. Rail, as a system for moving people, is usually more cost competitive than private road transport, unless the rail system has low loading factors, or has some specific problems that make it very expensive. This is one of the key advantages of operating a rail system.

The reduction in cost to society in providing transport is one of the key benefits of the installation of any rail line entirely within one city. A reasonable heavily used metro line may move 100,000 people per day, and a typical trip distance is about 12 kilometres. On that basis, if passengers switch from private vehicle use to rail, then the cost saving is staggering, and can be over $100 million US per year, which is normally more than enough to justify the construction of a metro line, even without all the other benefits such as better air quality and safety included.

For HSR (High Speed Rail), the situation is a little different. Passenger numbers are lower, and the travel distances are much higher. HSR competes with road transport for shorter distances such as 200 – 300 kilometres, and with aircraft for large distances such as 700 – 1000 kilometres. Rail is seen as a premium service, and superior to air travel, and is priced accordingly. HSR systems are NOT installed to reduce the cost of travel, but for convenience, environmental reasons, and most importantly financial ones (i.e., profit), and so HSR systems are not judged the same way as short distance metros and light rail.

Commuter travel, from a suburb to the centre of a city, and then out again at the end of a working day, is an expensive service to provide, for a number of reasons. These include the need to provide seating to passengers which results in a lower capacity compared to a similar sized metro, the large central terminus that needs to be maintained for these trains to terminate at, and the difficulty with rostering rail staff to work on these trains. The cost per kilometre of a commuter system can be high, and normally a commuter system is not justified on the basis of cost reduction. Commuter systems are used where people in the regional area, or the distant suburb, want to travel by train as they don't want to drive long distances. Even in Australia, where driving 1.5 hours to and from work each day (so that's 3 hours per day) is seen as reasonable, people are reluctant to drive further than this, and prefer to take a train. The fatigue that arises from long distance driving can be very draining, and long distance commuter trains are far easier to travel on. Passengers commonly sleep on these trains, or eat, something that is either difficult or impossible to do whilst driving a car.

Chapter 6 Externalities

Introduction

A full and correct assessment of the economics of any rail system involves the calculation of the full economic benefits, including those for which there is no market. In many cases there are benefits other than the consumption of rail travel or rail freight associated with a rail system. These need to be included in the calculation of any economic benefits.

A rail system provides a whole host of different benefits. In many cases the benefits of a rail system are much larger than the benefits from the passenger travel. Road congestion is reduced, emissions reduced, less energy consumed, and near passenger stations property values increase. Passenger rail systems are very safe, and provide a much safer system than road travel. All of these benefits are real, and need to be included in any economic appraisal.

An externality is a cost or benefit that is generated by some activity, usually trade related, that is not included in the cost of production of a good or service. For example, a typical externality is pollution, which is generated by many different manufacturing processes, and if it is not controlled may cause negative health effects to those nearby, but may not be counted as a cost during the manufacturing process. In a rail environment, a common externality for rail operations is noise, as the generation of noise by a freight train creates no cost for the freight company, but a cost to the community as a whole, depending on where the noise is generated. Externalities may be counted in the finances of freight companies, depending on the country.

Externalities need to be accounted for separately when performing cost benefit analyses of transport projects. A large part of the economics of transport is the assessment of the value of externalities, and putting a value to society of them. Externalities are difficult to assess correctly, but externalities are very important for assessing any rail project, and not considering them reduces any economic appraisal to farce. The method of assessment of externalities can strongly influence the result of any economic appraisal.

Externalities may also need to be considered in markets that are related to rail transport. For example, the market for road freight is a related market, as it is a substitute for rail freight in many circumstances. A negative externality of road freight is congestion on roads, and where more road freight will take up space on roads, and where congestion already exists, add to this congestion. A rail project to take road freight off the road will impact on traffic congestion, in a positive way, so this benefit needs to be considered in any economic appraisal, even though the benefit is not actually in the rail freight market, but in a related market.

The problem with externalities is that there is no market for them, so assessing their impact to society gets quite difficult. There is no market for noise produced by a freight train, or for the benefits to road transport of getting more trucks off the road and onto trains, but a value needs to be assigned to them. As projects are assessed on a cost benefit basis, and costs are in money, then externalities need to be converted into money to be included as part of that analysis. In economics there is a method to complete this transformation, and it is briefly outlined below.

Some of the more common externalities and associated with rail and related markets include:
- Noise increase or reduction
- Reduced congestion on roads
- Reduction in carbon dioxide and toxic gas emissions
- Improvement in safety for motorists
- Wear and destruction of roads by trucks

Many of these benefits are not included in the price of the rail ticket, price to access a rail system, nor in the cost of supply. This makes them externalities, as they are outside of the pricing of rail tickets. No money from rail tickets, nor provision of the supply of the good, goes towards these benefits (usually). This makes the normal supply demand curve analysis so typical of many economic appraisals incomplete, and needing more information to make it representative.

Quantification of the benefits can be challenging. Many studies have been performed to attempt to understand the various intangible benefits. The transport economics field has researched this problem extensively, and many high quality references exist which can provide guidance on how to quantify the many externalities associated with rail transport.

Changes in Asset Values from Building Rail Lines

Passenger rail projects provide improved transport services for those who live near it. As stations are fixed and don't move, the presence of a rail station typically causes an increase in property values which should increase as rail services are introduced or improve. Any improvement should produce an increase in property values, such as faster services, more frequent services, or an increased number of possible destinations.

Asset value changes are externalities because there is a change in the economic position of members of society that is not included in the market for the good. The price of a rail ticket for passenger travel does not include any provision for changes in property values. Changes in property values can be significant for new rail lines, or even for changes in the frequency of rail services.

An increase in property values can be an argument for property levies to pay for new rail lines. A typical levy is a property tax on nearby properties, which should be levied in proportion to the increase in value of the property. Thorough studies into any increase in property values can be very helpful in convincing local residents to pay more taxes, especially if their overall wealth position improves.

In practice the situation is a bit more complicated that what it would seem. There are a number of reasons why property values may decline because of new rail services, and not increase, and these include:
- Areas of high wealth are often very exclusive, and are not easy to access, especially for the general public. Putting a station in the middle of an exclusive area may rob it of the exclusivity that makes it attractive. This situation arises often in Sydney, but arises in many cities with high wealth.
- A new rail system brings noise, especially where the system is used for both passenger and freight trains. Depending on the level of the noise, property values may decline significantly

- Many freight trains carry materials that are dangerous, such as chlorine, or highly flammable, such as LPG or fuel. A new rail line may increase safety risks to local residents
- Many rail services are priced very cheaply, and crime may be much higher near a station compared to locations away from the station. In some parts of Asia such as Singapore, there is very little crime so this issue is not a problem, but in the US with their very high crime rates rail systems and stations may bring a lot of crime, which will reduce the value of property in the area
- The rail system is not needed, so there is no increase in property prices as local residents are indifferent to the introduction of the new rail line
- The rail system is poorly designed, so the travel times are too high for the rail line to be used by large numbers of people, and so the rail line is poorly patronised
- With each rail line includes some stabling, maintenance centres, freight yards, and intermodal terminals that are needed somewhere, and these facilities are ugly and visually intrusive. Any property next to these facilities may drop in value substantially.

On the other hand, there are many situations where the introduction of rail services provides a large increase in property values. If the increase in property values can be maximised, this is ideal for any rail project, and something that should be encouraged. Some of the situations where property values might rise quickly include where:
- The new rail service is very high quality, fast, frequent, or cheap. If the rail service provides a very efficient connection to highly desirable locations, then this is attractive and will increase property values
- If as part of the rail project other facilities are included in the project, such as shopping centres or parks. Areas with good quality facilities are more attractive to live in
- Remote locations with poor transport connections can be completely revitalised where vastly improved transport is provided. This sometimes occurs where old dockland or port land is revitalised, and a rail line included as part of the process. Access becomes very good, and property prices changes accordingly

- Regional centres that are connected with High Speed Rail often experience a renaissance, and grow. The availability of high quality transport allows people to line in that location and work in others, which is very desirable.
- Large cities with very high congestion can be difficult to move around in, especially by any transport that uses roads, such as buses, taxis or cars. Building a rail line allows people to get in and out of the area much more efficiently, avoiding traffic, and getting to work and other activities more quickly.

So it would seem that the increase in property values will depend on the situation and the needs of local residents. Certainly it is a very difficult relationship between land and property values, and calculating any future increases is not easy at all.

A number of reports completed in Hong Kong have assessed the increase in property values, and found a relationship between several variables and increase in property values. Some of these reports are very detailed, and assessed the benefit of improved train frequency, for example. The highest increase in property values in these reports for Hong Kong was about 10%, and this was for good quality properties very close to the rail line, with a highly frequent service. Certainly the increase in property value was not 100%, but really quite modest.

It must be kept in mind of course that even in Hong Kong, a city with a very well run metro system, has the highest property values in a place called "the Peak", which is on top of Hong Kong Island, and has no rail line at all (other than the cable car, a tourist rail system). The property there is some of the most expensive in the world, so it is possible for high value property to exist even in places with virtually no public transport.

The Pricing of Road Congestion

Road congestion is relevant to a rail system because building a rail line is one of the solutions to relieve congestion. Road congestion in a large or even a moderately sized city is a major issue, and has substantial economic, environmental and social impacts. Road congestion is seen as a great negative, and something that should be avoided if at all possible. As the construction of a rail system can substantially reduce congestion, the benefits of reduced road congestion is often included as part of the assessment of any rail project. Reducing road congestion can provide substantial economic benefits for any city or country, and this can be used to justify large rail projects.

Typically congestion is not a word commonly used for rail systems, but as a concept is very applicable. Rail systems can behave in a similar way to road ones when there are too many trains. Rail and road systems both slow down when the number of vehicles increases beyond a certain critical point, but the solutions for each can be quite different. Congestion in a rail system would normally be the result of the capacity of the network being inadequate for the number of trains, which can be often remedied with structural changes to the network, which is discussed extensively in other chapters in this book. Whilst conceptually this is the same for roads, the engineering solutions can be quite different.

Road congestion in any large city or region can have a powerful and very negative effect on business. Costs increase as businesses need more drivers and vehicles to get product around to their customers. Operating costs of trucks and light vehicles increases with the frequent starting and stopping that is typical in highly congested road systems, and fuel consumption is higher per kilometre travelled. Furthermore, in areas with high traffic congestion, the variability of the time of any travel increases, so that additional drivers and vehicles are needed to guarantee delivery times.

Perhaps the largest impact to business is the loss of scale, and this needs to be explained further. Businesses in areas of heavy road congestion will have a reduced area for customers, as there will be limits on the distances that can be effectively reached in a reasonable time throughout any busy city with deliveries. In a city with an excellent and effective road system, one business may be able to provide services to the entire city, and so have a large volume of business over which to spread their fixed costs. Where congestion is very bad, a large number of business supplying the same goods will be needed to cover each small part of the city, which will be less efficient, and need to charge higher prices. Competition will be reduced, as congestion will convert a free market into a series of tiny monopolies, in which suppliers of goods can charge higher prices.

Property prices will also be negatively impacted by road congestion. Roads with large amounts of traffic are very unpleasant to live near, they are noisy and smelly, and the noise from trucks can continue well into the night. Crossing major roads is also dangerous, and takes time. Property prices may be 10 – 20% lower in areas with heavy road congestion compared to similar areas without any congestion, and the loss of wealth is a serious factor that needs to be considered. Alternatively, when congestion is reduced there should be an increase in property values. Amenity is increased when road traffic declines, because the area is now more pleasant to live in.

For the travelling public, the use of taxis in a heavily congested road system is problematic. As taxi fares are calculated either on the distance travelled, or in congestion, by time, the cost of any taxi fares can be very large. Even short distances in heavy traffic can be very costly for any passengers, and this is unfortunate as taxis are another form of public transportation that should be encouraged.

In the context of economic appraisals of rail projects, it is often necessary to assess the benefits of providing more rail transportation, and hence the theory is that there will be fewer cars on the roads. The benefit of removing cars from roads needs to be assessed, and included in any assessment of the merits of rail projects. The benefits of removing cars from roads, as mentioned above, falls into four major categories:
- The time saving resulting from less cars on the roads to other road users
- The financial cost saving of operating less cars and more trains
- The improvement in air quality from operating less cars and more trains. The benefit is especially pronounced with freight trucks and replacing them with trains
- The gain in wealth from the improved rail service, and the reduction in unpleasant road congestion near places where people live

In economics, the overuse of public roads, and the resulting traffic jams, is sometimes referred to as the "tragedy of the commons". Roads are mostly free to use, and once a person enters the road system then typically there are no further charges. This situation leads to overuse, as the public good is free, and the price rationing mechanism of capitalist economics cannot be used because roads are free to use. There are of course strategies to avoid this problem, such as tolls, congestion charges, and setting licenses costs at a level to eliminate congestion. These strategies, all quite nasty and unpleasant, which involve in taxing people for just wanting to drive down the street, can be avoided by building a rail line that reduces the congestion on roads, without the need to damage people financially.

As with all economic analysis, benefits accruing from rail projects should be quantified in terms of dollars, so that comparisons can be made. Once again this means that the benefits of rail projects need to be quantified in dollars, and for travel times this is relatively straight forward. If the average trip is, say 40 minutes, and there is a reduction in the travel time, then this can be translated into dollars. A common way to make this conversion is to use the average wage in an area, and to multiply this by the time saving. So the formula for the reduction in travel time for a rail project is:

$$Economic\ benefit = avg\ wages \times trips\ per\ day \times \left(\frac{Dis}{Sp_1} - \frac{Dis}{Sp_2} \right)$$

Where:

Dis = average trip distance
Sp_1 = average traffic speed before the rail project
Sp_2 = average traffic speed after the rail project

This formula represents a rough but useful approximation.

Emissions from vehicles is a topic which is very contentious. Cars, in burning fuel, produce a number of quite nasty compounds and particles, and these include:
- CO_2, carbon dioxide, which is a greenhouse gas and causes global warming
- NO_x, which includes NO and NO_2, and these two gases are nitrous oxides. These gases can cause breathing problems, such as emphysema, and also potentially heart attacks
- CO, which is carbon monoxide. This odourless and colourless gas can cause brain damage and in severe cases death.
- Ozone, which has the chemical symbol O_3. Ozone is helpful for the upper atmosphere where is blocks ultraviolet light and protects animals and plants living on the surface, but at ground level can cause lung inflammation and induce asthma attacks.
- Particulate matter, given the abbreviation PM, which refers to tiny grains of organic material. The smaller the material, the more likely it is to get into the lungs, or the bloodstream and

cause damage. Particulate matter is referred to either as PM_{10} or $PM_{2.5}$, which means the particle is this size or less in microns. Particulate matter is considered to be particularly nasty to people's health.
- Lead, which is was an additive commonly used in fuel, now banned in many countries. Lead in the atmosphere causes reductions in IQ in children
- Sulphur oxides, given the chemical symbol SO_x, which can cause acid rain.
- Highly toxic organic compounds, such as benzene, which is carcinogenic.

We note that there are a large number of different unpleasant gases and other products from gasoline burnt to power motor vehicles. Combined these emissions seem to be quite dangerous, and there is research to suggest that, even in the developed world, the number of deaths from car emissions is in the tens of thousands. Particulate matter is considered to be particularly dangerous, and something that countries should avoid producing.

There are two ways that a rail project can reduce the level of toxic emissions; by reducing the number of kilometres driven by road vehicles, and by increasing the average speed at which road vehicles move. The graph below shows the basic idea, and many different versions of this graph have been published. The basic premise is that the emissions per unit time change based on the speed of the vehicle. As the vehicle slows down, not only is the travel time longer, but the efficiency of the engine drops, and more toxic gases are produced. Vehicle speeds need to be above 30 kms/hr (or 20 mph), so that the engine of the vehicle avoids producing large quantities of toxic gases.

The same applies for high speeds, once a vehicle travels at over 100 kms/hr, emissions tend to increase. A key question is: do all of the nasties in the emissions increase evenly as the overall emissions increase, and the answer seems to be yes. A small number of studies, quoted at the end of this chapter, have investigated this question, and it seems that as a rough approximation that each component tends to increase fairly uniformly.

Gas Emissions and Speed

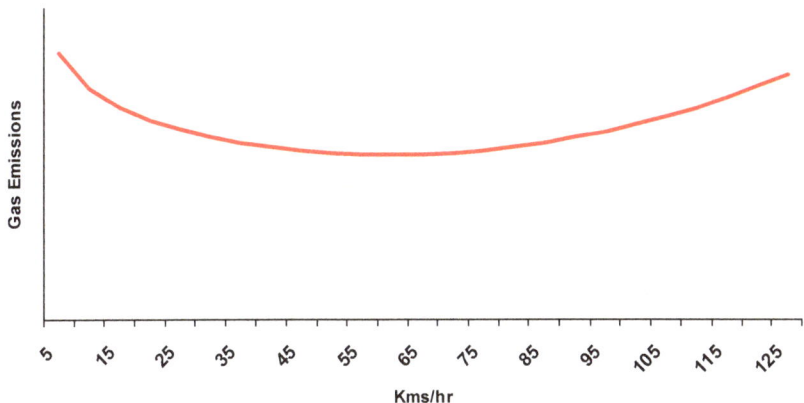

So getting back to the economic appraisal, and the inclusion of road traffic congestion, it is traditional to assign a cost per kilometre to the negative externality of traffic pollution. A cost of about US 5¢ per kilometre per vehicle seems to be about the right number (in 2012), which, the astute reader will notice, is quite a large amount. The cost per kilometre of providing metro services is often around 10¢ per kilometre, so the economic benefit of eliminating road trips is comparatively quite large. This is particularly so where the average traffic speed is below 30 kms/hr, and the movement of these trips from road to rail will mean that the remaining road vehicles are more efficient, so the economic benefit will be even larger. This figure includes all the different gases, but it is also possible to separate out all the different gases and apply a figure to each one, and then tally them. This approach is acceptable, but more complex, and it is left to the reader to choose which approach is the best.

In most large countries there will be a government department that determines the cost per kilometre that should be used in any economic appraisal that reduces the number of road trips.

The Economics of Safety Benefits

Rail is much safety as a transport mode than road transport. Often overlooked, rail transport is vastly safer, and per distance travelled the number of deaths is much lower. This safety benefit is quiet significant, and should be included in any economic appraisal of the benefits of building rail lines.

Statistics on the death rates of different types of transport modes are commonly available. There are a number of very good websites that provide this information, and the reader can use these very effectively. In the US there are a number of government bodies that publish statistics on transport modes, and their comparative safety, and these are also very helpful. It should be noted that there has been consistent action on safety in most developed countries for many years, and that the death rate per distance travelled is constantly falling. The numbers presented below should be taken only as a guide, and current figures should always be used when writing economic appraisals for new rail projects.

The unit of measurement adopted here is deaths per 100 million kilometres. This measure was chosen because it can be used to compare across different transport modes, which is the purpose of this section. Other measures include deaths per 100,000 people per year, and deaths per number of road vehicles owned. These measures are commonly quoted in different papers and documents, but are difficult to use for comparative purposes.

Of course the numbers presented here do not include suicides. Sadly in some countries suicide on the rail system is quiet common, and Australia is one of those countries. Whilst it is often difficult to implement a solution to prevent suicides, platform screen doors can be very effective in eliminating attempted suicides from platforms. The experience in Australia has been that the riskiest place for suicides is express trains passing platforms at high speed, where the train is not stopping, and the platform can be accessed when no trains are stopping there.

The numbers listed in the table below are useful for comparison purposes. It should be noted that these death rates per kilometre are appropriate for countries in the OECD, or countries in Western Europe. These numbers are not appropriate for use in countries like India, where the death rate is extremely high. The same can be said for China, where the number of road deaths per kilometre is much higher than in Australia/UK and Canada.

Externalities

Comparison Table Road and Rail Related Transport Deaths – English Speaking World only

Transport Mode	Death Rate	Place and year
Trucks, road freight	1.69 per 100 million kilometres	US, 2002
Buses/coaches	0.7 per 100 million kilometres	Australia 1999
Rail (all types)	0.15 per 100 million kilometres	NSW 2012
Motorcycles	25.3 per 100 million kilometres	Australia 1993
General aviation	8.5 per 100 million kilometres	1985 Australia
Large passenger jets (domestic in the US)	0.004 per 100 million kilometres	US, 2010
Cycling	7 per 100 million kilometres	NSW Australia, 1985
Walking	36.2 per 100 million kilometres	US, 1995
Road (all vehicles)	0.7 per 100 millions kilometres travelled	Australia 2009
Road (all vehicles)	0.6 per 100 millions kilometres travelled	UK 2009
Road (all vehicles)	0.8 per 100 millions kilometres travelled	USA 2009

General aviation refers to the many different types of small aircraft that might be used to transport people, or perform some sort of commercial function. Crop dusting falls under the heading of general aviation, and can be quite dangerous. Helicopters are more dangerous then general aviation. The death rate in Australia for large domestic passenger is 0, and has been since Qantas was founded in 1921. The death rate used for large jets for passenger traffic was the US domestic figure.

Trucks have a surprisingly high number of fatal crashes. A majority of the deaths from truck accidents are the occupants of the other vehicle that is hit when the truck impacts another vehicle. Trucks thus represent a major hazard to other road users. In Australia in 1996 almost two thirds of the people killed in accidents involving trucks were in the other vehicle. The death rate associated with articulated trucks is even higher, and the larger the vehicle the greater the death rate. Rigid trucks are far safer than articulated ones, on a per kilometre basis.

The Relationship between Property Values and Freight Systems

Rail freight systems are dirty and messy, and often noisy. They are beneficially environmentally compared to moving freight with trucks, but that is small comfort to anyone living alongside one. Houses alongside a freight line may also be exposed to the risk that there will be a derailment and a train crash into a house, or a derailed train release a poisonous chemical that injures or even kills anyone near it. Freight trains often operate late into the night, and so anyone that is a light sleeper will have difficulty sleeping when living next to a busy freight yard or line.

The drop in property prices around a freight line seems to be about 5-7%. This range is taken from a study done in Ohio, but seems consistent with studies in Hong Kong showing an equivalent rise in property values of this amount when a metro station is placed next to housing. The more freight trains that pass through an area, the greater the reduction in property prices.

Particularly irritating to those living nearby is the use of horns on trains. Trains, like cars, have horns to sound if they approach a level crossing or other area where there is likely to be a safety risk. The horn is a warning to other users of nearby roads that trains are near. The use of horns for trains is sometimes banned, as it is so noisy, but this increases the safety risk for rail freight movements.

In countries where property values are very high, any government action which results in reductions to property values is met with very determined and vigorous resistance. Whilst a rail freight line will reduce traffic congestion overall, the local residents alongside the new rail freight line will lose out as their property prices fall. Any government that plans to implement a transport plan that reduces property values, and the rail project is not desperately needed is likely to experience a lot of trouble. Even a 10% reduction in property values can translate to enormous amounts of money where average property values are over US $1 million per property (like it is in Sydney, Singapore or Hong Kong). Thousands of properties may be affected.

So how can this situation be managed? What controls or measures can the transport planner make to allow for this reduction in property values? So what possible solutions exist? Some of them include:
- Putting rail freight into industrial areas where noise from container terminals won't be noticed, or next to other industrial sites such as oil refineries
- Developing an area with the freight terminal on it before houses are built
- Putting freight terminals onto islands away from people. This solution is surprising common
- Banning, or limiting the use of horns on freight trains
- Putting sound barriers up around rail lines with freight
- Moving freight yards from high value areas to low value ones.
- Perhaps even shutting down freight operations, and moving all freight onto road vehicles, as was done in Hong Kong
- Relocating freight into freight corridors where the impact of the noise and unsightliness of trains is reduced
- Where possible, moving freight terminals away from areas where people live
- Electrifying rail freight lines, as electric locomotives are quieter

Freight lines are rarely put into tunnels, as diesel locomotives emit a lot of fumes. Freight lines in tunnels may seem a sensible option, as the noise from the train will not penetrate through the ground to the houses above, but in practice this solution is rarely implemented. In many situations is may be difficult or even impossible to reduce the negative impact of freight trains on property values, and a freight tunnel underground built. At present freight tunnels are limited to water crossings and tunnels under mountain ranges, but there is no technical reason why more freight tunnels cannot be constructed.

Chapter 7 Freight

Introduction

Goods need to be moved around from where they are created to where they are consumed. Freight performs this function and so is an important part of the economy of any country, and the efficient fast and cost effective movement of goods is critical to productivity and maintaining low prices for goods, and hence international competitiveness. Rail freight went through something of a decline in the 60's and 70's, and despite reports of the death of the rail freight industry, it is still alive and well, albeit a bit smaller in percentage terms compared to road transport.

In Australia, as in many developed countries, there was a boom in constructing railways from around 1850 to 1920. Rail technology was invented before automobiles, or before automobiles could move freight in any kind of significant economic way, and so was the standard for the movement of freight for decades. The development of many industrialised economies depended on the creation of large very comprehensive freight systems, and countries like Canada and the US were criss-crossed by rail lines. The growth of large rail companies was one of the drivers that led to the creation of common stock companies, ways of raising money for investment into large enterprises. The rail industry in many countries, such as Germany, the UK, France and Australia expanded very quickly, becoming very large.

As trucks improved, and road freight became cheaper and more efficient, rail started losing its competitive advantage, and through the 60's and 70's rail freight in most developed countries dramatically contracted. Rail lines were closed, and much of the freight moved to road transport. As road transport was cheaper, and more flexible, the maintenance of expensive rail infrastructure could not be justified, and many freight lines were closed. In Australia the closure of rail lines was particularly dramatic, and freight corridors were converted into walking paths, housing, light rail, roads, etc. Large freight yards next to old disused wharves were also common, and these freight yards became quiet as rail lost its ability to compete. As part of this process, and the development of new technology that made rail services more productive and require less staff, there were dramatic contractions in the number of employees working in rail companies. This contraction was also very pronounced in British Rail.

In many cases rail freight stopped operating entirely in some areas, such as in Hong Kong. In others rail freight become something of a niche player, and catered only for small markets with very specific needs. The cost advantage of rail systems for bulk materials such as coal and grain guaranteed their survival, but many goods that were previously moved by rail were rarely moved this way. In Australia wool was very commonly moved by rail, but now, or even since the eighties, is almost never moved with the rail freight mode. Also the development of the "road train", a truck/traction unit with a large number of trailers, allowed the movement of large amount of goods by road. Road trains can be extremely large, and large ones are not permitted to enter urban areas. The record for the largest number of trailers pulled by one large truck is apparently 112.

This great contraction in rail freight has left many rail lines either underutilised, or many freight yards are almost empty. Large numbers of freight lines were closed, and many rail systems shrank. In the US things seems to be a little better, and through very prompt action rail freight has survived in a much more substantial way there than in many other countries. This contraction has had a profound effect on the rail freight industry, with many deserted yards, little used freight wagons, and old rail freight lines covered with grass.

One advantage rail freight has is its fuel efficiency. Road vehicles such as trucks and articulated vehicles require more fuel than rail, so for intensely used freight corridors, rail freight can still be viable. For mines with large amount of material to be moved, rail freight works quite well, and so large rail lines often service mines. For non-bulk materials, the picture is more bleak, and even in areas where it has survived, there is relatively little moved by rail. In Australia, rail freight has about 20% of the market for non-bulk freight, in the UK it is about 10% and in the US about 40%. Rail has genuinely struggled to compete, but has survived nonetheless.

One of the main challenges with rail freight is the need to provide specialised infrastructure. Rail freight requires rail corridors, and rail tracks, which need to be built and maintained. The cost of rail freight infrastructure needs to be at least partly recovered, and so there are charges for the use of rail infrastructure. In many parts of the world, and Australia is no different, use of roads by trucks and road freight is taxed in a preferential way, or the full cost of the damage to roads is not covered in the cost of licenses, so rail freight needs to compete with road when it is paying for the infrastructure, and road freight is not. This is a very difficult situation, and one that is problem for the rail industry.

Rail freight is almost always heavy rail. Heavy rail is a rail system where the loads are very large and the trains very long. High speed rail for example is a heavy rail system, because of the large locomotives and the weight of the train. Some freight systems are however light rail, and sugarcane railways are a light rail freight system.

Despite the contraction of rail freight 50 years ago, and the difficulty of competing with road freight, rail freight is now perceived as being superior to road in many countries. Rail freight has many advantages, including the low level of emissions, its better safety, the benefits to urban spaces in terms of amenity and quality of life from removing road freight from roads, and the reduction in damage to roads. Many countries are encouraging rail freight through subsidies to the rail industry, taxes on road freight, and projects to improve the efficiency of rail freight. This level of support has been very beneficial to improving the amount of freight moved.

Much of the research and reports on rail freight focus on getting as much freight as possible onto the rail system and off roads. All sorts of different strategies have been investigated, and these are discussed below. Rail freight is seen as not being able to compete with road freight, but a commonly held view is that rail freight is something that should be encouraged. This view, coupled with constant study of rail freight systems, has provided a wealth of information on freight and how it is managed, and what is needed to improve it.

Overview of Freight Systems

Almost anything can be moved by rail freight, and almost any item that is sold or manufactured can be moved by rail. For example, washing machines could be moved by rail, or milk, or books, almost anything. What can be moved by road or air can be moved by rail. The choice of transport mode is an important one for any freight system, and this decision can have a large impact upon costs, delivery times, and punctuality.

To provide the reader with an idea of the broad range of goods that can be moved, consider the list of different goods below. It is not at all an exclusive list, but provides some indication of the broad range of goods that an be moved by rail:
- Whitegoods and furniture
- Food products
- Livestock
- Animal products, such as wool
- Bulk food products such as wheat or milk powder
- Petroleum products
- Gases of all types such as chlorine
- Liquids used in production process such as ethanol or methanol
- Bitumen or other organic compounds
- Lumber
- Minerals and bulk materials such as coal, iron ore or sand
- Parcels
- Weapons, such as tanks or missiles
- Road vehicles, cars and trucks
- Mail
- Industrial machinery
- Sugarcane

Many different products can be moved by rail. In competition with rail, the main transport modes are:
- Road freight, which means mostly trucks. Road freight is more flexible than rail, and often suited to short distances or small numbers of shipments
- Air freight, which is used for long distance freight, and where the item is needed to be transported quickly. Air freight is very expensive and struggles to compete with other transport modes
- By ship, which are mostly ocean going. This transport mode is frequently the only serious way to transport goods from one country to another that is not linked by land.
- By barge, a type of boat that is suitable for large navigable rivers. Barge transport depends on the location of suitable rivers, and whilst not common in Australia is still common in the US.
- Other more unusual means of transporting products, including dedicated pipelines, or conveyors.

Freight trains are quite different to passenger trains, although some of the design concepts are the same. Some of the key differences are:
- Freight trains accelerate and brake much more slowly than passenger trains
- Freight trains are almost always much longer than passenger trains, and are often over 1 km long
- Freight trains can be diesel or electric, in Australia freight is mostly diesel
- Freight trains have difficulty climbing grades, and even small grades can be a problem
- Passenger trains often have powered passenger cars (EMUs), freight trains are almost always powered by separate locomotives
- Passenger trains are rarely divided and amalgamated, freight trains are often split and recombined
- Freight trains are mostly much noisier than passenger trains
- Freight trains are almost always much heavier than passenger trains, and frequently do much more damage to infrastructure than passenger trains, particularly track infrastructure
- Freight trains are limited to an economic speed of about 100 kms/hr, although there are exceptions to this rule. Passenger trains often are much quicker than freight trains.

Australia has a number of very successful freight rail systems, which are able to survive and thrive because of the high price of coal (which at the time of publishing this book has changed substantially), and the energy efficiency of moving bulk materials by rail. Successful rail freight companies, which in Australia can even generate enough revenue to pay for the infrastructure and signalling, move very large quantities of coal for export to overseas markets, mainly China and Japan (in that order). The volumes of material moved are truly extraordinary, and by weight rail is by far the most commonly used mode of transport for freight in Australia.

The photo below shows a typical freight locomotive. Large and extremely powerful, these locomotives can be combined together to be able to generate the motive force to move large number of wagons. The fuel consumption of diesel locomotives can be very large, although it should be noted that freight trains can be very fuel efficient compared to the loads they are moving.

A Freight Locomotive

Freight trains are often barred from entering a rail passenger network during peak times, when there are large numbers of passengers moving around the system. As freight trains are slow moving, and accelerate and decelerate slowly, putting them into a passenger system in peak times causes problems. The most common effect of mixing these two rail modes is that the total capacity of the system is reduced, and top speeds are lower. To mitigate these problems, a rail system may impose a curfew, which is a blackout period where freight trains are not permitted to enter a rail system. Curfews have a profoundly negative impact of freight movements, and should only be implemented where absolutely necessary.

Maintainers of rail infrastructure tend to dislike rail freight, and this is because of the changes in infrastructure needed to accommodate freight trains. Broadly, more infrastructure is required, and some of the infrastructure required is different to what is normally required for passenger services. Some of the changes/additions to rail infrastructure include:
- The spacing between signals is increased, so the headway increases, even for passenger trains. This can be extremely inconvenient when a small headway is needed
- The track structure needs to be stronger to accept freight loads that are normally much heavier than passenger loads
- Freight trains have paths through the rail system that are different from passenger trains, and normally more junctions will be needed to accommodate those paths. For example, passenger trains, especially commuter train, operate from the city to the outskirts of large cities, but freight services may move from one remote part of the city, to another remote part, in a direction completely different from the passenger traffic.

These different direction may require substantial amounts of additional infrastructure (turnouts commonly)
- Some sort of billing system is needed for the freight trains, as access to the network is often based on the number of wagons and the weight of the train. Whilst in theory it might seem ok to trust the freight company when they provide data on what trains went where, experience in Australia has shown that freight companies will understate the loads on their trains. Weighbridges are needed to weight trains are they enter the rail network to accurately bill freight companies for the trip through the rail system
- Freight companies will need marshalling yards, where wagons are combined into trains, and where locomotives are stored awaiting use. Marshalling yards can be very large, and are not pretty to look at, and so any rail network with large amounts of freight will need to have at least, and maybe several of different sizes
- Freight trains are often not as reliable as passenger trains. This is frequently because passenger trains use electric power, and operate as EMUs, and so have natural advantage compared to freight trains. This means that they break down more frequently, and there needs to be a system of "recovery" or "rescue" of broken down trains. A normal high powered locomotive is often enough to rescue a broken down freight train, but there are also speciality rail vehicles that perform a similar function. Rescue is often provided at a fee, and a failed freight locomotive will block the rail line in at least one direction, depending on where it has broken down. This needs to be considered in the design of any freight system
- Freight trains pull wagons that can have a bearing failure, which can derail the freight train. Special infra-red cameras are available to look for heat in a rail wagon, and this system is often called a "hot box" detector. These will be needed in strategic places around the network to prevent large derailments
- Facilities will be needed to store freight trains when faster moving passenger trains need to pass. Alternatively, the freight train may need to wait to get access to a freight terminal, because it is full, or there is a curfew that prevents the freight train from entering a certain area of the network at a certain time. Freight trains seem to spend a lot of time waiting, and

sidings, or sometimes called a refuge will be needed at strategic places in the network. Passing loops can also be used.
- Special precautions may be needed before hills to ensure that freight trains do not stop before a hill. Whilst freight trains will be able to start moving on level ground, and climb moderately steep grades, if they stop on a high grade they may not be able to pull the load up the grade. Special signals may be needed to ensure that once a freight train enters a section of track before a steep grade, that there is nothing to stop the train on the grade, until the track is in a place where the grade is lower. A freight train may need 10 kilometres of clear track to ascend a particularly steep grade, and stopping halfway through the climb can mean that the freight trains gets "stuck". In Australia this special type of signal is called a "tonnage signal", which will tell the driver of a freight train that the road (ie the rail track) is clear and that it is ok to proceed at normal speed for several kilometres.
- Freight trains are often diesel hauled locomotives, and these produce diesel fumes. Whilst this is fine in the open air, in a tunnel the fumes can rapidly build up and create a toxic environment. In a narrow tunnel the diesel fumes will need to be removed, and this means additional ventilation. A rail tunnel with mixed freight and passenger traffic will need very good ventilation systems to ensure that the air is acceptable to the passengers, and not smell or be full of soot. Ventilation systems in tunnels are expensive
- Modern intermodal container freight trains are often "double stacked", where a second set of containers is placed on top of the first. Where this is done the height of any overhead wiring will above the containers will need to be extremely high, maybe as high as 7.5 metres, and this can impose a substantial cost to have either the overhead wiring moved higher, or built high when first installed.

The damage caused to a rail system from freight can be quite significant, especially where the rail freight is very heavy. The main damage to the rail system is the rail and supporting infrastructure, which will be "pounded" by the heavier loads. Damage to the infrastructure consists of :
- The top of the rail will develop metal defects, such as flat spots and cracks

- Trains carrying bulk loads will often drop some of their load onto the rail track, fouling the ballast and filling points/turnouts with coal or grain or whatever material is being carried. This can cause many problems, especially with the points filling with this unwanted material, and this if often a problem at the entrance to the final terminal where the bulk material is unloaded.
- The track infrastructure will degrade with the constant passage of heavy trains, and need more frequent maintenance

Many types of passenger rail systems cannot accept freight onto their system. If anything freight on a rail system is becoming less common for a variety of reasons discussed below. Some of the rail systems that cannot accept freight, or rarely do, are:
- Metro systems, where the high frequency of service makes it almost impossible to schedule freight trains in between passenger services
- Light rail, where the track structure is rarely strong enough to take large freight trains, and freight trains are rarely suited for running down the middle of streets (although freight trams still exist and were common in Australia and many other countries for decades)
- Monorails, which are utterly unsuited for freight trains, unless the monorail has been specifically designed to accept freight
- High speed rail, where the slow speed of freight trains will not permit HSR trains to operate at their normal commercial speed. HSR freight is something that does exist, but is quite rare.
- Some specialised rail systems, especially medium capacity metros that operate with rubber tyres, are not suited for freight

Some of the passenger rail systems that are better suited to accepting freight are:
- Commuter systems, where the heavy commuter trains run on infrastructure that is often the same as what is required for freight
- Long distance and overnight trains, which are often not high speed, and so can intermingle with freight trains quite effectively.

Large cities may need freight movements from one part of the city to another. A very large city may be 40 kilometres across, and so large that freight trains are needed to move freight from one side to another. Sydney has this type of freight traffic, and normally the rail freight originates from somewhere on the outskirts of the city, and then moves to the port. This situation arises in part because of severe road congestion, and trucks moving containers may take long periods to get to the port and back again. In theory containers can be moved around at night when roads are empty, but in practice is seems that most intermodal traffic that is short distance needs to take place during business hours. This requirement gives intermodal traffic a chance to be competitive in a rail system even over short distances in very large cities.

Some of the different types of freight are:
- Bulk materials, such as coal, iron ore, grain, milk, fuel, sand, flour, gypsum, etc
- Intermodal freight which consists of large metal containers. Intermodal freight is very important, because this is how most items are shipped around the world today
- Other more unusual freight types, such as steel coils, or road vehicles. In theory many different types of large materials may be moved, should a freight wagon be designed to move it.

The photo below shows some of the different types of freight wagons that can be used. At the front are flat cars, in the middle hoppers for powder of different types, and then after that tank wagons for transporting liquids.

A Freight Yard

There are a number of useful numerical terms that can applied to a freight system. These can be used to describe many aspects of a rail freight system, and some of the key parameters are:

- Axle load. This measure normally has the units of tonnes, and there are mostly 4 axles per freight wagon, so the axle load is the weight of the wagon divided by 4. Freight companies often want to operate with the highest possible axle load, as this increases their efficiency, and reduces the number of trains needed. A typical limit for the axle load would be about 20 tonnes, depending on the freight network of course. In Australia some railways have been able to achieve up to 40 tonnes per axle.
- MGT, which stands for Million Gross Tonnes, which is one measure of the number of tonnes that have been moved through the network in any given year. The measure is made at one point, and the same network will normally have different MGT figures throughout the network. A network with a low number of freight trains may only have an MGT of about 5, and with a moderate amount may have 10 to 15 MGT, Some freight systems in Australia have only 100 MGT, or even over 200, which is a very large amount
- GTK, which stands for Gross Tonne Kilometres. The GTK represents the weight and the distance that freight has been moved, and it is the multiplication of the number of kilometres travelled, by the distance the train has travelled. GTK numbers are often very large, and so are commonly quoted in millions of GTK. A rail network with only a small number of trains may still be able to have a large GTK figure if their trains travel large distances.

A freight corridor is a dedicated rail freight line that does not have any passenger traffic. Freight corridors can move large quantities of freight, and are very popular with freight operators. The safety risk of freight is much lower than for passenger trains, a freight train can have a derailment where many of the wagons are derailed and destroyed, and there is no loss of life because the freight locomotives are the only places where there are any people. Freight corridors are a very effective infrastructure strategy, and can be spectacularly successful in increasing rail freight movements. Many of the problems associated with moving freight are eliminated, the higher priority given to passenger trains, the lack of network capacity, and curfews that are often placed on freight movements are all eliminated as types of problems.

One problem that commonly arises in freight networks is balancing loads between destinations. It is common for intermodal trains to operate between only 2 destinations, and pick and deliver at both ends. What is desirable is for the loads and freight traffic to be balanced, and so the same number of intermodal containers, or really any other freight traffic, to be the same in both directions. This will reduce cost as the cost of the train is spread over a larger number of containers. In practice things are rarely so nice, and often there is a much higher flow of freight in one direction than in another, and so in one direction trains operate at capacity an in the other are only partly full.

Bulk materials freight almost always has fully loaded wagons and trains moving in one direction, and empty ones in the other. In Australia trains make their way from mines to ports, so that raw materials can be exported, and there is nothing to bring back from the port to the mine. As a result bulk material trains almost always operate half the time full, and the other half empty. This is very difficult to avoid.

A derailment is when train wheels no longer sit on top of the rails, and in severe cases can lose contact with the rail entirely. Derailments are one of the major safety risks for any railway, and for passenger trains this risk should be kept to an absolute minimum. For freight systems derailments have a much lower risk, as the locomotive will rarely derail, but wagons can and often do, especially towards the back of the train. Derailments are much more common for freight trains than for passenger trains. Many freight systems have dozens of derailments per year, and this is because the risk associated with the derailment is so much lower, so mitigations to prevent derailments are not as commonly applied as for passenger trains. Given the relative frequency of derailments, any significant freight system needs to have a method or re-railing any derailed freight train. There are a number of methods for doing this, and a common and easy one is to use jacks to lift freight trains up and back onto tracks.

Freight trains are almost always driven by a human driver. Many freight drivers consider the driving of a freight train to be an art, and requires a special skill. Recall that freight drivers mainly control the speed and braking of a train, and mostly cannot control direction.

Managing the acceleration of a freight train is apparently quite difficult, and mistakes can result in separated trains, damage to rail, slow movements of freight, and safety risks. In Australia there have been attempts to automate the driving of freight trains, especially in large mines in the desert where salaries are very high, and up until the writing of this book these attempts have been almost entirely unsuccessful. This may change in the future, as research is continuing into this topic.

Different Types of Freight

Bulk Material Freight

Bulk materials includes bauxite, coal, iron ore, sand, wheat, etc. In Australia the three largest bulk materials moved by rail freight are coal, iron ore, and grain. Bulk materials are particularly easy to load and unload into wagons as they can be poured, rather than lifted with a crane or individually handled into the train or onto a wagon.

Below is a photo of a coal train passing through suburban Sydney. This particular train is empty, and notice that it is quite long and the end of the train cannot be seen. Also note that it is passing a suburban rail station, and there are occasionally injuries to passengers who attempt to "touch" the passing freight train.

Coal Freight Wagons

The coal, or similar bulk material, can be poured, using gravity as the motive force. Not all bulk freight moved is solid, some is liquid. The freight wagon in the photo below was used for moving milk, although based on its condition has not been moved or used for a while. Sometimes the freight wagon below is called a tank wagon. This one is quite old, at least 30 years, and has seen a lot of use.

Liquid Wagon for Freight

Bulk material freight is often more economic and profitable than intermodal freight. The relative wealth of companies who move bulk materials means that they operate their rail operations differently; their trains are often in much better condition than intermodal locomotives, they can brake more quickly and have a superior braking curve, and can pay higher prices for paths through complex networks.

Intermodal Freight

After World War II increasing trade volumes placed great pressure on ports and transport systems, and there was a need to develop a better way of moving goods from one place to another. In the 1950 a trucking company owner called Malcolm McLean developed the modern shipping container, which was a standard size and can be used to move a large variety of different goods. The key advantage of the shipping container was its standard size, which meant that trucks, rail wagons, and ships could be specially adapted to move the containers.

Shipping containers, also called intermodal containers, can be moved on almost any transport mode. The containers are strong, durable, and can survive bad weather and rain. They are easy to move and transport, and can be placed on top of one another. Each corner of the intermodal container has a locking mechanism called a "twistlock", that allows containers to be secured to each other when they sit on top of each other. The twistlock mechanism also allows the container to be placed onto transport, such as ships, trains, and trucks, and then locked into place so that it does not fall off when the vehicle bounces around of passes through heavy seas. The introduction of the intermodal container has been one of the great successes of the 20th century, and has revolutionised the movement of freight worldwide.

Intermodal containers come in many different types. Whilst the early versions were little more than steel boxes, modern intermodal containers can be quite different to one another. Intermodal containers can be refrigerated, for the shipment of ice cream, and other foods that need to be frozen. Containers can also have air conditioning, or ventilation. Bulk containers are also available, suitable for moving bulk materials much like the specialised wagons in the section above. Also available are container to move dangerous goods, which have special flooring to contain spills, may be have special insulation, and of course have different signage.

Intermodal freight is a very important part of any modern economy. Whilst in Australia intermodal freight is often seen as the poor cousin of bulk material freight, in many countries and especially the US, intermodal freight is a very central part of the transport system. The US has a high rail intermodal freight share, with rail moving 35-40% of all intermodal containers countrywide.

Intermodal containers come in many different sizes, but are classified according to their volume. The standard intermodal container is 20 feet long, and 8 feet wide and 8 feet high. In metric units this corresponds to a length of about 6 metres, and a width and height of about 2.44 metres. Intermodal containers are wider than rail gauges, and so will overhang the rail gauge. Recall from chapter 8 that trams are typically 2.45 metres wide, and light rail 2.65, and metros about 3 metres (9.8 feet), so intermodal containers are about the same width as a tram. High shipping containers are also available, and these are about 2.9 metres in height.

Intermodal containers seem to be limited to carrying about 28-30 metric tonnes of goods, regardless of their length or height. Containers often weigh about 3 to 4 tonnes, so the gross weight of a container should not exceed 32 tonnes. For most rail systems that is not a lot of weight, and most railways should be easily able to accommodate this amount of weight on one wagon. Where double staking is employed, even 64 metric tonnes is easily carried by the right rail wagon, and with 4 axles on the rail wagon this corresponds to a per axle load of about 16 tonnes, not a large amount for most heavy rail systems.

It is a commonly held view that moving intermodal containers by rail is only economically viable when the transport distances are very large. By large this can mean over 500 (around 310 miles) kilometres, or even further, over 800 kms. This is quite a large distance, and many countries and not this wide or long, especially in Europe where many countries are very small. In the US, Australia and Canada this is not a particularly large distance, and freight movements of this distance are common. In Europe a 1000km (620 miles) freight movement would almost definitely require transport through 2 or more countries, or in some cases more than 5.

Below is a photo of an intermodal container loaded onto a train. This particular one is quite unremarkable, and seems to be relatively old. Notice that the container is a nice square shape, and it's quite long, so probably 40 feet in length.

An Intermodal Wagon

One each corner of the container is a device called a "twistlock". It is on the corner that containers are secured to each other, and onto other objects. To secure a container effectively requires a matching unit underneath the container, and if needed, on top.

Intermodal containers are rated according to units of Twenty foot Equivalent Units (TEUs). The standard intermodal container is 20 feet long, so a 40 foot long intermodal container would represent 2 TEU's. Most containers now moved worldwide seem to be the 40 foot or longer container, rather than the shorter containers.

The table below shows the TEU rating of different sizes of containers.

Container size and TEU rating	
8 feet high x 8 feet side by 20 feet long	1 TEU
8 feet high x 8 feet side by 40 feet long	2 TEU or 2.25
8 feet high x 9 foot 6 inches side by 20 feet long	1 TEU
8 feet high x 8 feet side by 48 feet long	2.4 TEU
8 feet high x 8 feet side by 54 feet long	2.65 TEU

The TEU is a very important unit of measure for intermodal shipping. Trains and terminals are rated in terms of the number of TEUs moved. A typical intermodal terminal might move 100,000 containers per year. This does not mean that 100,000 containers were moved, only that the total TEU ratings of all the containers add up to that figure

Intermodal containers are often stacked on top of a rail wagon called a flat car. Flat cars, as the name would suggest, are entirely flat, and can be an excellent way of transporting many types of goods, in addition to intermodal containers. The photo below shows a modified flat car that is used for moving intermodal containers.

A Flat Car

Double stacking

Double stacking is a method of transporting more intermodal containers for a given train length. A second layer of containers is stacked on top of the first layer, and so more containers can be moved than a single stack. Double stacking is very common in the US, where it is widely considered to have dramatically improved productivity. In the US it is common for governments and private companies to have considered investing in their local rail systems to allow double stacking, and many of these reports have been published to the internet.

Double stacking is not as straightforward as it might seem. There are many different configurations of stacking that just simply don't work, and can't be used. In practice special software, deployed in the terminal where the trains are loaded, is often used to allow the efficient and safe double stacking of containers, and avoid many of the unacceptable configurations that cannot be used. The effort involving double stacking means that it is sometimes more economical to not double stack, especially where trip distances are short.

One of the main advantages of double stacking is the reduction in cost. As more containers can be moved, and the weight of containers is normally not that high, for a given locomotive it is often possible to move more containers. This increase in volume moved per locomotive results in a cost decrease, which for the highly competitive freight market is very important.

Overall the effect of double stacking is to either reduce train lengths or to increase the capacity of trains. It is not the case that introducing double stacking can reduce the length of trains by 50%, in practice there is a reduction of maybe 25-30% in train length, as not all intermodal containers can fit together or sit on top of one another. Some of the more heavy containers cannot sit on top of lightweight or weak containers, as it cannot be guaranteed that the lower container won't be damaged. The table below shows which configurations are acceptable and which are not.

Often the sidings where freight trains are loaded with containers is not the ideal length, and too short. Double stacking allows an increase in capacity for a train of a given length, and this can be very important where sidings are too short. In remote areas land will often be very abundant, and so rail sidings can be almost any length, but around ports the length of sidings may be very restricted. Allowing double stacking is one way of making more efficient use of scarce land around ports, as a train of a given length can move more containers when double stacked.

Double stacking requires higher structure and loading gauges than single stacked trains, and this is the major reason why double stacking is so difficult to achieve in practice. Typically the height/structure gauge required is about 6.5 metres (21 feet), although a loading gauge of 5.9 metres(19.3 feet) will also allow two standard height containers to be placed one on top of the other. Even a loading gauge of 5.9 metres is quite a lot, and the loading gauges of many rail networks is about 4 to 4.5 metres. Increase the loading gauge is not cheap, and an increase of 2 metres (6.5 feet) is a large amount.

Sugarcane Railways

This type of freight operation is common in some parts of the world, especially where sugar cane is grown in large quantities. Sugar cane railways are a form of light rail, and move much lower tonnages and quantities than say a freight train moving iron ore or sand. They are normally built on 2 foot gauge (61 cm) and radiate out from the sugar mill and the system length can be very large.

The sugarcane railways in Australia are very large and run for over 4000 kilometres (2500 miles). Sugarcane is more economically transported by rail when volumes are large, and the ground is very flat. There are also some large sugarcane railways in Egypt, as well as a number of other countries.

The photo below shows two locomotives coupled together to pull sugar cane wagons back to the mill. These locomotives are always diesel, and need to be built to the 2 foot gauge. Notice the unharvested sugar cane on the left of the photo.

Sugar Railways Locomotives

Below is a photo of some sugar cane wagons waiting to unload their sugarcane to the mill. The mill can be seen in the background with the smoke stacks. Notice the very small size of the wagons, which are completely unpowered and unbraked.

Sugar Cane Wagons

The total weight of sugarcane moved in Australia was 36 MGT in 2007, or about the same as weight of all intermodal traffic moved in Japan for that year. Despite being a light rail freight system, the volume of material moved can still be quite large

In some cases where sugarcane is no longer grown in some countries or areas, the railways has been converted to run as a tourist railway, and even as a passenger railway. There are tourist railways in Taiwan and Fiji that use the old converted 2 foot gauge tracks.

Other types of Freight

It is possible to move many other types of freight, other than bulk materials and intermodal containers. Rail wagons can be customised to move almost any type of freight, and in Australia the main type of freight that is moved is steel products and coils. The steel coil is manufactured in a large steel mill and then shipped for final processing or for export. The photo below shows steel soils waiting to be shipped Australia, in a custom designed rail wagon.

Steel Coils Moved by Rail Freight

Piggyback operation is a type of freight system where semi-trailers (lorries) which are carrying freight are themselves put onto the train, and then transported. The driver of the truck or semi-trailer will get out of the vehicle and then sit in a special rail car where many drivers can sit. This type of system is rail in the Chunnel, the rail tunnel that runs from the UK to France.

Rail Freight Terminals

Modern intermodal terminals can perform some of the functions of international border clearance, such as customs and quarantine. It is more efficient, and better for the senders of the containers, for these government checks to be performed at the same place as where the container is dropped off and delivered to. Intermodal terminals might also offer ancillary services, such as cleaning of containers, or repairing them if they are damaged. Some containers may need to be disinfected, and this service can also be offered for a fee. Perhaps the most important service is to store intermodal containers, as they are not expensive to buy, and companies often buy too many, or have procured some for freight movements that only occur occasionally. The storage of shipping containers does not generate much revenue, but it is an important function in support of intermodal freight.

Freight terminal are often linked to ports, where goods can be exported and imported. In rare cases goods may be taken to a port to ship to another port in the same country, although for reasons that are not clear this is unusual in Australia. Small countries will normally have only a small number of ports, and would not ship containers from one port located close to one another.

Bulk material freight terminals are often located outside large cities, in a regional area. Material shipment such as coal or grain, destined for export, does not need to pass through a major city, and doing so only adds cost and time. On the other hand intermodal traffic is often destined for major cities, much of the contents of intermodal containers are consumer goods, and these end their journey in a shop or retailer.

Freight terminals that move intermodal containers can be classified on the basis of the number of containers moved through the terminal per year. Some references discussing intermodal freight traffic distinguish between terminals that move more than 10,000 TEU's per year, and those lower than that being a small terminal. Some major intermodal terminals handle millions of TEU's per year, and a terminal that handles less than 10 thousand is really quite small.

The photo below is of the intermodal terminal in Yennora in Sydney. The train sits in between the two long gantries, and the gantry crane moves along the length of the train to remove or place intermodal containers onto the train. This type of lifting arrangement is more efficient than a diesel powered container forklift, but more expensive to construct.

A Intermodal Freight Terminal and Gantry Crane

Below is a photo of the coal bulk terminal no 1 in Newcastle. This terminal is structured as a giant loop, and freight trains arrive, move around the loop, and unload their coal onto a conveyor, which moves the coal to where it is stored. Many of the coal freight terminals in Australia have some limited storage capacity, called a stockpile, where coal can be stored for a short time until loaded unto a ship for transport to the final consumers. This particular coal terminal loads ships with coal, and they are not in this photograph. The large orange machines are coal loaders.

A Coal Freight Terminal

Many terminals have restrictions placed upon them by government as to their hours of operation. Many terminals in Australia are required to close at certain hours. The placement of a terminal, especially if it is placed in an industrial area that has no housing, will give the terminal a better chance of being permitted to operate longer hours.

REFERENCES

1. Wardrop, A and Suess, P, *Strategies to Increase Line Capacity and Reduce Travel Time in a Mixed Passenger and Freight Corridor*, The Institution of Railway Signal Engineers Inc Australasian Section Incorporated, Nov 2009

2. Gifford, J. & Moore, T. *Axle Counters – For Heavy Rail Applications*, The Institution of Railway Signal Engineers Inc Australasian Section Incorporated, March 2007

3. Andersonn, M. *Marginal cost of railway infrastructure wear and tear for freight and passenger trains in Sweden*, Swedish National Road and Transport Research Institute (VTI), Department of Transport Economics, 2011

4. Hassan A *The Role of Light Railway in Sugarcane Transport in Egypt*, Infrastructure Design, Signalling and Security in Railway, Chapter 1

5. Wardrop, A. & Suess, P. *Strategies to Increase Line Capacity and Reduce Travel Time in a Mixed Passenger and Freight Corridor*, IRSE Australasia Technical Meeting – Sydney, Nov 2009

6. Joint Transport Research Centre of the OECD *Survey on price and demand elasticity in terms of reliability in freight railway services*, International Transport Forum, May 2008

7. West, R. et al *Identification and Evaluation of Freight Demand Factors*, National Cooperative Freight Research Program, Sept 2011

8. Beuthe, M. *Freight transportation demand elasticities: a geographical multimodal transportation network analysis*, Transportation Research Part E 37 (2001) 253 - 266

9. Troche, G. *High-speed rail freight*, KT Railway Group, Stockholm 2005

10. Shughart, L. *Trends and Issues in Container Transport*, TRF Annual Meeting, March 2012

11. Lin, CY. *Causal Analysis of Passenger Train Accidents on Freight Rail Corridors*, 2013 World Congress on Railway Research, November 2013, Sydney Australia

12. ABC Containers *ABC Container Guide*, http://www.abccontainers.com.au/downloads/abc-refrigerated-container-guide

13. Department of Infrastructure, *Transport, Regional Development & Local Government Adelaide Rail Freight Movements Study*, Oct 2009

14. Bureau of Infrastructure, Transport and Regional Economies, *Information Sheet 34 Road and Rail Freight, Competitors or Complements*, April 2009

14. Bureau of Infrastructure, Transport and Regional Economies, *Information Sheet 65 Australian Container Ports in an International Context*, Sept 2009

15. Woodburn, A. *The role of rail in port-based container freight flows*, Maritime Policy Management, Aug 2007, Vol 34, No 4, 311-330

16. Piyaatrapoomi, N et al Freight Intermodal Terminal Systems for Port of Brisbane, Melbourne, and Sydney, 2006, http://eprints.qut.edu.au

17. van Geldermalsen, T. & Leviny, D. Viability of Providing Double Stack Access on Railway Lines in SouthEast Australia, 28th Australasian Transport Research Forum,

http://www.atrf.info/papers/2005/2005_vangeldermalsen_leviny.pdf

18. Rahall, N. Central Corridor Double-Stack Initiative Final Report, Appalachian Transportation Institute, Feb 2003

19. Yang, Q. *How to Improve the Efficiency of Railway Freight Transport in the Urban Area?*, Service Operations and Logistics, and Infomatics, 2008

20. Freight Infrastructure Advisory Board *Railing Port Botany's Containers*, July 2005

21. Shipping Australia Ltd *Metropolitan Intermodal Terminal Study 2011*, http://www.transport.nsw.gov.au/sites/default/files/b2b/freight/rail-access-review-shipping-aust-mits-attachment.pdf

22. Iawasa, K. Rail *Freight in Japan – The Situation Today and Challenges for Tomorrow*, Japan Railway and Transport Review 26, Feb 2001

23. Sydney Ports Corporation *Intermodal Terminal Guide Metropolitan & Regional New South Wales*, October 2009

24. Colliers International *The National Intermodal Terminal Challenge*, 2010, www.colliers.com.au/research

25. BSL Management Consultants GmbH & Co. KG *Survey on price and demand elasticity in terms of reliability in freight railway services*, Hamburg May 2008

26. Bureau of Infrastructure, Transport and Regional Economies, *Report 114 Optimising harmonisation in the Australian railway industry*, 2006

27. Park, H. *Rail Freight Transport in NSW Briefing Paper No 8/09*, November 2009

28. Radosavljevic, A. *Measurement of train traction characteristics*, Proceedings of the Institution of Mechanical Engineers; Sept 2006; 220, F3; Proquest Central

29. Lukaszewicz, A. *Running resistance – results and analysis of full-scale tests with passenger and freight trains in Sweden*, Proceedings of the Institute of Mechanical Engineers; Jun 2007; 221, F2; Proquest Central

30. Andersson, M. *Marginal cost of railway infrastructure wear and tear for freight and passenger trains in Sweden*, European Transport no 48, (2011): 3 – 23

Chapter 8 Economics of Rail Freight

Introduction

Price is very much the most important factor for influencing freight originators as to which mode to choose. Freight as a transport mode is very price sensitive, and this can be a useful thing for economists. Changing the pricing of rail freight can make it more or less attractive, which is a mechanism governments can use to achieve their overall objectives.

It is through an economic analysis of a freight market that estimates can be made of freight demand when changes are made to a freight system. Rail freight is very price sensitive, and this can be used to generate forecasts of future rail freight demand. This makes an understanding of the economics important.

The Supply Demand Model Applied to Externalities

Externalities are not always a large factor in any project justification. In Australia there are some freight rail lines that pass through large deserts, and there is no local community to be effected by an externality because no one lives near the rail line. For a number of mining railways in Australia this is the case, and there are many rail freight lines all over the world where the consideration of externalities is necessary but not quite as important. Some externalities should still be considered such as for greenhouse gas emissions.

Private companies need to perform a financial appraisal of any new project which involves large expenditures. Project justification is quite different for the private sector compared to the public, as private companies are motivated by profit, and will often not include any externalities in any project appraisal. Having said that, some private companies do include externalities in their project evaluation, but this seems to be unusual. Project justification, which normally means a business case, will need to demonstrate a rate of return that a private company is prepared to accept. Many large private companies have an internal benchmark for the acceptable rate of return, and any project that is being considered for approval will need to at least reach the required rate of return, but preferably achieve a much higher rate of return than what is required.

The discussion on externalities leads to the topic of regulation of the rail freight industry. Once externalities are calculated a government may be able to estimate what taxes to impose and how much support to provide to freight companies. Once externalities are estimated, then the level of financial support, of support through regulation, as an optimum, can be determined. Freight should not be supported to the extent that the government is excessively supporting it, and costs for the public for transport is excessive.

Governments often have targets to increase the mode share of rail freight compared to road. It is because of the externalities that they want to do this, rail freight is considered to be much more beneficial to society and the community at large, and it's a noble thing that needs to be supported. Governments create targets for rail freight, and then need to implement these targets, and yet many freight companies are privately owned, and there is a real reluctance to mandate that freight MUST travel by rail. So this presents a problem; how to increase the mode share of rail freight without mandating it.

In some limited circumstances it is acceptable to mandate the use of rail freight, and some crossing of the Alps in Europe there are such rules. Also there is no road freight through the Chunnel, and trucks need to piggyback onto trains. However overall these cases are exceptions, and governments need to convince freight operators to use rail without actually forcing them to do it. There is one main mechanism to achieve this, adjusting the cost of the rail freight. Cost is an extremely important motivator for freight companies. The demand for rail freight is often considered to be highly elastic, which means that there are large changes in demand for small changes in price.

Some of the ways that governments can influence the cost of freight transport, for both rail and road freight, include:
- Setting the level of access charges for trains to operate on networks
- Setting the cost of buying licenses for vehicles and drivers
- Setting the cost of taxation on fuel, and in Australia there is a very large differential on taxes for fuel for road compared to rail, with "rail" fuel being much cheaper
- Setting tolls on roads for trucks

- Imposing taxes on direct transport movements
- Offering subsidies for freight transport

The question arises when applying these taxes and subsidies as to what level to set them at. Any level of taxation will always offend someone, and so there needs to be some level of support for what taxes to impose. For this reason many governments, and the EU, have commissioned dozens of reports in the appropriate level of taxation for different modes of freight. Many of these reports are published online, and provide different transport economists with a constant stream of work (which is greatly needed of course)! The primary method of allocating taxes preferentially to one transport mode over the other is as follows:
- Identify the different externalities that are relevant
- Perform an analysis on the cost to society of these externalities
- Identify which of the different transport modes generates what externality, and within transport modes which is worse or better than the others (for example, B doubles are more efficient than rigid trucks)

Determine what cost/taxes to apply to different vehicles, and when the taxes should apply, and how they should be calculated

Price Elasticity for Rail Freight Used for Forecasting

Price elasticity is a standard concept for relating changes in quantity demanded to price. However it is also used in a very similar way for forecasting changes to markets when price is changed. A price elasticity is very important for economic appraisals, as this is the technique used to estimate the change in freight if the price of moving freight changes. Often rail transport projects aim to improve the efficiency of infrastructure, by increasing the capacity of freight services, or quicker, or require less resources to complete a freight movement, and so the cost of providing the service falls. A cost change can, with some effort, be translated into a change in quantity of rail freight demanded.

Governments, when making investment decisions, want to know how much of a change their project will make. If a $200 million rail freight project is to be approved, then in the press release the media and public will be expecting to know what is going to change. Details are needed of the changes, and so this is where the price elasticity of freight is useful. Using price elasticises to forecast future demand is a very standard technique for estimating the benefits of rail infrastructure projects.

Freight elasticises are very important in assessing infrastructure projects. They allow the determination of the change in freight movements when transport projects are completed. The standard process for determining the change in freight movements or tonnages is:

- As assessment is made of the freight operation, it costs, speeds and frequency
- A number of options are identified for changing the freight network, and their cost assessed
- The new costs, frequencies, capacity, and loads are assessed for the completed project. It is almost always possible to determine what the new network capacity will be.
- The changed freight network will have improved performance characteristics. For example, the cost per movement of freight will change.
- The change in performance of the freight network is converted to a change in the number of freight movements through a demand elasticity.
- The change in freight movements is assessed on an economic basis, with the externalities and financial benefits included.
- The ratio of costs to benefits determined, to assess the benefit to society. Benefits should be higher than costs, and the greater the ratio of benefits to costs, the more likely a project will proceed

Governments of major countries will normally have determined a set of transport elasticises for different transport modes, and these should be used where possible. Smaller countries may not have any standard elasticises, so in producing any economic analysis recourse may be needed to some official government reports produced in the US or Europe, or maybe even Australia. These reports are numerous, and very easy to find on the internet.

Freight elasticises will change, depending on where they were conducted, and what industry is assessed. Rail freight industries the world over are not the same, and their economic characteristics may vary significantly. This is why it is important to use freight elasticises that are generated from the actual country in which the proposed project will take place. Where this is not available, then a comparable country should be used. For example, Canada and Australia would be reasonably comparable, being large in size, with resource based economies. Using freight transport elasticises for a country like Belgium, and then applying it to an African country, may be less wise.

Recall that the formula for elasticity of demand is:

$$E = \frac{(Q_2 - Q)_1 / Q_1}{(P_2 - P)_1 / P_1}$$

Where:

Q_1 = old quantity demanded
Q_2 = new quantity demanded
P1 = old price level
P2 = new price level

It is useful to include a summary of useful price elasticises in this book, but the exercise was difficult. Different studies produce dramatically different results, and there is very little consistency between them. Freight elasticises can be dramatically different between different commodities, even within the same country.

Freight Elasticities for Price		
Parameter	**Lower bound**	**Upper Bound**
Price (coal only)	-.1	-0.4
Price (wheat, corn)	-.5	-1.2
Other commodities	-0.4	-1.2

And yes, strictly speaking, the upper bound is in fact the lower bound as the numbers are negative. The reason the elasticises are negative is because a price increase results in a decrease of the amount of freight moved. The short term elasticises would all be much lower in absolute value than the ones presented above.

The above formula for price elasticity uses only price to determine future demand. This concept has been extended to apply to a wide variety of different measures and parameters, many of which are not denominated in dollars. The variable for price are replaced with others, for example, travel time, or punctuality. The underlying theory behind this substitution is a little shady, but it seems to be a common practice for forecasting future demand.

So the formula for future demand can then be written:

$$Q_2 = Q_1 \left(E \frac{(Pa_2 - Pa_1)}{Pa_1} + 1 \right)$$

Where:

Pa = any parameter relevant to the market

Economic/financial Performance of Rail Freight

Regardless of the taxation and support regime offered to rail freight, the financial and cost structure of a rail freight operation are also very important. Broadly, rail freight is more economical when more freight can be moved from one point to another, rather than road freight where freight can be moved in an almost infinite number of different paths. Rail freight thrives with consistent and regular loads, from one fixed destination to another. Rail freight has much higher fixed costs than road freight, and with any business with high fixed costs, large volumes are needed to spread the fixed costs out over many different freight movements.

Rail freight has a number of economic advantages of road transport, which are quite significant. These are:
- When purchased new, rail freight wagons have a much longer operating life than a truck. A truck may have a useful life of 10 years, depending on where it is used, and how often it is used, whereas rail wagons can last over 20 years, and in some cases 30 years. Trucks cannot last 30 years when used frequently

- Per dollar, rail wagons are able to carry far higher loads. Per tonne of capacity rail wagons are much cheaper than trucks, perhaps only half the cost or even lower.
- A one or two train crew, depending on the rules in the relevant railway, can move far greater amounts of freight than a truck driver. Many freight trains are over 1 kilometre long, and it is not unusual for an intermodal train to move 80 TEUs in one movement, and with double stacking even more
- The energy costs of rail freight movements are much lower, the energy required to move freight is a small fraction of the energy required to move freight on roads

Road transport does have many advantages over rail freight, and the main one is the lower handling costs, and terminal costs. The cost of loading a full intermodal train can be quite high, and this cost needs to be offset against the lower operating costs of the train per tonne per kilometre travelled. For longer trips, rail freight starts to become more cost competitive. Road transport is also far more flexible, and a truck loaded with a intermodal container can go almost anywhere, whereas rail freight is limited to terminals with rail connections.

It should be remembered that many customers and recipients of intermodal containers are not located next to rail terminals. This varies from country to country, and even within individual countries can vary significantly. Normally intermodal containers are trucked from one destination to another, or if travelling by rail, trucked from the origin to the rail hub, put onto a train, moved by rail to another terminus, and then unloaded and the trucked to its destination. Rail freight has two additional handling movements that are justified only if the cost of rail transport is much cheaper than road transport. Short distances seem to be almost impossible for rail transport unless there is some mitigating factor that makes rail more competitive.

The graph below shows the conventional wisdom on the cost of moving intermodal freight, based on the distance travelled. The point at which rail becomes more competitive than road freight will change for different countries, especially where there are government policies designed to encourage rail freight. Also the fuel price can have a large impact on the relative costs, with higher fuel prices tending to favour rail transport over road.

Cost Road Freight vs Rail Freight

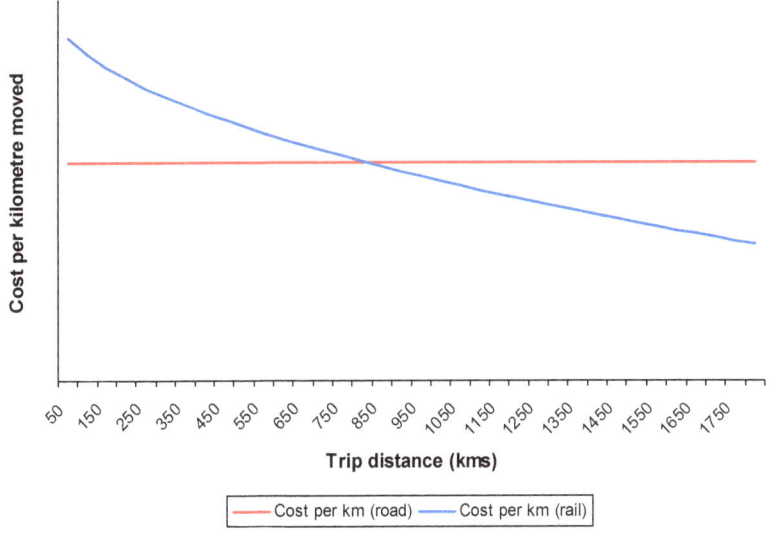

The major disadvantage of rail freight compared to road transport is flexibility. Road transport is very flexible, can go to almost any location, and is not dependent on timetables nor getting access to passenger networks for getting to the destination. This flexibility is the reason why road transport companies have captured such a large part of the intermodal container market, and why governments, even when spending large amounts of money in large capital projects, have such difficulty in increasing the modal share of rail freight companies.

Valuing Capacity of a Freight System

A freight system will have a finite capacity per hour, based on the number of tracks, the signalling system installed, and the terminal capacity on the system. Capacity on a rail system has a definite value, and the greater the capacity, the higher the value. This value is strongly linked to the value of the freight that is moved on the freight line, a freight line that has no freight at all, or almost none, is worth almost nothing.

It is useful to think of the capacity of a freight line in terms of its value. Freight lines with a high volume of freight, say over 50 MGT per year, can be valued in terms of capacity. The cost of capacity upgrades can be compared to the total value of the line, and if the value of the line can be increased with projects that cost less than that increase, then the project is justifiable, and should be approved. The value of a freight line will also depend on the speed at which trains can traverse the network, and the maximum permitted axle loads.

Many freight lines are provided as a community service to remote areas, and the value of the freight line is very low. There are many thinly used rail lines in Australia, and many of these lines move wheat. During harvest many rail lines may only move 1 or 2 trains per day, which is a small number. Outside harvest times there may be no traffic at all, and the use of the rail line may be seasonal. Capacity on these lines has a very low value.

Many projects can be identified to upgrade the capacity of large freight systems, and a large number of different projects are available. Different signalling systems, improvements to rollingstock, better terminal design, passing loops, or larger loading gauges are all possibilities. Freight companies, and the companies that manage the infrastructure, will be able to identify bottlenecks to the system, and then upgrade that part of the system. Once a bottleneck is removed, then another part of the system will become a bottleneck, and this can be removed, moving the bottleneck to another place, and so on. For each project there is a cost, and so the incremental improvement in a rail freight system can be valued. An analysis of the cost of each project will generate a estimate of the cost of generating that capacity. Where that cost is less than the value of the capacity, the project should be approved, all things being equal.

Construction of New Rail Freight Lines

Any major changes to a rail system need to pass through some sort of economic appraisal, or a justification process involving a business case. As part of that process, at attempt is made to predict or forecast the increase in freight traffic from the project. The most common, and best, way of doing this is described above with elasticises. Using elasticises means examining the current freight levels, and then attempting to identify the incremental change in freight traffic.

For new rail lines, this very sensible approach may not be able to be followed, because the increase is not incremental to an existing rail line, but is a new service in a new place. An entirely new rail line will require something different other than price elasticises. An alternative is to use information provided by freight operators, or sometimes the owners of businesses that generate freight. Many of those businesses are very large, and have the resources to estimate any change in traffic that occurs when they build new mines or factories and then connect a rail line to them. They will often make an approach to government, and attempt to convince government to build the infrastructure. As part of that approach, they may even offer a cost contribution to the construction cost, as a reward for government for completing the project. This type of offer can be very attractive to government.

Freight, mining and industrial companies often band together and form an industry body, which lobbies government for improvements to their infrastructure. The industry body will have some spokesperson that gives interviews, and appears on local or national television to promote their industry. They will also commission reports into infrastructure, which detail how things would be better if this of that is done. These reports are an extremely valuable source of information for any rail transport planner, and can contain a lot of information about the local rail system. These reports should not be discounted, even if the grammar is a little strange or the tone a little irate.

Governments also conduct large reviews of freight infrastructure, and during most reviews will call for submissions. This is a particularly useful time for freight companies to express an opinion, and the content of the submissions is very important. Key transport needs should be identified in these submissions, and any constraints that inhibit the successful movement of freight clearly explained. Once again these submissions are a useful source of information for the rail transport planner. Of course once the review is complete, then there will be some sort of report, and this also is very useful.

In rare cases an industry body may suggest improvements to rail freight systems without providing much detail. For well funded industries this will be rare, but for less affluent ones it may occur. In Australia this happens with wheat lines, which move only small amounts of traffic, and the wheat farmers do not have enough money to do any kind of review, or lobby government using spokespeople. This situation creates some real difficulties, as estimates of any future rail freight demand can be difficult to generate.

These types of freight lines, thinly used, present problems for the rail transport planner. They are rarely economically viable, and often survive with very limited funding, and sometimes even second hand rail materials discarded by other railways. Where worn rails are given to a thinly used rail line and then put into service, this is called "cascading", and it done for some rail lines that really have very little money at all. The best way to assess the value of these lines is to conduct a study into the minimum cost required to move the materials from farms, or whatever the origin of the freight is, to their final destination. If the minimum cost involves rail, then the government should use the rail system.

The process for this kind of review, for rarely used freight lines, is:
- Identifying the freight that needs to be moved, from origin to destination
- Identify any future trends for this freight market; it is going to grow, or shrink, or remain stable?
- Identify the different freight options that can serve the need
- Clearly identify the responsibilities of government in the movement of this freight, if any. Governmental responsibilities will vary with the industry and the region
- Perform some cost calculations to determine which transport mode is the cheapest to provide this service
- Identify the investment and consequently the cash flow required to provide this service. Governments may want to keep the costs low, but if large investments are required up front they may struggle to find the money
- Draw a conclusion on which transport mode should move the freight

This type of report can be completed by either consultants, or a government department. It is often filled with calculations on the damage caused to roads by trucks carrying the freight.

REFERENCES

1. Wardrop, A and Suess, P, *Strategies to Increase Line Capacity and Reduce Travel Time in a Mixed Passenger and Freight Corridor*, The Institution of Railway Signal Engineers Inc Australasian Section Incorporated, Nov 2009

2. Gifford, J. & Moore, T. *Axle Counters – For Heavy Rail Applications*, The Institution of Railway Signal Engineers Inc Australasian Section Incorporated, March 2007

3. Andersonn, M. *Marginal cost of railway infrastructure wear and tear for freight and passenger trains in Sweden*, Swedish National Road and Transport Research Institute (VTI), Department of Transport Economics, 2011

4. Hassan A *The Role of Light Railway in Sugarcane Transport in Egypt*, Infrastructure Design, Signalling and Security in Railway, Chapter 1

5. Wardrop, A. & Suess, P. *Strategies to Increase Line Capacity and Reduce Travel Time in a Mixed Passenger and Freight Corridor*, IRSE Australasia Technical Meeting – Sydney, Nov 2009

6. Joint Transport Research Centre of the OECD *Survey on price and demand elasticity in terms of reliability in freight railway services*, International Transport Forum, May 2008

7. West, R. et al *Identification and Evaluation of Freight Demand Factors*, National Cooperative Freight Research Program, Sept 2011

8. Beuthe, M. *Freight transportation demand elasticises: a geographical multimodal transportation network analysis*, Transportation Research Part E 37 (2001) 253 - 266

9. Troche, G. *High-speed rail freight*, KT Railway Group, Stockholm 2005

10. Shughart, L. *Trends and Issues in Container Transport*, TRF Annual Meeting, March 2012

11. Lin, CY. *Causal Analysis of Passenger Train Accidents on Freight Rail Corridors*, 2013 World Congress on Railway Research, November 2013, Sydney Australia

12. ABC Containers *ABC Container Guide*, http://www.abccontainers.com.au/downloads/abc-refrigerated-container-guide

13. Department of Infrastructure, *Transport, Regional Development & Local Government Adelaide Rail Freight Movements Study*, Oct 2009

14. Bureau of Infrastructure, Transport and Regional Economies, *Information Sheet 34 Road and Rail Freight, Competitors or Complements*, April 2009

14. Bureau of Infrastructure, Transport and Regional Economies, *Information Sheet 65 Australian Container Ports in an International Context*, Sept 2009

15. Woodburn, A. *The role of rail in port-based container freight flows*, Maritime Policy Management, Aug 2007, Vol 34, No 4, 311-330

16. Piyaatrapoomi, N et al Freight Intermodal Terminal Systems for Port of Brisbane, Melbourne, and Sydney, 2006, http://eprints.qut.edu.au

17. van Geldermalsen, T. & Leviny, D. Viability of Providing Double Stack Access on Railway Lines in SouthEast Australia, 28th Australasian Transport Research Forum,

http://www.atrf.info/papers/2005/2005_vangeldermalsen_leviny.pdf

18. Rahall, N. *Central Corridor Double-Stack Initiative Final Report*, Appalachian Transportation Institute, Feb 2003

19. Yang, Q. *How to Improve the Efficiency of Railway Freight Transport in the Urban Area?*, Service Operations and Logistics, and Infomatics, 2008

20. Freight Infrastructure Advisory Board *Railing Port Botany's Containers*, July 2005

21. Shipping Australia Ltd *Metropolitan Intermodal Terminal Study 2011*, http://www.transport.nsw.gov.au/sites/default/files/b2b/freight/rail-access-review-shipping-aust-mits-attachment.pdf

22. Iawasa, K. Rail *Freight in Japan – The Situation Today and Challenges for Tomorrow*, Japan Railway and Transport Review 26, Feb 2001

23. Sydney Ports Corporation *Intermodal Terminal Guide Metropolitan & Regional New South Wales*, October 2009

24. Colliers International *The National Intermodal Terminal Challenge*, 2010, www.colliers.com.au/research

25. BSL Management Consultants GmbH & Co. KG *Survey on price and demand elasticity in terms of reliability in freight railway services*, Hamburg May 2008

26. Bureau of Infrastructure, Transport and Regional Economies, *Report 114 Optimising harmonisation in the Australian railway industry*, 2006

27. Park, H. *Rail Freight Transport in NSW Briefing Paper No 8/09*, November 2009

28. Radosavljevic, A. *Measurement of train traction characteristics*, Proceedings of the Institution of Mechanical Engineers; Sept 2006; 220, F3; Proquest Central

29. Lukaszewicz, A. *Running resistance – results and analysis of full-scale tests with passenger and freight trains in Sweden*, Proceedings of the Institute of Mechanical Engineers; Jun 2007; 221, F2; Proquest Central

30. Andersson, M. *Marginal cost of railway infrastructure wear and tear for freight and passenger trains in Sweden*, European Transport no 48, (2011): 3 – 23

Chapter 9 Emissions and Rail Systems

Introduction

Trains require energy to move, and it is important for any transport system that energy consumption is managed as efficiently as possible. The consumption of energy is expensive, and there are negative effects from its consumption. Emissions from energy consumption are directly and linearly linked to the amount of energy consumed. There is much to be said about energy consumption for trains, and how to best manage it.

Much has been written about this topic, and power consumption by different modes of transport has been extensively studied. There has been a very high level of interest in energy consumption, for obvious reasons, and the internet abounds with many high quality research materials on the topic. Should the reader wish to learn more on this topic, then there are many high quality references available free of charge on the internet.

Almost all trains are powered by either electricity or diesel fuel. Electricity required for propulsion is almost always provided through physical contact with a wire or other lump of metal, and flows all the way from a power station to the train. Diesel locomotives and DMUs store the diesel fuel on the train, and it is burnt to produce the energy required to move the train. The process of burning the fuel, called combustion, produces CO_2 gas, which is a gas that contributes towards global warning. Both of these methods of producing power have their advantages and disadvantages. More unusual methods of driving trains exist, such as rollingstock being pulled by cables, or steam power.

Power is also consumed in trains in managing and providing auxiliary services. This includes air conditioning, which can consume quite of lot of power. In hot environments, such as South East Asia, air condition is greatly desired on trains by the local population, and many of the rail systems in that area are fully air conditioned. Depending on the weather, weight and speed of the train, air conditioning can be quite a large part of the power consumption of any train. Other systems in a train that carries passengers can also consume power, such as doors, lights, CCTV cameras, and other systems.

Steam power is almost never used any more for power for trains, despite its popularity and sex appeal. Steam trains were very difficult and time consuming to maintain, and expensive to operate. Steam engines needed to be constantly supplied with water, and less frequently with sand, and of course coal. Steam as a power source is no longer used in any significant way worldwide.

Where trains are powered by electricity, then it needs to be generated somewhere and then moved to where trains are operating. Power is created at an electricity generator, and then moved using transmission lines, or cables, to where the trains are. The engineering of moving electricity from a generator to a place where it is used is quite complex, but this technology is mature and standard, and mostly operates efficiently without much fuss. The generator of power can be many different types, and which type it is determines the level of output of carbon dioxide. This is sometimes referred to as the mix of power generation.

One question that commonly arises is; which produces more CO_2 gas; diesel or electric power? At first blush it would seem obvious that diesel power produces more CO_2 than electric power, but this depends almost entirely on the method of electricity production. Countries that rely heavily on coal to produce electricity have a very high level of emissions per unit of energy generated, and those that rely on renewable sources or nuclear power have very low levels of emissions. The mix of power generation in a country is a powerful factor in determining the level of emissions for the rail mode of transport.

The main different types of power generation are:
- Coal fired
- Gas turbines
- Solar
- Nuclear
- Wind
- Hydroelectric
- Oil

Power consumption is often converted into a total emissions figure, and to do this requires an estimate of the amount of power that a rail system consumes, and then how much was the volume of greenhouse gas that was released. Electric trains produce no emissions on their own, they consume electrical energy, which when consumed produces no CO_2. The process of producing electricity for consumption by a rail system does produce emissions, and so to calculate the level of emissions a link is needed between the electricity consumed and the level of emissions. This is easy where a rail system possesses its own electricity generation, but this is now rare, and mostly rail systems buy their power from the local power grid. Almost all power grids are a combination of many different electricity producers and suppliers, and it is customary not to separate out any one industry as being better than another when they are all connected to the same power grid. For this reason the rail industry is almost always assessed as producing emissions at the same level as the local power grid.

It's useful to make an attempt to compare the energy used for diesel trains with that from electricity. In theory this is possible, because in both cases the energy is used to move the train along, so a direct comparison should be possible. Unfortunately things are not that easy, and these comparisons usually produce some very strange outcomes. The problem is that diesel fuel contains a lot of energy, and it is converted into useful work at a rate that changes depending on the efficiency of the diesel motor. Only a small percentage of the energy in diesel can be converted to useful work, but the release of CO_2 is correlated to the amount of energy released, regardless of the efficiency of any motor. This can make comparisons rather unfair.

Another problem is estimating power losses in the electricity network that feeds any rail system. This includes any power stations or generators. Generating electricity is not perfect, and as it is generated some of the power is wasted as heat and noise. These losses need to be included otherwise the comparison is unfair once again. There are also power losses in any transmission network, and again, these need to be included. Not including all of these factors generates the impression that electric power is always far more preferable to diesel, which is not the case.

An attempt is made in this chapter to compare the different modes of transportation, and the power they consume. Included in this attempt are some calculations on the emissions generated per seat kilometre, and per passenger. There are many challenges with this kind of approach, and the major ones are:
- Stations and other facilities also consume a lot of power, and depending on the study and the railway these may or may not

be included. Up to half the power in any railway and potentially even more can be devoted to other rail related facilities, and their inclusion can dramatically change any calculation. As many studies in this area do not specify whether the power consumption for these facilities are included, direct comparisons are difficult. Rail systems often include power hungry facilities such as maintenance centres, or washing sheds.
- Some studies only analyse peak passenger loads. Passenger loading has a powerful effect on the efficiency of a transport mode, and rail is no exception. Are all rail services included in any analysis, or only the ones on weekdays or during the peak? Again, this is not made clear in the many studies published in this area
- The on-selling of electricity is common for rail systems, as they consume power in large volumes, it is cheap for railways to buy power, and then just as convenient to on sell it. In some cases remote towns or villages might be entirely powered by "rail" power, where the railway buys the power and distributes it, and then bills consumers. Surprisingly this is the case in NSW, where a number of small towns receive almost all their power from a railway. This can distort the energy figures substantially

So direct comparisons are difficult, and perhaps comparisons within studies are the best way to examine the power consumption of different modes of transportation. An attempt is made below to create a "league table" of different transport modes, and the quantity of power they consume in comparison to one another. But first some definitions and equations are needed.

Formulas and Calculations for Energy Consumption

The basic unit of energy is called the Joule, and is given the letter J. One thousand Joules is one kilo Joule, and this is given the abbreviation kJ. An even larger unit for energy is the Mega Joule, or 1 million Joules, and this is given the unit MJ.

The first law of thermodynamics states that energy is conserved, and cannot be created or destroyed. When used energy is converted to other forms, and electrical energy is often converted into heat. When it is said that energy is lost or consumed, it is actually converted into a different form and no longer usable.

Power is defined as the rate at which energy is consumed, or the total energy divided by the time it takes to use the energy. The formula for power is:

$$Power = \frac{Energy\ consumed}{time}$$

The units of energy of course are Joules, and time is seconds. The units of power are Watts, named after the Scottish engineer who dramatically improved the steam engine.

The most commonly used units for power are the kilowatt, which is one thousand watts. The physical meaning of this unit is the use of 1000 watts per second.

Energy consumption is often expressed in Kilowatt hours. Kilowatt hours are calculated by finding the amount of energy that is used at a rate of 1 kilowatt for 1 hour. In Joules, one kilowatt is:

$$1\ kilowatt\ hour = 3.6\ x\ 10^6\ Joules$$

As the kilowatt hour is the standard unit for billing for power, this is what is commonly used for power comparisons. Notice that it is a very large unit in terms of Joules.

There are a number of measures for power consumption per distance travelled, and these are listed below.

For electric trains:

$$Energy\ consumed\ per\ kilometre = \frac{Energy\ consumed}{Distance\ travelled}$$

$$Energy\ per\ seat\ kilometre = \frac{Energy\ consumed\ per\ km}{Number\ of\ seats\ in\ the\ train}$$

$$\text{Energy per unit capacity} = \frac{\text{Energy consumed per km}}{\text{No seats + No standing spaces}}$$

Energy per passenger kilometre
$$= \text{loading factor} \times \frac{\text{Energy consumed per km}}{\text{Number of seats in the train}}$$

Energy cost per seat km = Cost per kilowatt hour x energy per seat km

For diesel trains:

$$\text{Fuel consumed per seat kilometre} = \frac{\text{Fuel consumed per km}}{\text{Number of seats in the train}}$$

$$\text{Fuel consumed per unit capacity} = \frac{\text{Fuel consumed per km}}{\text{No seats + No standing spaces}}$$

Fuel consumed per passenger kilometre
$$= \text{loading factor} \times \frac{\text{Fuel consumed per km}}{\text{Number of seats in the train}}$$

Fuel cost per seat km = fuel cost per litre x fuel consumed per seat kilometre

Note that sometimes attempts are made to calculate the energy consumed for a diesel train per kilometre. It is not recommended to perform this comparison, as the energy content of diesel fuel is very high, so the figures for diesel are always extremely high in comparison to electric powered trains. A much better way to compare is to use CO_2 emissions, and the formulas for this are presented below.

For emissions, for electric trains:

CO_2 emissions per pass kilometre = CO_2 per kilowatt x Energy per passenger kilometre

For emissions, for diesel trains:

$$CO_2\ emissions\ per\ pass\ kilometre = CO_2\ per\ litre\ of\ fuel \times Fuel\ per\ passenger\ kilometre$$

It's best when calculating power consumption to use metric units, such as Joules, rather than such units as BTUs and others.

For freight, the standard unit is CO_2 emissions per tonne kilometre, which can be calculated from the formula below:

$$CO_2\ emissions\ per\ tonne\ kilometre = CO_2\ per\ litre\ of\ fuel \times \frac{fuel\ consumed\ per\ km}{tonnes\ moved}$$

As freight is mostly moved with diesel locomotives, this is normally how emissions are calculated for freight. There are of course some exceptions to this, and there is a coal line is Australia that is electrified and moves bulk freight to port, so it is possible for freight to be moved with electric power. Nonetheless in this chapter diesel will be assumed to be the standard fuel source for freight trains.

CO_2 Emissions per Kilowatt hour per Country

The emissions per kilowatt hr varies substantially from country to country. As mentioned above, this can impact upon rail planning decisions as it is desirable for a rail system to produce as low emissions as possible. There are tables published in reports on the emissions per kilowatt hr, and extracted below are some of those. These numbers were current around 2012. The differences between countries can be ascribed to a variety of reasons, such as the availability of fuel, the number of rivers that can be dammed to use for hydroelectricity, and a range of other factors.

| Emissions Per Kilowatt Hour ||||
Country	Grams CO_2 per kilowatt hr	Country	Grams CO_2 per kilowatt hr
Canada	186	Germany	461
Mexico	455	Iceland	0
USA	522	Poland	781
Australia	841	Spain	238
Israel	689	UK	457
Japan	416	Russia	639
Korea	533	China	766
New Zealand	150	Taiwan	768
Austria	188	India	912
France	79	Hong Kong	723
Malaysia	727	Singapore	499

The data was extracted from "IEA Statistics", 2012 edition, International Energy Agency.

The country with the highest emissions per kilowatt hour is India, with its heavy dependence on coal. The emissions per kilowatt hour is really dependent on the fuel source used to generate the electricity, coal produces a lot of emissions, and hydroelectricity and nuclear power produce nothing. Many countries have a mix of these energy sources, which is why there is such a large range in the emissions per kilowatt hour.

Power Consumption and the Population Density of Cities

Global warming is a serious issue, and the emission of global warming gases is something that, as much as possible, countries should attempt to avoid. Railways are a key part of this situation, and are a very effective way for entire cities and countries to reduce their emissions.

Encouraging citizens, residents and visitors to use public transport can be a very effective way of reducing emissions. The emissions from cars and private vehicles is far higher than for public transport, and moving people into public transport will reduce emissions. There is however much more to this story, and the population density of any city is also very important. If a city builds apartments, and high rise buildings, then the population density of the city is higher, and the overall size of the city is lower. This makes public transportation much more attractive, and much easier to use. A higher population density makes public transport much easier to economically justify, and a smaller number of lines will be more effective in moving people around the city.

The population density of a city is for some, in countries like Canada and Australia, a passionate issue. Whilst in Asia and Europe cities typically have very high population densities, this is uncommon in Australia, Canada and the US. The internet has many discussion pages where arguments are made for low population densities, and this is not seen as a problem for providing cost effective public transportation. These public discussions sometimes get very heated.

The reality is of course that more dense cities require less energy for transportation, and public transportation works much better with people concentrated into small areas. The graph below was extracted from a paper called *"Transport Energy Use and Greenhouses in Urban Passenger Transport Systems: A Study of 84 Global Cities"*, and demonstrates the concept quite well. This graph shows the energy consumed for transportation based on a large number of cities, and there was a clear relationship between the population density and the energy consumed.

Energy Consumer per Person (MJoules)

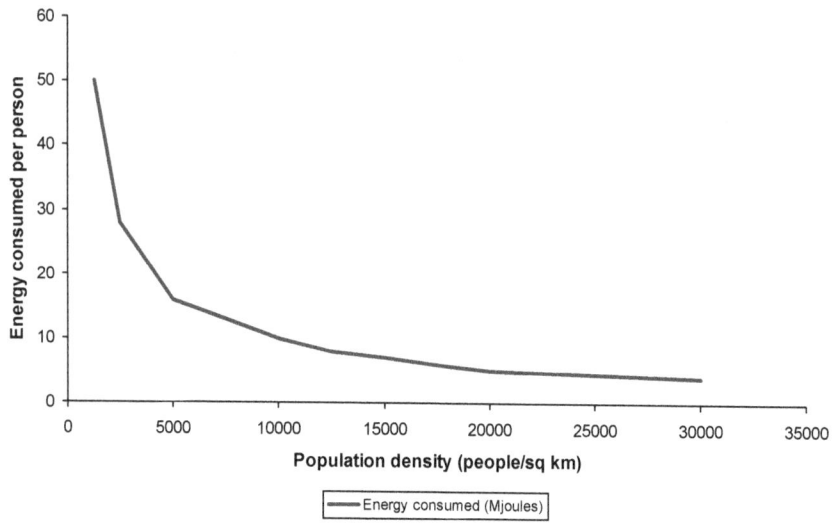

This data was calculated for 84 cities, and represents real data, not a theoretical calculation. We can see that the energy consumed per person falls dramatically as the population density increases. Most of this benefit is realised for cities where the population density is over 10,000 people per square kilometre.

There are two reasons why the energy consumed per person drops so rapidly, and these are:
- The city is smaller in size, as a higher population density means that trips throughout the city are much shorter in distance
- Public transport becomes more efficient, and the smaller size of the city means that the rail or bus system reaches more people

Many cities in Canada, Australia, and the US have population densities of less than 2000 per square kilometre. This is very low, and it is difficult to provide effective public transport in cities of this size. Brisbane in Queensland has a population density of only 350 people per square kilometre, and this ludicrously low number makes rail transport difficult to provide economically.

We note that cities with population densities of less than 2000 people per square kilometre can be very large. Australian cities are enormous, and a trip from one end to another takes hours. Even very large numbers of stations and rail lines are not enough to remove many of the cars from city streets, and the traffic every where is terrible. Rail transport planning in this environment can be a nightmare, because there are never enough people to justify the large expenditure required to build a rail line or system, and HSR systems are impossible because the urban area is large and too expensive to build through. And of course the emissions per person are very high, and the entire situation is really very unpleasant.

Note that this type of city is not only confined to Australia, the US, and Canada. The Chinese city of Ningbo has a low population density, about 770 people per square kilometre, and is similarly spread out over a very large area. Ningbo has 7 million people in it, so a city with a population density this low will have a very large urban area.

REFERENCES

1. Bombardier, *EcoActive Technologies Mitrac Energy Saver*, www.bombardier.com

2. Kenworthy, J. *Transport Energy Use and Greenhouse Gases in Urban Passenger Transport Systems: A Study of 84 Global Cities, Institute for Sustainability and Technology Policy*, Murdoch University

3. Dearien, J. *Ultralight Rail and Energy Use*, Encyclopaedia of Energy, Elsevier Publishing, March 2004

4. Romo, L.& Turner, D. & NG, L.S. Brian *Cutting Traction Power Costs with Wayside Energy Storage Systems in Rail Transit Systems*, Proceedings of JRC2005, Joint Rail Conference, March 2005

5. Halcrow, *Energy Efficiency Opportunities Study Driving Style Modelling* ED-003-012, April 2011

6. World Nuclear Organisation, *Comparison of Lifecycle Greenhouse Gas Emissions of Various Electricity Generation Sources*, http://www.world-nuclear.org/uploadedFiles/org/WNA/Publications/Working_Group_Reports/comparison_of_lifecycle.pdf

7. Jernbaneverket, *Environmental Analysis Energy Consumption – Norwegian High Speed Railway Project Phase 3*, Dec 2011

8. Network Rail, *Comparing the environmental impact of conventional and high speed rail*, www.networkrail.co.uk/5878

9. Leung Michael KH *Carbon Emission Factors for Public Transportation in Metropolitan*, International Conference on Carbon Reduction, Sept 2010

10. Carruthers, J.J. et al *The application of a systematic approach to material selection for the lightweighting of metro vehicles*, Proc. IMechE Vol. 223 Part F: J. Rail and Rapid Transit, May 2009

11. Falvo, M.C. *Energy Saving in Metro-Transit Systems: Impact of Braking Energy Management*, SPEEDAM 2010, International Symposium on Power Electronics, Electrical Drives, Automation and Motion

12. RATP Group 2012 Sustainability Report, http://www.ratp.fr/en/ratp/c_5367/our-essential-documents/

13. Win van Beek The Effects of Speed Measures on Air Pollution and Traffic Safety, The Association for European Transport, 2008

14. Yangzhen, Z et al *A Simulation Model of Energy Efficient Automatic Train Control* (ATC 1999), http://citeseerx.ist.psu.edu/viewdoc/summary?doi=10.1.1.508.9800

15. Kemp, R. *T618 – Traction Energy Metrics*, No 2, Rail Safety and Standards Board, Engineering, Dec 2007

16. International Energy Agency, *Transport Energy and CO_2*, 2009, https://www.iea.org/publications/freepublications/publication/transport2009.pdf

17. Defra, *2012 Guidelines to Defra/DECC's GHG Conversion Factors for Company Reporting*, https://www.gov.uk/government/uploads/system/uploads/attachment_data/file/69554/pb13773-ghg-conversion-factors-2012.pdf

18. Lang, P. *Emission Cuts Realities – Electricity Generation*, Jan 2010, http://bravenewclimate.com/2010/01/09/emission-cuts-realities/

19. Commissioner for Environmental Sustainability Victoria, *Public transport's role in reducing greenhouse gas emissions*, July 2008

20. Dearien, J. *Ultralight Rail and Energy Use*, Encyclopedia of Energy, Elsevier Publishing, Cutler J. Cleveland, Editor-in-Chief, March 2004

21. Romo, L. et al *Cutting Traction Power Costs with Wayside Energy Storage Systems in Rail Transit Systems*, Proceedings of the JRC 2005 Conference March 2005 Colorado

22. Williams, M. & Schmid, L. *The Effect of Rail Running Surface Irregularities on Energy Consumption*, Railway Engineering Conference Newcastle Australia Oct 1993

23. Bae, C.H. et al *Simulation Study of Regenerative Inverter for DC Traction Substation*, Electrical Machines and Systems, 2005, ICEMs

24. Griffiths, M. *Energy management of traction power substations on the Dallas Area Rapid Transit System*, Proceedings of the 1999 ASME/IEEE Joint Railroad Conference , 1999

25. Henning, U. et al *Ultra low emission traction drive system for hybrid light rail*, SPEEDHAM 2006, International Symposium on Power Electronics, Electric Drives, Automation and Motion

26. Jong, J.C. & Chang, E.F. *Models for Estimating Energy Consumption of Electric Trains*, Journal of the Eastern Asia Society for Transportation Studies, Vol 6, pp 278 – 291, 2005

27. Tourism and Transport Forum Public Transport and Climate Change, Nov 2009, http://www.ttf.org.au/Content/ptclimatechange.aspx

28. Thong, M. & Cheong, A. *Energy Efficiency in Singapore's Rapid Transit System*, Journeys May 2012

29. Hong, W. & Kim, S. *A study on the energy consumption unit of subway stations in Korea*, Building and Environment 39 (2004) 1497 – 1503

30. Kennedy, C. *A comparison of the sustainability of public and private transportation systems: Study of the Greater Toronto Area*, Transportation 29: 459 – 493, 2002

31. Viswanathan, C.N et al *Energy Conservation in Subway Systems by Controlled Acceleration and Deceleration*, Energy Research, Vol 2, 133 – 151 (1978)

32. Oak Ridge National Laboratory, *Transportation Energy Data Book, Edition 29*, July 2010, cta.ornl.gov/data

Chapter 10 Power Consumption

Introduction

Rail systems are very energy efficient, and the use of a rail system will normally consume far less power than any other transport system for the same purpose. Rail systems require far less energy to perform the same function.

The lower power consumption is one of the great advantages of rail. In performing an economic assessment of the benefits of rail, special consideration should be made of the lower energy consumption. Depending on the government policy at the time, this may or may not be important to the decision maker for a new rail project. It is a real benefit, and should have significant value placed upon it.

Typical Values for Power Consumption

Below are summarised the results of many reports that have examined the energy consumption of different types of transport modes. An attempt has been made to summarise many different reports into a ranking of power consumption per passenger, or per seat kilometre. Problems abound with this approach, but for rail planning it's a necessary step. Many of the papers available are of varying quality, and separating out fact from fiction was not an easy process.

Technology has been improving, and the power consumption per passenger kilometre, and the fuel consumed per kilometre, has been dropping. This improvement has been steady for at least the past 20 years, so the power consumption and fuel figures listed below will change over time, and improve. References and reports produced more than 15 years ago often quote higher consumption figures, and the drop in power consumption per vehicle, and per passenger, has been quite substantial. No doubt in the future improvements will continue to be made, so it seems likely that the rankings in the tables below may change into the future.

Transport Modes Typical Values

Mode	Metric	Typical Value
Electricity		
Metro	Energy per pass km	14 - 60 watt hrs per pass km
Light rail	Energy per pass km	33 – 115 watt hrs per pass km
Tram	Energy per pass km	33 - 150 watt hrs per pass km
Intermediate capacity metro	Energy per pass km	20 – 200 watt hrs per pass km
HSR	Energy per pass km	30 – 55 watts hrs per pass km
Commuter rail	Energy per pass km	30 – 100 watt hrs per pass km
Diesel		
Bus	Fuel per pass km	12 – 60 ml per pass km
Minibus	Fuel per pass km	22.77 ml per pass km
Ferry	Fuel per pass km	850 ml per pass km
Regional train	Fuel per pass km	10 – 70 ml per pass km
Commuter rail	Fuel per pass km	10 – 40 ml per pass km

The numbers above should be treated with a great deal of caution. The power consumed by any railway per person can very by an enormous amount, and the rankings above are really only a rough guide. Nonetheless some important points should be made:

- A heavily loaded metro will always be the most power efficient per person, as people stand and many metros operate fully loaded
- Air and sea transport is wasteful of energy in comparison to rail, and is always less efficient
- High Speed rail is surprisingly efficient, and very similar to commuter and regional rail systems

There are an enormous number of factors that could potentially change the energy consumption per person. Perhaps the most important is the loading factor, which can substantially change the energy efficiency per person, because most of the weight of trains is in the body of the train, and the weight of passengers is small in comparison, so increasing the number of people always improves the energy efficiency. So it is always energy efficient to pack as many people as possible into each vehicle.

The table below is a list of the different types of rail systems and how they are powered. Electric systems will draw their power from the location power grid, and diesel systems use fuel. As diesel fuel is largely standard between different countries, emissions from diesel are vary little from system to system. Alternatively emissions from electric trains varies enormously, and the same train with the same number of passengers can different emissions, even on the same trip from one country to another.

Type of power used to Drive Transport Mode	
Transport Mode	**Power source**
Metro train	Electric
Intermediate capacity metro	Electric
Commuter/regional	Electric or diesel
High Speed Rail	Mostly electric
Light rail	Mostly electric
Trams	Mostly electric
Buses	Mostly diesel or LPG, some electric
Minibus	Mostly diesel or LPG
Long haul air travel	Aviation fuel
Taxi	Petrol or LPG
Short haul air travel	Aviation fuel
Ferries	Almost all diesel

It is sometimes suggested in papers on power consumption for transport that countries that have high emissions per kilowatt should stick to diesel, and those with very low emissions per kilowatt convert to electric powered trains. Whilst this argument is very convincing, the emissions of any country can change, and with an investment programme will change, and so it may be a little premature to commit to one fuel source or another where the input power generation mix may change. This may not the case for countries with large coal reserves, such as Australia or India, where it is highly likely that this dependence on coal for power generation will continue for decades.

Typical values for a variety of different measures are shown below. Notice again the large ranges for each different transport mode. The table below lists typical values for CO_2 emissions for different transport modes.

Transport Modes CO_2 Emissions Typical Values	
Mode	**Typical Value**
Metro	7 - 30 grams per pass km
Light rail	15 – 70 grams per pass km
Tram	17 – 75 grams per pass km
Intermediate capacity metro	12 – 100 grams per pass km
HSR	15 – 30 grams per pass km
Bus	30 – 100 grams per pass km
Minibus	60 grams per pass km
Ferry	2250 grams per pass km
Regional train	25 – 200 grams per pass km
Commuter rail	25 – 105 grams per pass km
Road Vehicles	
Small road vehicle < 1.4 litre engine (petrol)	153 grams per km
Medium road vehicle 1.4 – 2.0 litre engine (petrol)	190 grams per km
Large road vehicle > 2.0 litre engine (petrol)	260 grams per km
Aircraft	
Long distance air travel	100 grams per pass km
Short distance air travel	150 grams per pass km

Some commentary is needed for emissions for intermediate capacity metros. The technology of intermediate capacity metros is well developed, and very efficient, and it is possible to have a very efficient metro system using these smaller trains and stations. Where intermediate capacity systems have large numbers of passengers, and the loading factor is high, then they can be just as efficient as a full metro system. In practice however, the emissions of these systems is often terrible, and the system in Porto in Portugal and the Vancouver Skytrain, as well as the Docklands Light Rail are all very energy intensive, and very poor energy performers. These systems are very well designed, and should be highly efficient, and yet seem to be very wasteful with energy.

The answer seems to be the loading factors of the trains. As intermediate capacity metros are mostly driverless, they can operate at very high frequency. As a result, the loading factor of these systems is extremely low, and 20% seems to be a common figure. This is particularly so for the light rail system in Porto, and the Vancouver Skytrain. The high frequency of trains means that the capacity of the system is quite high, and can be 8,000 to 10,000 per hour, and this can be maintained outside of peak times because there are no driver salaries to be paid. Whilst these numbers are small compared to metros, they are large compared to almost all other rail systems, for example, for intensively used commuter systems even 6,000 per hour is high. The result seems to be that most of these rail systems operate almost empty, and the author's experience on the intermediate capacity metro in Malaysia was the same. The grim truth for many of these systems is that they probably didn't have the passenger numbers in nearby areas to justify the service when constructed, and the aim of building the system was to create demand by providing the service. This can mean that when calculating the energy efficiency of intermediate capacity metros they can rate very poorly.

Intermediate capacity metros can also serve a purpose of encouraging rail demand in an area. As the trains and stations are small, and often driverless, providing the service can be cheap enough to run a high frequency system that encourages people to use the system more. A very high frequency rail system can be very attractive to people living in that area, and over time the system will attract more passengers. Nonetheless, in the interim, the energy consumption figures for intermediate capacity systems can be rather poor.

Regional trains have an enormous range for emissions and this is because again of the loading factor. Many regional trains are operated as a public service, and can be almost empty. Governments often want to support regional areas, and one way of doing this is providing uneconomic rail services to areas with little passenger traffic. This might sound harsh, and the benefit of this is that remote regional areas can have good quality transport services without large numbers of people. Because of the policy implications of providing services, energy consumption is not considered to be a priority and so energy efficiency can be a little low.

As an overall trend rail systems in Asia tend to be very efficient, and those in the English speaking world less so. Rail systems in Canada are quite efficient, and the country with the worst energy consumption per person seems to be the US. This difference between these countries is another of the reasons why the range for power consumption for even the same type of rail vehicle is so large.

Power Consumption for Freight

The following tables were extracted from an English report (listed in the references), and show the relativities quite well for the different transport modes for freight.

CO_2 emissions per Tonne Kilometre	
Transport Mode	**CO_2 emissions per Tonne Km**
Rigid van, 3.5 to 7.5 tonnes	591 grams CO_2 per tonne km
Rigid van, 7.5 to 17 tonnes	336 grams CO_2 per tonne km
Rigid van, > 17 tonnes	187 grams CO_2 per tonne km
Articulated van < 33 tonnes	163 grams CO_2 per tonne km
Articulated van > 33 tonnes	82 grams CO_2 per tonne km
Rail	21 grams CO_2 per tonne km
Small bulk carrier (marine)	11 grams CO_2 per tonne km
Large bulk carrier (marine)	7 grams CO_2 per tonne km
Small container vessel	15 grams CO_2 per tonne km
Large container vessel	13 grams CO_2 per tonne km

For air freight, the same report produced these figures:

CO$_2$ emissions per Tonne Kilometre	
Transport Mode	**CO$_2$ emissions per Tonne Km**
Domestic flights (UK)	1900 grams CO$_2$ per tonne km
Short haul flights	1320 grams CO$_2$ per tonne km
Long haul flights	1480 grams CO$_2$ per tonne km

Emissions for freight for flights is extremely high, and air freight is normally only used where the freight is very light or speed of delivery is required.

The numbers used here are drawn from *"2008 Guidelines to Defra's GHG Conversion factors: Methodology Paper for Transport Emissions Factors"*, written by the department of energy in the UK.

High Speed Rail and Energy Consumption

The energy consumed by high speed rail (HSR) is very important. As HSR trains travel large distances, and large numbers of people are moved, then it is critical to know how much power an HSR train will consume. The energy cost of moving large numbers of people with HSR is quite significant. Whilst this question is easy to propose, getting the answer is quite difficult.

The conventional wisdom is that HSR trains should consume large amounts of energy. Pushing against the air, at high speeds, should require large amounts of energy, and the faster trains go then the greater the energy consumption. It would be easy to assume that a trains travelling at 250 kms/hr would consume more power than one travelling at 100 kms/hr. Often, experiments have been performed that calculate the forces on trains, and they are almost expressed as a function of speed, and they always look like:

$$Force = a + bv + cv^2$$

Each of the terms in the above equation represent some part of the resistance to movement for each train, for example, the cv^2 part of the equation is often though to be related to aerodynamic drag, which is important at high speeds. The other terms are related to friction in the train, bogies, and wheels, which does not change with the speed of the train (or shouldn't anyway).

We also know that *Work = Force x distance*, and work is measured in Joules, so as the force increases then the energy consumed should also increase. So it is easy to expect that the energy consumed by HSR trains is very high, even at relatively moderate speeds.

In practice this is not the case. As surprising as it may seem, HSR trains travelling at 250 kms/hr consume the same energy per person as a regional or commuter train travelling at 100 kms/hr. The author, after first calculating this result refused to believe it, but there is no question that it is true. This value of energy consumption is one of the key reasons why HSR systems and technology are so desirable, and why many countries are considering installing them. But why, how can this be?

The author suggests the following reasons for the energy efficiency of HSR systems, and it is difficult to know which factor is more important than any other:
- HSR trains are aggressively streamlined, and so the aerodynamic drag is much lower than a conventional train
- HSR systems mostly are built on open ground, so energy is not wasted pushing air along a long tube
- HSR systems have very few stops, often 6 to 10 on one line, so stopping and starting occurs infrequently
- HSR trains are often able to maintain constant speeds from one end of the line to the other, so acceleration and deceleration is limited
- There are no large vertical curves in HSR systems, so trains rarely climb and descend hills, which can waste power, especially if the station is at the bottom of a hill
- HSR trains are very long, so the drag from the train per unit length will be lower for a longer train, as drag is mostly calculated relative the frontal cross-sectional area. IN practice a longer trains will have a higher aerodynamic drag, but a longer trains is always more energy efficient than two trains that add to the same length. One HSR trains may be the same length as three regional trains.

So for these reasons, energy consumption of HSR trains is similar to commuter and regional trains, and maybe a little more efficient. From an energy consumption perspective, this makes HSR trains very attractive.

The Shinkansen is the most energy efficient HSR train at the time of writing of this book (2012), and it seems that a number of innovations were employed to get the drag as low as possible, and these include:
- Further streamlining the front of the train
- Putting aerodynamic covers on everything underneath the train
- Making the outside of the train as smooth as possible, including the area where carriages are coupled together
- Reducing the number of pantographs from 8 to 2
- Designing a low drag pantograph, with a specially designed cover
- Even redesigning the windscreen wiper for the front of the train

The Japanese were partially motivated by the desire to reduce emissions, but also were motivated by the desire to reduce noise from the train, as much of the Japanese HSR system is built on slab concrete track, and that's noisy, so there was great political pressure to reduce the noise. As it turns out, reducing the noise is almost the same thing as reducing power consumption, so the Shinkansen trains became very energy efficient.

The graph below shows a comparison of the running resistance for two types of Shinkansen, the 300 series and the 700 series. This information was extracted from a paper published in 2000 called *"Improvement to the Aerodynamic Characteristics of Rollingstock"*. It shows the benefits of improved technology to the drag of HSR trains, and how reducing the drag effectively increases the maximum speed of the train. Since this paper was published the Japanese have built the E5 series Shinkansen train, and this train is even more streamlined than the 700 series.

Shinkansen and Drag

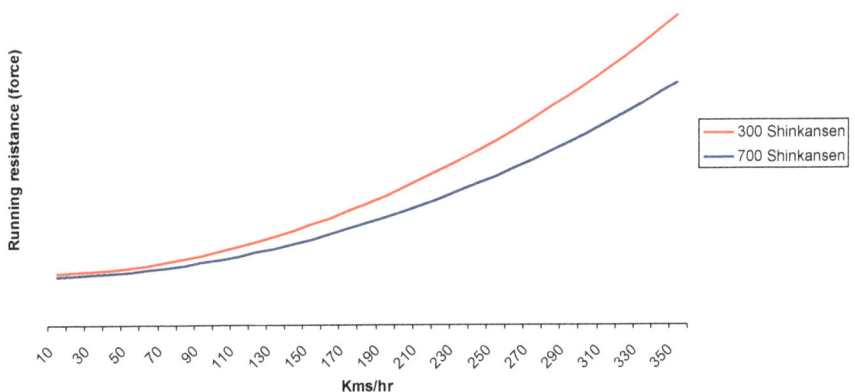

Notice that the running resistance increases at the power of 2 compared to the velocity.

It seems that the Japanese have settled on a energy consumption value of around 30 watts per seat kilometre. As their technology improves, they are able to increase the speed of their trains, but are currently limited to about 320 kms/hr. Their trains could probably go much faster than this, and modern European trains can do 350 -360 kms/hr, but as mentioned above, the noise restrictions on HSR trains within Japan means that they are not permitted to travel above these speeds. European trains seem to average about 50 watts per seat kilometre, which is a little high but not excessively so.

So what about the length of the HSR train, does this help with reducing the drag? Is this a more energy efficient option? It seems that increasing the length of the train does actually help, and the equation below shows the relationship between the different variables.

We start with the formula for the aerodynamic drag for a train:

$$D = \frac{1}{2}\rho A v^2 \left(C + \frac{\lambda}{d_h} l \right)$$

Where:

D = aerodynamic drag
ρ = density of air
v = velocity of the train
C = constant based on the drag caused by the front and back of the train
λ = constant for the drag from the surface of the side of the train
d_h = the hydraulic diameter of the train

The hydraulic diameter is a standard term used in flow calculations, for produced a diameter that is roughly the same, in terms of fluid flow, as the equivalent diameter for a round object. It is normally defined as follows:

$$d_h = \frac{4A}{P}$$

Where A = area, and P = the perimeter.

The only terms for this equation that could be found were for the Shinkansen 100 series train, which at the time of writing is an obsolete model and has been removed from service in Japan. Nonetheless, for the purposes of the analysis, we can assume that the relative weights of the drag coefficients are similar comparable to more modern trains. The numbers for this equation were:

$$D = \frac{1}{2}\rho A v^2 (0.15 + 0.004521)$$

From this equation we can see that drag increases linearly with length, but is quite large to begin with. The longer the train, the drag increases, but there is a large constant term, so per passenger, it's always better to make the train as long as possible. A length of 200 metres, from this equation, seems to be a reasonable compromise, and anything lower than this would be energy inefficient. A 300 metre train is better than a 200 metre one, and the energy consumed per person will be lower. Of course it would be helpful to have these coefficients for more modern trains.

So does HSR travel compare well with air travel? Above we saw that the figure to use for comparison with HSR for air travel was an emissions level of about 158 grams of CO_2 per passenger km. For the purposes of comparison, the table below shows all the different scenarios under which an HSR system might operate, and what the comparable emissions might be.

HSR type	Emissions	Load factor	Grams CO_2 per km per passenger km
European	High	30%	133
European	Low	30%	67
European	High	50%	80
European	Low	50%	40
Japanese	High	30%	80
Japanese	Low	30%	40
Japanese	High	50%	48
Japanese	Low	50%	24

Scenario Analysis – HSR – High and Low loading factors

The assumption was made that the Europeans have not improved their HSR technology so that it's similar with the Japanese, but it is likely that this gap in efficiency will soon close. A value of 800 grams per kilowatt hour was used for high emissions, and 400 grams per kilowatt hour for low. A value of 50 watts per seat kilometre was used for European HSR trains.

There is a lot to be said about this table. We can see that even the worst emitting HSR system produces less CO_2 than a domestic flight in the UK.

Also note that increasing the load factor is very helpful in reducing emissions. The graph below shows the effect of increasing the load factor on emissions per passenger km, and it's very helpful. We note that even the worst emitting train performs extremely well when it's full of passengers.

Emissions per Passenger Kilometre 700 Shinkansen

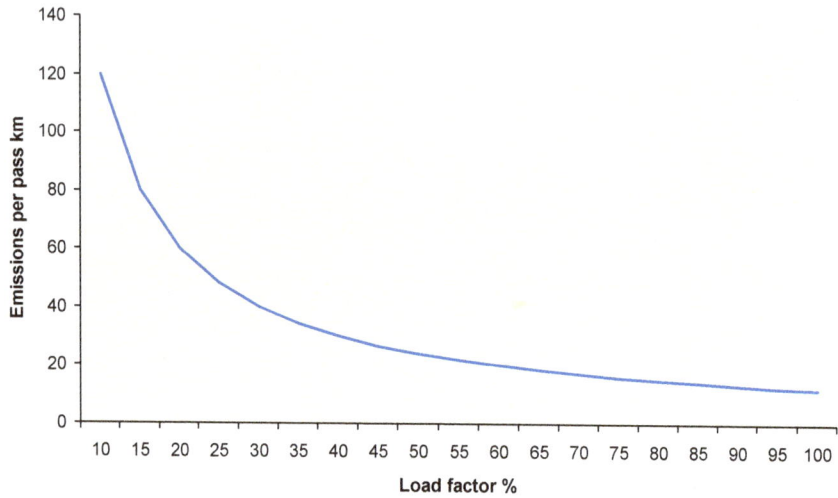

From this graph we see that a rail system really needs at least 30 – 40 % loads to be energy efficient, and for a well-designed rail system this should be no problem.

Diesel Vs Electric

Diesel powered trains have the advantage that they require less infrastructure. Overhead wiring, or alternatively a third rail, is not needed. To supply power to either the overhead or third rail systems, substantial infrastructure is needed, such as substations, transmission lines, and cabling running everywhere. This infrastructure requires a significant number of people to maintain, and the engineering skill set both difficult to trains for and retain, so the cost of wages for the maintainers is often quite high. The question is often asked; is this all worth it?

Electric power systems have a lot of problems associated with them, and these include:
- Anyone who touches the third rail or the overhead is usually killed instantly
- When performing maintenance, especially for track maintenance (i.e. fixing track geometry), the power needs to be switched off

- Accidental contact between equipment such as cranes and the overhead does happen, and this is a safety risk
- Substations, where the electricity is converted to the right voltage, sometimes catch fire and explode
- The presence of electricity in the rail corridor can cause electrolysis and other bizarre problems
- Electric overhead power line (the catenary and contact wire) are often considered ugly and unpleasant to look at

So if electric power is so problematic, then why is it installed? There are some advantages, and these include:
- In areas of large numbers of train movements, it's cheaper
- Tunnels and diesel trains are a bad combination, the smoke produced from diesel motors is unpleasant, and nasty to breathe in
- HSR diesel trains are limited to 200 kms/hr as a top speed
- Diesel motors are often considered to be dangerous to use in tunnels, and may require more infrastructure to accommodate their presence in the tunnel. In particular diesel trains introduce a fuel source into a tunnel, and it is possible for a poorly maintained diesel motor to explode
- In countries with low emissions per kilowatt hour, using electricity produces less emissions than diesel motors

One of the key questions for deciding to use electric powered trains, is the environment, and emissions. It's another important factor in the decision making. The commonly held view is that diesel trains are more polluting than electric trains, but this is not necessarily the case.

An attempt is made below to compare consumption of diesel and electric trains. Typical values are used to demonstrate which fuel source produces less emissions under certain circumstances. For the graph below it is assumed that 10 millilitres of diesel fuel is used for each seat kilometre, and 35 watts for each seat kilometre for electric trains. The CO_2 emitted for electric trains is calculated, and this is based on the amount of CO_2 emitted per kilowatt hr.

The quantity of CO_2 produced from a litre of diesel fuel is often assumed to be 2.65 kilograms of CO_2 per litre of diesel fuel. This number comes from an EU directive, 1999/100/EC, which is a directive concerning the level of emissions produced when testing cars. This number is specified in this directive, and it has become the defacto standard for the quality of CO_2 produced from diesel. In practice the actual figure can vary depending on the type of fuel and its source, but as a standard figure this one is useful.

Emissions Comparison Diesel vs Electric

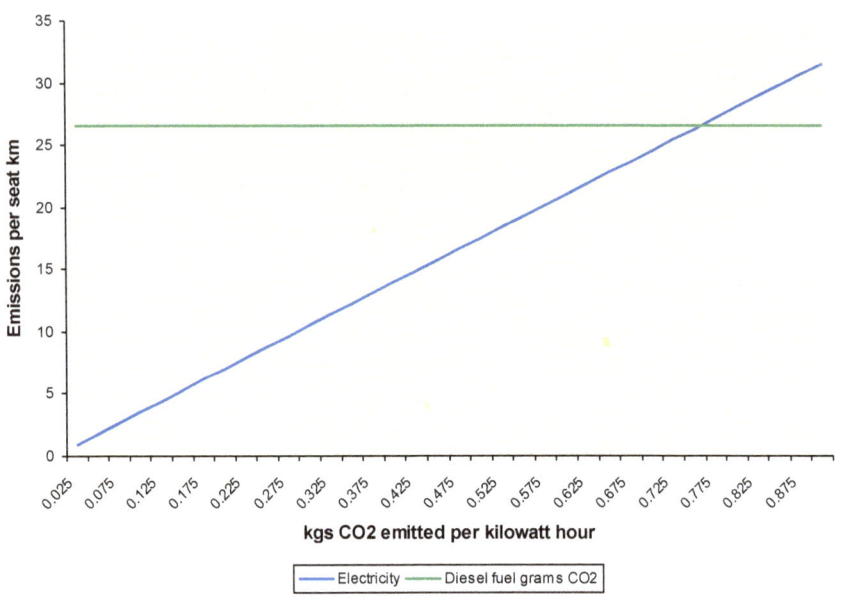

The blue line represents the emissions per seat kilometre with differing levels of emissions per kilowatt hr. Notice that for most of the graph that the blue line is lower than the green, and at very high values of emissions per kilowatt, it is possible for diesel trains to actually be more environmentally friendly than electric trains. This situation will be confined to countries where energy produced is dependent almost entirely on coal, such as Australia and India.

Overall most countries can reduce their emissions by changing their trains from diesel to electric.

Driving Trains Efficiency

It is possible for railways to minimise their power consumption through driving trains differently or more efficiently. For a railway that has already been built and commissioned this represents one of the few ways that power consumption can be reduced. Obviously changing driver behaviour is relatively cheap, so railways will always be interested in reducing power consumption this way.

There are two main ways to reduce power consumption, through driver behaviour. These are:
- Driving more slowly
- Driving the train in an efficient way

Driving the train in an efficient way refers to the way that a driver applies the power to the motor in the train. As with any motor, there are a number of settings for the amount of power applied to a motor, and the output of the motor increases as the power applies is increased. A number of studies have been performed to examine how to drive the train the best, and an optimal speed profile has been developed. Essentially, the best way to drive a train is to accelerate as hard as possible, and then coast until time to decelerate, and then decelerate as quickly as permitted for passenger comfort. This optimal speed profile is shown in the figure below.

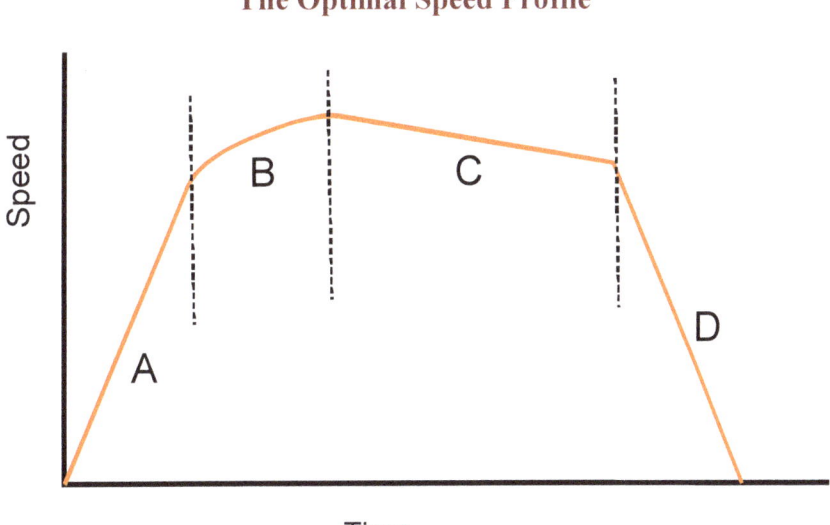

This graph has speed on the vertical axis, and time on the horizontal. As a train leaves a station it speeds up, and then slows its acceleration, coasts, and then decelerates. The time to get from one station to another as shown above may be only 1 or 2 minutes, or could be substantially longer.

Each of the stages in the speed profile are:
- A: acceleration away from the station
- B: tapering off of acceleration
- C: coasting, where no power is applied
- D: deceleration and stop

The height of the profile, ie, the final speed reached when leaving the station, as well as the acceleration, will determine how long the train takes to reach the next station.

It is particularly important that the train does not apply power throughout the entire distance, or until the end of section C.

The optimal speed profile can be calculated ahead of time, and then speed boards placed at the correct places alongside the track to indicate to drivers when to accelerate, stop accelerating and coast, and then decelerate. Without some guidance it may be a little difficult for all drivers to know when to apply power or to coast. One of the benefits of an ATP system is that it can, when designed to allow this, provide a target speed to the driver so that the motor and brakes can be applied at the correct time. Significant power savings are available for implementing this type of system, but it is unlikely to be a saving more than 10% of total power consumption.

Top speed is also very relevant, and has a profound effect on the energy consumed to drive trains. The energy and hence power consumed for a train, for short distances, can be very roughly approximated using the formula for kinetic energy, which is:

$$Kinetic\ energy = \frac{1}{2}mv^2$$

Where m = mass, and v = velocity in ms^{-1}. As the velocity increases, then the energy stored in the movement of the vehicle increases with the square of the velocity, so the energy consumed increases very quickly. This equation is rarely used for energy and power calculations for rolling stock, but does neatly illustrate the point, that increased speed increases power and energy consumption substantially. In practice there are losses associated with almost all aspects of transferring power from a power station to a train, and these would need to be considered as well to improve the accuracy of this equation.

So driving trains more slowly almost always reduces the power consumption, but from a customer perspective, is often unacceptable. It is sometimes possible to increase the acceleration of a train to compensate for a lower top speed, as acceleration is not a term in the above equation. For any given railway this may or may not be possible, as many different types of trains are limited in their maximum acceleration, or for passenger comfort purposes there are limits on the maximum acceleration. Nonetheless increasing the acceleration and reducing the velocity of a passenger train should reduce power consumption.

Power Consumed in Stations and other Facilities

The power consumed in stations, workshops, shops and cleaning equipment, can be a significant percentage of the power consumption for a railway. Certainly in Sydney the power consumed at stations is relatively low, as the pleasant and comfortable weather means that air conditioning at stations is rarely needed, something that consumes a lot of power. In Singapore on the other hand on some lines the power consumed in stations is greater than the power used for moving trains, and this is probably because of the need to air condition stations in that country. It is possible to achieve reductions in power consumption in stations, and below are some fairly standard measures that can be implemented in stations to reduce the power consumption:

- Platform screen doors retain the air conditioned air within the station. The are particularly effective in cities where the temperature is either very hold or cold
- Special lighting systems can reduce the power needed for lighting by about 30%. There are a number of different technologies, including voltage regulation and special types of fluorescent tubes
- Reducing the number of entrances and exits into the station
- Installing escalators that slow down when no one is using them. These escalators can detect when passengers step onto them
- Special types of lifts consume less power moving people up and down

- Overall the energy consumption of a station is usually proportional to its floor area, so smaller stations consume less energy
- Smaller numbers of escalators and lifts
- Installing solar panels on the rooves of outdoor stations
- Technology in stations, especially the air conditioning system, that can air condition the station more efficiently

These initiatives can reduce the power consumption in stations by up to 50%, and should be implemented where economically feasible to do so.

Much larger railways may have other facilities to which they need to provide power. Maintenance depots, or large facilities such as washing sheds, can be run from railways power. In some cases workshops, and machine tools such as lathes, can also be run from railways power. This is especially true where the workshop is located in a rail corridor, and away from any other power source or the local power provider.

Providing power to shops on stations is common in Australia, and is a good way to supplement income derived from leasing out parts of the station. It is not possible to find any publicly available information on what railways do in other parts of the world as regards on-selling power, but we can probably make some educated guesses on the conditions that increase the probability that railways on-sell power:
- Railways that consume large amounts of electricity are better equipped to on-sell electricity, those with only diesel trains may not be in a position to do so
- railways would on sell power to shops located on platforms, or wholly within the paid area
- where stations are located in places where there are no other buildings, then the railway is likely to provide the power
- where it is technically challenging to provide power to shops, ie, in a very strange place, the railway may provide the power as the local power company does not have the skills to do it

There are occasionally special situations where a railway may be required to supply power to facilities where there are no other providers. Examples include army facilities, hospitals, hotels and mines located in places where there is no other supply of power. In these cases the railway may need to supply power, and bill for its provision.

It is very difficult to reduce or even manage the power consumed by external parties, towns, workshops, or maintenance facilities. Where the power is supplied, it is not the railway's concern as to the size of the power consumption, unless the power consumed overloads the rail system power grid, in which case the something needs to be done. For reporting purposes any power on-sold should be excluded from any analysis of power consumption. Railways often set targets for energy consumption reduction, and including these makes things very difficult indeed.

Being more efficient with Power Consumption

It is important for a railway to attempt to minimising the consumption of power, and to be as energy efficient as possible. There are lots of things that can be done to reduce power consumption, and some are easy to implement, and some of them are politically difficult, or difficult to implement. These include:

- Reducing the mass of rollingstock, by using lighter materials such as aluminium
- As mentioned above, driving slower. A very unpopular option
- Operating trains with a high loading factor, which either means fewer services, or shorter trains. Neither of these options are popular with passengers
- Limiting the maximum speed of the train, and procuring trains designed for lower speeds
- Using special lubricants on top of the rail to reduce friction, and save power
- Using better electrical infrastructure with fewer energy losses
- Closing stations, or designed rail lines with fewer stations, so that trains do not need to accelerate or decelerate as often
- Operating a metro style system, where people stand, so only a small number of seats are needed
- Installing regenerative braking on rollingstock, or buying trains with this feature included
- Removing any grade crossings, ie, so that trains can accelerate and decelerate smoothly
- Streamlining rollingstock so that drag is minimised
- Increasing the length of carriages, so that the average weight per metre is reduced
- Single bore rather than twin bore tunnels

The best time to plan and implement any energy initiatives is when the railway is being constructed. Once a railway is built, it is very difficult to change the energy consumed. Most passengers will not accept slower travel times in exchange for lower power consumption, passengers are very sensitive to travel times, and so not want them increased. In some countries perhaps with very strong environmental sentiments, it may be possible politically to do this, but the author recommends not doing so. Rail as a system is a solution to reduce emissions and power consumption, and slowing trains down to save a small amount of power undermines one of the main benefits of the system by discouraging people from using the system.

It's really important for any rail system to reduce the weight of its rollingstock. Heavier trains require more power to move, so lighter trains are more energy efficient. Modern trains are a little lighter than trains 30 years ago, and much of this has been achieved by using more aluminium. It is possible to design the trains with lower weight by redesigning many of the fittings inside the train. Beware however that in many cases the weight of trains is increasing in some countries, as heavier trains are more crash resistant, and in the US and Australia some trains are heavier than a comparable train on the same rail line with the same stopping pattern than 20 years ago.

Streamlining is common on all modern rollingstock. Trains more recently manufactured have become progressively more and more streamlined, and this has reduced the drag they experience as they move. The appearance of many modern trains has changed as the streamlining has become more pronounced. Streamlining may even include the underneath of the train, and may include the bogies and the underside of the train. Significant energy efficiencies can be gained by streamlining the front of the train, especially low in front of the bogies. This is especially true of high speed trains, where streamlining underneath the train is common.

One thing that is commonly done is to the track at stations slightly raised in comparison to the track between stations, so that when the train comes to stop at the station, gravity assists. When the train departs from the station, it is assisted again by gravity, which pushes the train down. London Underground has this design on some of its lines. This is shown below.

Surprisingly only a few metres of depth between stations is needed to reduce the power consumption dramatically. To use the correct physics terms, when the train climbs to get to the station, energy is transferred from kinetic energy to potential energy, and when the train leaves the station, it is converted from potential to kinetic.

Raising the track at stations was a common practice even 50 years ago. Some water stations for steam trains were designed in this way, and placed at the top of hills.

Regenerative braking has become very popular with new rail systems. This type of braking involves storing kinetic energy from the moving train when the train brakes and comes to a stop. Until very recently when trains braked the energy was converted almost entirely into heat, and wasted. Modern trains are often equipped with regenerative braking, where the energy is "regenerated" and essentially can be used again. There are a number of different regenerative braking systems, and the most common is to use capacitors to store energy as a train comes to a stop. Once the train resumes motion, this stored energy may be used to accelerate the train.

Regenerative braking needs to be distinguished from dynamic braking, and occasionally these two things are confused. Dynamic braking is a type of braking where the kinetic energy is dissipated by using the motor to generate electricity when braking, and then sending this energy into a bank of resistors. It is a particularly efficient form of braking, but as with friction braking, the energy is wasted.

There are a number of different types of systems of energy storage used in regenerative braking, and it is also possible to put the energy back into this electricity grid, which is discussed below. Capacitors are commonly used for energy storage, and they need to be very high performance to be able store the power needed, and sometimes these capacitors used are called super capacitors. Capacitors electrically wear, and come with all sorts of problems, but many of these engineering problems seem to have been overcome.

Another way of storing the power generated in braking is to use flywheels. This is a mechanical system with spinning wheels, and they are heavy, and as the train decelerates the wheels spin faster and faster, storing the energy as rotational energy. If the train sits at a station for a long period of time, the flywheel will slow down and energy will be wasted, so it's a system that is more efficient where the train accelerates away from the station fairly quickly after coming to a stop.

As with any type of regenerative braking, energy is lost in the conversion from one type of energy to another. Energy is also lost if the train does not resume its motion as quickly as possible, and the stored energy is slowly dissipated as time progresses. There are also some potential risks with energy stored in batteries or similar, as very rarely batteries may explode, particularly when they are not handled correctly or properly maintained.

Another form of regenerative braking is to put the energy back into the power grid. Electrically powered trains can put energy back into the overhead wiring or third rail, so that it can be used by either other trains or in stations. Whilst in theory this idea is very good, in practice the energy put back into the overhead or third rail needs to be used by a train in the nearby area, i.e., at most a few kilometres away. A train on its own with no other trains or stations nearby, if it puts power back into the railway power system, will not achieve anything and the power will be wasted.

It is often not possible to put power back into the city or country power grid. One obvious way to deal with the power generated from regenerative braking is to put the power into the grid that supplies local houses and businesses. Whilst on paper this seems like a good idea, in practice it is often not possible. Railway power is often very dirty, and the quality of the power is low. In technical terms, the power is full of harmonics, which can damage or destroy electrical equipment. Railway power is often so dirty that only the railway itself will accept using for any purpose, and even then special equipment is needed to manage the power. This is unfortunate, as the often occurs that a lone train is passing through the country or regional area, and putting its braking energy back into the power grid would solve a lot of problems. This is especially true of trains powered with DC power.

It should be noted that regenerative braking can only save around 10-20% of the power consumed. It might seem that much more than this can be saved, but no. Losses in conversion of the energy are significant, but more importantly, regenerative braking only works at moderate to high speeds, and at low speeds traditional friction brakes are needed. Regenerative braking is often used in combination with friction brakes, and almost never used on their own.

Twin bore tunnels are less energy efficient than single bore. In the paper *"Twin-tube, Single track high speed rail tunnels and consequences for aerodynamics, climate, equipment and ventilation"* a graph is provided that would suggest that energy consumption in a single bore tunnel is about 20% lower than that of a twin bore tunnel. The key to reducing the power consumed in a tunnel would be to decrease the blockage ratio, which is the ratio of the train area to the area of the tunnel. A smaller area will mean less energy is wasted accelerating air in the tunnel when a train passes through, and hence is more energy efficient.

It is also possible to reduce the power consumption by applying lubricants to the top of the rail. This very interesting area offers opportunities to reduce the power consumption with just applying oils and grease to the top and side of the rail. A device exists called a rail lubricator, and it stores and pumps out lubricant as trains pass over the rail. It's a standard and common technology. This is typically done for freight traffic rather than passenger, and in freight systems so doing is common. Whilst there is a lot of argument in several papers on this topic as to the exact benefit, and the existence of any kind of benefit seems controversial, an energy saving of 10% seems typical. The benefit for a passenger rail system seems to be less than that of a freight system.

REFERENCES

1. Bombardier, *EcoActive Technologies Mitrac Energy Saver*, www.bombardier.com

2. Kenworthy, J. *Transport Energy Use and Greenhouse Gases in Urban Passenger Transport Systems: A Study of 84 Global Cities, Institute for Sustainability and Technology Policy*, Murdoch University

3. Dearien, J. *Ultralight Rail and Energy Use*, Encyclopaedia of Energy, Elsevier Publishing, March 2004

4. Romo, L.& Turner, D. & NG, L.S. Brian *Cutting Traction Power Costs with Wayside Energy Storage Systems in Rail Transit Systems*, Proceedings of JRC2005, Joint Rail Conference, March 2005

5. Halcrow, *Energy Efficiency Opportunities Study Driving Style Modelling* ED-003-012, April 2011

6. World Nuclear Organisation, *Comparison of Lifecycle Greenhouse Gas Emissions of Various Electricity Generation Sources*, http://www.world-nuclear.org/uploadedFiles/org/WNA/Publications/Working_Group_Reports/comparison_of_lifecycle.pdf

7. Jernbaneverket, *Environmental Analysis Energy Consumption – Norwegian High Speed Railway Project Phase 3*, Dec 2011

8. Network Rail, *Comparing the environmental impact of conventional and high speed rail*, www.networkrail.co.uk/5878

9. Leung Michael KH *Carbon Emission Factors for Public Transportation in Metropolitan*, International Conference on Carbon Reduction, Sept 2010

10. Carruthers, J.J. et al *The application of a systematic approach to material selection for the lightweighting of metro vehicles*, Proc. IMechE Vol. 223 Part F: J. Rail and Rapid Transit, May 2009

11. Falvo, M.C. *Energy Saving in Metro-Transit Systems: Impact of Braking Energy Management*, SPEEDAM 2010, International Symposium on Power Electronics, Electrical Drives, Automation and Motion

12. RATP Group 2012 Sustainability Report, http://www.ratp.fr/en/ratp/c_5367/our-essential-documents/

13. Win van Beek The Effects of Speed Measures on Air Pollution and Traffic Safety, The Association for European Transport, 2008

14. Yangzhen, Z et al *A Simulation Model of Energy Efficient Automatic Train Control* (ATC 1999), http://citeseerx.ist.psu.edu/viewdoc/summary?doi=10.1.1.508.9800

15. Kemp, R. *T618 – Traction Energy Metrics*, No 2, Rail Safety and Standards Board, Engineering, Dec 2007

16. International Energy Agency, *Transport Energy and CO_2*, 2009, https://www.iea.org/publications/freepublications/publication/transport2009.pdf

17. Defra, *2012 Guidelines to Defra/DECC's GHG Conversion Factors for Company Reporting*, https://www.gov.uk/government/uploads/system/uploads/attachment_data/file/69554/pb13773-ghg-conversion-factors-2012.pdf

18. Lang, P. *Emission Cuts Realities – Electricity Generation*, Jan 2010, http://bravenewclimate.com/2010/01/09/emission-cuts-realities/

19. Commissioner for Environmental Sustainability Victoria, *Public transport's role in reducing greenhouse gas emissions*, July 2008

20. Dearien, J. *Ultralight Rail and Energy Use*, Encyclopedia of Energy, Elsevier Publishing, Cutler J. Cleveland, Editor-in-Chief, March 2004

21. Romo, L. et al *Cutting Traction Power Costs with Wayside Energy Storage Systems in Rail Transit Systems*, Proceedings of the JRC 2005 Conference March 2005 Colorado

22. Williams, M. & Schmid, L. *The Effect of Rail Running Surface Irregularities on Energy Consumption*, Railway Engineering Conference Newcastle Australia Oct 1993

23. Bae, C.H. et al *Simulation Study of Regenerative Inverter for DC Traction Substation*, Electrical Machines and Systems, 2005, ICEMs

24. Griffiths, M. *Energy management of traction power substations on the Dallas Area Rapid Transit System*, Proceedings of the 1999 ASME/IEEE Joint Railroad Conference , 1999

25. Henning, U. et al *Ultra low emission traction drive system for hybrid light rail*, SPEEDHAM 2006, International Symposium on Power Electronics, Electric Drives, Automation and Motion

26. Jong, J.C. & Chang, E.F. *Models for Estimating Energy Consumption of Electric Trains*, Journal of the Eastern Asia Society for Transportation Studies, Vol 6, pp 278 – 291, 2005

27. Tourism and Transport Forum Public Transport and Climate Change, Nov 2009, http://www.ttf.org.au/Content/ptclimatechange.aspx

28. Thong, M. & Cheong, A. *Energy Efficiency in Singapore's Rapid Transit System*, Journeys May 2012

29. Hong, W. & Kim, S. *A study on the energy consumption unit of subway stations in Korea*, Building and Environment 39 (2004) 1497 – 1503

30. Kennedy, C. *A comparison of the sustainability of public and private transportation systems: Study of the Greater Toronto Area*, Transportation 29: 459 – 493, 2002

31. Viswanathan, C.N et al *Energy Conservation in Subway Systems by Controlled Acceleration and Deceleration*, Energy Research, Vol 2, 133 – 151 (1978)

32. Oak Ridge National Laboratory, *Transportation Energy Data Book, Edition 29*, July 2010, cta.ornl.gov/data

Chapter 11 Frequencies of Trains and Service Hours

One of the most important decisions for any rail system is the service frequency, and the hours of operations of any new line or rail service, be it for passenger or freight. Service frequency and hours of operation are important variables, and strongly influence the perception of success or failure of a rail system. A railway that has only a small number of rail services per day may be perceived to be a failure. Likewise, where trains are strongly limited on the hours they can operate, again, this may defeat the purpose of the construction of any rail line.

Service frequency should be made on the basis of the greatest benefit to society, and hence this topic is in this book. The economic benefit to society should be maximised through the provision of rail services at the right frequency.

There is rarely any engineering reason why trains cannot run 24 hours a day, 7 days a week, most of the time. There will however need to be times when maintenance is performed, and this will act as a limitor on the maximum possible service hours. In many cases this limit will never reached, as the demand for rail will not require trains to operate at all hours of the day and week. Sometimes, however, very in demand rail services will need to be interrupted for essential maintenance to be performed. Otherwise the rail system will degrade and be unable to provide service at all, or under heavily degraded conditions.

Once a rail system or line is constructed the maximum service frequency is limited to what was designed and installed, and without a major project to change it, this is what the rail line can offer. Great care needs to be exercised in determining what the design headways should be for any rail line. In many other cases however, the maximum is never reached, and the total number of services is limited by other factors, such as the number of passengers, or the economic benefit of operating rail services, or the amount of rollingstock available. This is especially the case outside of peak periods, where there may not be enough passengers to run services at a high frequency.

Network design too can play a large role in limiting the number of services. For rail systems where multiple lines combine into one more busy rail line, often in a flat junction, then the limit on the number of services will be the most congested line. Here network design is key, and a poor design will limit the number of services that are needed in busy areas. For the commuter railways in Australia this is often the case, and the limiting factor is the maximum possible frequency of trains through the city centre. Questions about the economic frequency of services rarely arises, but sometimes this question is asked about the number of services away from peak periods. In smaller towns the formulas presented here are very useful.

What this chapter is about is determining the service hours and frequency of a rail system where there other limits on the number of rail services has not been reached, and an economic decision is needed on how many trains to operate, or more accurately, the train frequency. In this specific case there are economic formulas to use to determine this answer, and these are discussed and applied.

Recall that many passenger service rail lines have something called a peak period, and road traffic in large cities has peak periods as well. Peak times are when the number of rail services are at a maximum and is at the maximum possible level as per the headway, or sometimes even more. A term that is sometimes used is the "shoulder period", and it represents a time before and after a peak period where service frequency is still high, but not as high as the peak period. Outside of these two times is the off-peak period, where there are limited numbers of services. The last remaining time period is the one where there are no services at all.

For rail systems where passenger services are mixed with freight, they may be a curfew period where freight trains are prohibited from entering the rail system until the peak period has ended. Curfews are extremely irritating for freight companies, and they limit the efficiency of the freight operation. Curfew periods affect the profitability of their rail operations significantly, and a late running freight train can be held in the most awkward position waiting for the curfew to end. Curfews are also sometimes imposed because freight trains are very noisy. In any event, where curfews are imposed then this needs to be clear in the planning stage of any new rail line.

So how to describe the frequency of trains? When the question is asked, how to respond? Well, the type of information that is normally provided is:
- When the peak period is, between what times?
- The number of services per hour, in peak periods. This is also called the frequency
- Any curfews for freight, if there are any
- Service periods, when trains are operational, and when the line is closed.
- The mix of traffic, the number of express services and all stopping services

This is usually enough information to explain how many services will operate and when they will operate.

Choosing a train frequency (and headway)

Setting the frequencies of trains for an already constructed rail line is normally the responsibility of the operational railway, and this decision is made based on operational reasons. Factors affecting this decision includes the number of passengers who wish to travel, the number of train sets available, or where to stable these trains, or a number of other reasons. For example, the railway might have only limited number of trains available, or providing there are limitations to the amount of power that can be provided to move trains around. Rostering of crews and drivers may also be difficult. Other issues such as decanting of toilets on trains, or cleaning of trains, can be important as well.

Remember that the maximum number of trains that can move down a rail line is determined by the headway, but it is not necessary for a railway to send the maximum number of trains all day. Where passenger loads are lighter, then there is every reason to reduce the number of trains. When moving from a peak to non-peak period, a number of trains may be removed from operation, and stabled somewhere.

Passengers always want the maximum service frequency, as this speeds their journey, and is more convenient. Railways often want a low service frequency, requiring a smaller number of trains, fewer staff, more efficient operation, and lower power consumption. Rollingstock wears when it is used, wheels wear down, the carbon strip on the pantograph will wear away, and generally there is a lot more maintenance to do on a train that moves around all the time. So there is a conflict between passengers who want more services, and rail operators who want to be more efficient and provide less. A decision is needed on the number, and it's best to have a clear process to determine how many trains should operate, and some methods to do this are listed below.

Remember that during the design and construction of a rail line that the minimum headway will be determined. Higher headways are much cheaper to build and maintain, and less equipment is needed, so there will be a temptation to increase the headway as much as possible. It would be a terrible shame however for the headway to be too high for what is needed on the line, so some care is needed in choosing what the headway should be. A common headway is about 3 minutes, which is related to the type of signalling equipment installed.

Many rail systems, especially metros, operate without a publicly available timetable, and this is often seen as being an efficient way to operate. The rail operator naturally will have their own internal timetable, called a working timetable, but only the rail operator and staff will be able to view it. So even without a publicly available timetable, the service frequency is still known and controlled. It would be ridiculous for a railway without a timetable to send trains randomly down a rail line, even if passengers cannot check to see what trains should be arriving, a rail operator should know when and where trains are and how many are needed to meet service frequency requirements.

Creating a timetable for a complex rail system is a messy and expensive business, and once created then the railway needs to monitor how closely train operations match the timetable. Timetables are a big topic, are complex to create. Avoiding the need to create a complex timetable is one of the reasons why metros can operate so efficiently. A rail system with more services and flat junctions will have a more complex timetable than one with separated rail lines.

As a general rule trains services need to be very frequent to not have a publicly available timetable. A frequency of one train every ten minutes should be considered the absolute maximum time between trains, to operate without a passenger timetable. Metros operate normally with one train every 3 to 5 minutes, and this is much more appropriate for train services without a timetable.

For rail lines where there are only one or two trains per hour, then a timetable is essential. Passengers need to plan their day around when the train arrives at the station, and this can be helped with a timetable. Where the service frequency drops too low then a publicly available timetable will be needed. Stations with low patronage will mean a low service frequency, and this will lead to a timetable. For everyone, it's best if there are lots of passengers, as this results in a better rail service.

In comparison bus services can be changed easily, but rail services are much more inflexible. Rail service frequencies often remain unchanged for decades, because the infrastructure and headway places powerful limitations on how many trains can move through the network, and this limit remains in place for a very long time.

High speed rail lines always have a publicly available timetable, for operational reasons, even where the service frequency is very high. There are many reasons for this, including the need to provide passengers with information on when their two to four hour trip will end, and the ticketing system often requires seat reservations on specific trains, which means that a timetable is needed so passengers can meet the train that they have booked their seat on.

The table below has some typical service frequencies. These numbers are really only a very rough guide, and there are many exceptions.

Train Service Frequency - Typical	
Light rail	1 every 10 minutes
Trams	1 every 10 minutes, but can be extremely frequent
Metros	1 every 3 to 5 minutes
Commuter rail	1 every 15 to 30 minutes
Regional rail	1 every 1 to 3 hours, depending on the destination
High speed rail	Huge variety, but 1 every 15 minutes between very large cities
Overnight trains	1 or 2 per night

There are a number of different ways of choosing what the frequency of trains should be, and some of the better known ones are presented below.

1/ Using load factors

Perhaps the best way to plan rail service frequencies is to look at load factors. The reader will recall that load factors are a ratio of the number of passengers on a train, to the total number of seats. Whilst different services will have markedly different load factors, and trains in the peak usually will have much higher load factors, there is enormous variability in the load factors of trains, even ones that operate on the same lines following one another. Despite this, targeting a load factor is often a good and relatively simple way to determine train frequency, as it is clear and easy to apply.

Surveys can be done on the number of passengers on each line, and using the different services throughout the day. Once this is determined, the railway can set the service frequency to target either an average load factor, or a maximum one, depending on which is the most appropriate.

Rail systems with large numbers of people travelling for small numbers of stations are confronted with an interesting problem. The train may operate over a long distance, but between two stops there are large numbers of passengers, perhaps because the stations are large, or are very important interchanges. In this scenario, the train frequency will be chosen on the maximum load factor, and not the average one, because it is this trip between these two stations that is what passengers need and want to do. Setting train frequencies this way may mean that the trains operate for large sections with almost no one on board, which is very unfortunate.

The situation with metros is a little more interesting. Most metros have very few seats, and most passengers stand for most of their trip. The capacity of any metro train is determined based on the available places to stand, and this is a rubbery figure, as in theory a lot of people can stand closely together. A common number is 4 people per square metre, but other railways use 6, especially in Asia in very large cities. A political decision is needed on what exactly the capacity of a metro carriage is. The reader should remember that a small number of railways use 8 people per square metre, and in India it is possible to find trains with up to 14 people per square metre, a very high figure.

2/ Maximising the economic benefit to society

A formula commonly used to maximising the benefit to society for transportation, is given below, and can be used to determine the economic frequency of trains. This equation was first reported from the paper by H Mohring in 1971, and it is sometimes used in different textbooks on urban planning, often related to the frequency of bus services.

This formula works on the basis that the fixed costs of providing the rail service are not relevant, and that the decision on train frequency should be made on the basis of marginal costs. A marginal cost is similar to the direct cost often used in accounting, and represents the cost incurred through operating one additional train. This cost can be thought of as the cost of power, wages for drivers, and direct wear and tear on the train.

So let's define some terms:

EC = *economic cost to society*

T = *Travel time (hours)*

C = *cost per hour of operating a train*

p = *number of passengers boarding a train per hour*

VPM = *value of a passenger minute*

The two parameters we are interested in is the waiting time for passengers, and the direct cost of providing the train service. Whilst there are many other factors, it is these two that shall be used to determine the service frequency. We can express this relationship as follows:

Economic cost to society (train frequency) = *marginal cost running trains +*
cost of
passeng

ers waiting for trains

The marginal cost for operating trains on a rail line is:

*Marginal cost of running trains =
Cost per hour x train frequency x route length (hours)*

The cost of passengers waiting time

$$Passenger\ waiting\ cost = \frac{60 \times p \times VPM}{2f}$$

It's *2f* because on average passengers arrive half way between each train, and not immediately after a train has left. So, combining these terms, we get:

$$EC = TCf + \frac{60pVPM}{2f}$$

And to find the turning point, where the equation is minimised:

$$\frac{dEC}{df} = 0$$

So differentiating the above equation, we get:

$$\frac{dEC}{df} = TC - \frac{60pVPM}{2f^2} = 0$$

We can re-arrange this to obtain:

$$2f^2 = \frac{60pVPM}{TC}$$

And this gives for *f*:

$$f = \sqrt{\frac{60 pVPM}{2TC}}$$

To finish this equation, we note that:

Value passenger hour (VPH) = 60 x VPM

So we finally get:

$$f = \sqrt{\frac{pVPH}{2TC}}$$

This is the classic equation for the economic frequency of transport services.

Worked Example

For our example, let's use the following numbers.

The trip length is 45 minutes
The number of passengers per hour = 4000
The cost of operating a train is $150 per hour
The wages per hour in the area is $20 per hour

What is the economic frequency of trains?

T = 45/60 = 0.75 hours
p = 4000
C = $150
VPH = $20 per hour

Substituting into the equation gives:

$$f = \sqrt{\frac{4000 \times 20}{2 \times 0.75 \times 150}}$$

$$f = 18.8 \text{ trains per hour}$$

A frequency of 18.8 trains per hour is quite high, so we can observe that the equation above often provides a high number of trains per hour. The numbers used in the equation above are quite typical.

Something that should be considered is that where a train moves in one direction, typically it needs to move in the other direction as well (but not always). Where this is the case, then the calculation needs to take into account both directions of travel, especially where trains in one direction operate mostly empty.

Recall that for rail services, and many government organisations, the pricing and decision making points should use the marginal cost, rather than the average cost or the total cost.

3/ Community service obligations

Community service obligations refers to the provision of public transport when there are insufficient people to justify the service, but the government wishes the transport provider to provide it anyway. These types of agreements are common in Australia, as there are many places where the population numbers are low, and public transport such as trains run almost empty.

Community service obligations are sometimes abbreviated to CSO. A CSO agreement between the transport provider and government will stipulate the number of services per hour, the capacity, and the times over which this service will run. The areas covered, or a description of the bus or train services, is obviously very important to a CSO. This type of agreement will often also include payments from the government to the transport provider in compensation for providing the service. CSO agreements can be an important source of funding for a transport provider. In Australia most CSO agreements would be with bus companies, but they also exist with rail companies as well.

CSO agreements would be a very unusual thing to implement with a new rail line. CSO's are almost always implemented in areas where the train line has been there for decades, and where population densities are low. It would be unthinkable to build a new expensive rail line, and then have so few people that a CSO was needed. It is conceivable that a new rail freight line may operate with passenger traffic as well, and in this situation small numbers of passengers may be acceptable because the line is there to service the freight, but it is difficult to imagine any other scenario where a rail line would be constructed in parallel with a CSO.

Of course CSO's would rarely provide for a high level of passenger service, such as a train every 3 minutes. Common CSO train frequencies are 2 or 3 trains a day, or potentially 1 train an hour. The frequencies are quite low, but enough for people without a car to get around, should they need to. Trains provided under a CSO agreement are often quite short, only a couple of carriages, and operate at modest speeds. CSO services are often diesel, at least in Australia, as there is often no overhead wiring in areas with very limited traffic.

Looking at CSO's from the perspective of government, they are useful in providing services to places where there would otherwise be no public transport. Passengers who often use CSO services are the elderly, students and young people who are too young to drive, those with disabilities who can't drive, and others who for whatever reason can't buy a car. In car loving Australia, most people have access to cars, CSO services are often almost empty. Where there are lots of people who don't have cars, but not enough to warrant a profitable bus or train service, then a CSO can be a good way to help people with their transport needs. In Australia, in areas where CSO agreements are needed, there are often approaches from local community groups to government, requesting a subsidy for public transport.

4/ Other political reasons

Stations exist where the number of stops at the station is extremely small. In NSW there are some stations where there are only 1 or 2 stops per week. These stations are often only serviced to keep them open, and there may be political pressure to close them. The experience in the UK and Australia is that once a rail line is closed then is can never be returned to service, or it is often very difficult. Later the closure of a rail line is often regretted, and a political decision is sometimes made to keep the line open, and this sometimes means just one train per week.

Choosing Service Hours

Choosing service hours an important decision for any operational railway. Trains cannot run continuously over a stretch of track for 24 hours a day indefinitely, as the track will degrade and its condition will be very poor. Time is needed for maintenance, and this is often a very major factor in determining the hours in which a railway operates. Alternatively, there may not be the demand to operate trains throughout the entire day, and there may be periods where the passenger demand is so low that there is little need for services. Either way, almost all railways are confronted with the decision on what the hours of operation should be.

Many metros, light rail, and tram systems close at night. When they close there are normally maintenance people waiting to jump onto the track to perform maintenance, and this needs to be done. Whilst it is not necessary to perform maintenance every night, most nights something will be done, and this needs to be allowed for. A typical number of hours per night set aside for maintenance is 6 hours, and this seems to be a reasonable compromise. Both the Hong Kong metro and the Shanghai stop operating around 11pm.

The same can be said for commuter systems, and high speed rail. These systems also close at night, and maintenance people enter the rail corridor and start doing work.

It's really important for rail managers to set aside some time for maintenance work to be performed. If there is no time then track conditions will be poor, and any maintenance work that is performed will be hurried and poor quality. Increasing the number of work hours available in a block is a good way to reduce maintenance costs, and blocks of only 2 or 3 hours are difficult to use effectively. It is much better if the maintainers get solid blocks of at least 5 hours.

Of course it is not necessary to make a 6 hour block available every night (in most cases). It is acceptable to have little or no maintenance window for, say, Friday and Saturday nights, as this will give maintenance workers time off and 5 nights per week for maintenance is generally sufficient. Services can operate all night on Fridays and Saturdays, which are nights that are often much more busy than other nights.

Another alternative is to have a longer maintenance window on quiet nights, such as Tuesday and Wednesday nights. This is sometimes done for large work, such as resleepering. Services might end at 9:30 pm, and allow maintenance workers significantly more time to perform whatever work is needed.

Things are a little easier for rail lines with low levels of traffic. Service frequency here is chosen because of the number of people travelling, and where there are large gaps in services, no specific maintenance window is necessary. Maintenance workers can perform maintenance between train services.

High Speed Rail presents some interesting challenges for providing a maintenance window. HSR trips are typically 2 to 4 hours, so a 5 or 6 hour maintenance window means that train services will need to cease around 10pm or even earlier. Whilst in theory it is possible for rail workers to do work on one rail line and not another, having a HSR train pass at 300 kms/hr might be a little disturbing for rail workers and present some real safety risks. Maintenance workers for an HSR rail system will need the entire rail corridor in many cases to perform work, especially where it involves heavy equipment. Having said that there are maintenance vehicles that allow maintenance workers to work along a rail line alongside a working rail line.

REFERENCES

1. Rietveld, P. et al *Choice of Frequency and Vehicle Size in Rail Transport. Implications for Marginal Costs*, European Journal for Transport and Infrastructure Research, 2, no 2, (2002), pp 95 - 111

2. Wong, R. *Optimising Timetable Synchronisation for Rail Mass Transit*, Transportation Science Vol42, No 1, February 2008, 57 – 69

Chapter 12 Demand Estimation

Introduction

Demand estimation refers to any attempt to predict the patronage of a rail system either before it is built, or before changes are made to the system. Demand estimation for an existing line is often done via elasticises, which are very commonly used, researched and reported, and are discussed at length above in this chapter. Demand estimation for entirely new rail lines is much harder, as an estimate needs to be made for a service where presently none exists.

It should be noted that it is not always necessary to have a comprehensive model of the demand for a rail service. Some rail projects are built because of reasons in addition to moving lots of passengers, and some projects have a highly political nature and may not need large passenger numbers to be approved. Some of the projects in Hong Kong that connect the city to mainland China are being completed for integration purposes, and the number of passengers is not the primary consideration. However for most projects passenger numbers or freight movements are a key consideration.

It is not always possible to have access to detailed and complex demand forecasting models, and at early stages of project development these will not be available. As projects progress however, the expectations as regards passenger forecasts grow, and more detailed analysis is needed. Demand estimation will start very basic, and become more sophisticated as any project progresses. Many governments, before providing the substantial funding required for any rail project, will expect some pretty thorough research into passenger numbers to be completed. Demand modelling techniques that are quick and easy to perform are sometimes described as "sketch planning". This term refers to the need to create very simple demand estimates in the early stages of any demand estimation.

One of the key considerations for any the demand estimate for passengers is the time frame over which any analysis is performed. Demand for rail services changes over time, and mostly increases. In some cases the increase in demand can be quite dramatic, and increasing the size of the analysis window will often produce much better results. A typical time period for analysis may be 10 years, or 20, or 25. When comparing different project alternatives, it is important to use the same time window for comparison.

Demand estimation for a new freight line is quite different to that of a passenger line. Freight companies, and companies that produce items that need to be shipped, are often in a position to provide the transport planner with substantial information about what freight movements a new line will have. Freight companies often have industry bodies where the demand on new rail lines can be estimated with a good degree of certainty, and freight companies will have a good understanding of their demand patterns, it is easier to determine the freight movements on any new freight line. Unless otherwise stated, the discussion below excludes freight.

Different Techniques

There are a range of different techniques that can be employed to estimate the demand for new passenger lines. Some are very simple, others are very complex. What type of technique is used will depend on a number of factors, including the budget that is available, the technique that was used in past studies, and the information on hand at the time of the forecast. It should be remembered that all attempts to predict the future are fraught with difficulty, and no one technique can guarantee success.

So, from the most basic to the most complex, the types of forecasting of demand, for new rail lines, is:
- Statements about the potential for high demand for rail services, such as the number of people in an area, the demographics of those people, the number of trips, and other factors such as the income level or the number of cars owned. From a relatively simple analysis of these factors, much can be learned, and a competent planner can get a sense of the viability of a project or rail line
- Rules-of-thumb to generate a simple estimate of demand, such as comparing the location and type of service with a comparable service and location elsewhere that already has the service. There are many cities and regions worldwide with varying rail characteristics, and an observant rail planner can normally find one that is quite similar to the one being studied. The demand levels in the comparable place may very well be similar to the place where the rail line is being proposed

- Analysis of the rail travel patterns in a region that has a lot of rail, but where there are gaps in the rail service, and the proposal is to close those gaps. This situation may occur where a large city is seeking to build another metro line, and wants to estimate passenger numbers, and has a large number of other stations to study to determine what travel patterns are. A regression analysis may be performed on the number of passengers at existing stations, using variables such as the number of people in the surrounding area, location of schools, parks and shopping centres, available employment, incomes, etc. This type of analysis is recommended in this book because of it's accuracy, cost, and is relatively easy to complete
- Catchment analysis, where the number of people living nearby to the station is determined, and then multiplied by a factor that represents how many trips will be generated by each household per day by rail. The choice of factor is based on any previous study that estimated how many people used a rail service per day, who lived nearby to the station.
- Formulas for the percentage of travel expected based on travel time. This type of analysis is sometimes used for high speed rail, where travel times of over 4 hours will attract a low percentage of the total number of trips, and a travel time of 2 hours resulting in rail capturing almost 100% of all trips.
- Surveys of the people in the area surrounding where stations are proposed to be built. There is nothing wrong with launching a survey to determine what local people think of a new proposed project, but the results need to be interpreted with caution. In small towns people will rarely say no to a new rail line, but that does not mean that there will be adequate patronage of the rail line once it is built. Nonetheless, surveys are one way of obtaining a clear picture of the travel habits of the people near the rail line.
- Activity based modelling, where a model is built that contains estimates of the movements of every passenger in the relevant area. A model of the utility of the transport trip is created, and then applied to each different trip pattern. This modelling technique is particularly useful where new rail lines are to run along existing highways. This type of model is sometimes considered to be the best way to produce a forecast, but it is very resource hungry, and expensive and time consuming to produce. Where a strong modelling group in an area has built

one of these models, then it is possible to make use of their system, and for the privilege fees must be paid.

The type of demand modelling used can vary greatly, even for the same country, and for the same project. In the feasibility stage of any project to build a new rail service, it is likely that money is quite limited, and there will be relatively little information on the proposed new service. Not every project starts with a clear set of requirements, and for some projects the objectives and goals can be quite vague. In that situation demand planning using "sketch planning" is entirely appropriate.

Regardless of the type of model used to estimate demand, there are a number of key variables that need to be defined in order to determine what the demand will be. These include:
- Service frequency
- Cost of tickets
- Type of service
- Punctuality
- Number of rail interchanges to reach important destinations
- Crowding
- Travel speed and time

It's best if these variables are known, and as a project progresses more information will be known about a project. It is the author's experience that often projects may be publicized with high frequencies, high average speeds, and low costs, but as the project nears completion then some of these key assumptions may change, and the cost of tickets increase, the frequency of service might drop, and overall the project may not seem as rosy as when it was announced. Furthermore, punctuality figures almost never match those promised, and train delays, especially in a newly constructed rail system, will be lower than what was promised.

Activity based modelling, as mentioned above, is a way modelling the movements of people in a city or region. The results of a model using this technique can produce a lot of information, and this information centres on the trips that will occur when the transport project is completed. Some of the information that is produced about the trips includes:
- The purpose of trips in the area
- The time trips occur

- The origin and destination of all trips
- The travel mode, be it car, train, bus or any other mode
- The route that the trips take
- And the frequency of the trips

That's a lot of information. It is for this reason that activity based modelling is seen as the preferred way to model new transport projects, and produces far more information than how many people will use a particular station or transport service each day.

The underlying premise of any activity based modelling is that demand for transport is a "derived demand", which means that the service is not demanded for it's own sake, but is demanded as part of another activity. People rarely take trains without having any other purpose, but in some cases, especially on railways or on other speciality railways, then the trip itself is all that the consumer wants. Notwithstanding this, the vast majority of trips are related to work, buying groceries, social activities, or children going to school, and occur because of work, social activities, or educational requirements. As transport is related to other activities, it is possible to work out from the location of offices, places or work, school and shopping centres how many trips will be generated. It is this way that is the key to modelling transport in an activity based model.

Utility is a concept in economics that concerns the satisfaction of consuming a good. Utility is a different concept from cost, as the cost of a service or good may not be the same as the satisfaction of its use. For example, the cost of purchasing a good may be $10, but someone buying it may be prepared to pay much more, because their utility from the consumption of that good is far higher than the $10 that the good cost. Utility, as the satisfaction from consuming a good, is what economists use to model transport demand. Unfortunately, as utility is not the same as price, an activity based model that maximises consumer utility will need a lot of information about how consumers perceive utility, and then this should be entered into the model. Once again, as mentioned before, this requires a lot of groundwork, and this is one of the major barriers to creating an activity based model.

Sensitivity analysis is a term that is used to describe the analysis of options and input variables to any process. Transport planning is a process, and in planning for a new rail line, or modifications to one, input parameters such as the type of new line, frequency of trains, type of trains, and capacity of new rollingstock, are the input parameters to the process. The transport planner attempts to produce some outputs from the process, which is the number of passengers, the economic benefit to society from the transport project, the cost, etc. A sensitivity analysis attempts to determine how much the outputs change based on the inputs. A normal process, to perform a sensitivity analysis, is to modify the inputs a small amount, and then calculate the new outputs. How much the outputs change relative to the inputs, is what a sensitivity analysis is all about.

With a sensitivity analysis, it is possible for the transport planner to answer questions that are normally posed during the planning process; what happens if this is changed, how can costs be reduced, or how can the inputs be changed to increase the number of passengers. These sorts of questions are normal, and when asked indicate that the planning process is worked normally. These questions are not a sign that the planning process is under attack (usually!).

Demand Elasticises

A demand elasticity is the change in demand for a transport service given a change in the way the service is supplied, or in the nature of the service. Demand elasticises can be applied to changes in service frequency. If a rail service is very slow, then fewer passengers will want to use the service. A very quick and efficient service will result in higher number of passengers. From a rail transport planning perspective, it is necessary for an estimate to be made of the number of passengers who will use a service when transport times are either increased or decreased. This can happen when service frequency is increased or decreased, or when passengers need to interchange where previously services were direct. Changes to travel times are common in any rail system.

Elasticises are used in economics, and they describe the effect on demand of changing a variable on the quantity demanded of a good, and commonly the price is the variable that is changed. An elasticity is how much the demand changes, and an elasticity of more than 1 means the good is elastic, and small changes result in large changes in demand. An elasticity of less than one means that the good is inelastic, and that changes to price and other variables means that the quantity demanded will change only a little. Goods such as food and fuel are inelastic, as they are basic necessities and are needed regardless of the price. Goods that are discretionary are often strongly elastic.

Demand Estimation

This concept of elasticises is commonly applied to rail transport, and it is possible to develop a formula relating travel time to number of passengers. Much research has been done on establishing the relationship between travel time and passenger numbers, and this is presented below. This research often focuses on the value of the elasticity, rather than any other statistical parameter such as the correlation, or the shape of the curve that relates travel time to passenger.

So the basic variables are:

TT = *travel time*

P = *number of passengers*

η = *elasticity of demand*

The formula for the elasticity of demand assumes a base level of passengers is known, and the formula applies to changes from this base level. The classic formula for demand elasticity is:

$$\frac{\Delta Q}{Q} = E \times \frac{\Delta P}{P}$$

We modify this to account for changes in travel time, rather than price, and we obtain:

$$\frac{\Delta P}{P} = E \times \frac{\Delta TT}{TT}$$

We can express this differently as:

$$\frac{P_2 - P_1}{P_1} = E \times \frac{TT_2 - TT_1}{TT_1}$$

Where

P_2 = *number of passengers after the change*

TT_1 = *travel time before the change*

TT_2 = *travel time after the change*

Also note that the travel time is calculated from:

$$TT = \text{transit time in train(s)} + \text{interchange time} + \text{maximum waiting time}/2$$

The maximum waiting time is divided by 2 because it is assumed that passengers arrive randomly, and there will wait on average half the maximum waiting time.

One challenge applying this equation is that for any rail line passengers will be alighting and boarding at all the stations along the line. Passengers will have many different destination choices, so a change in frequency of service will impact upon passengers differently. In particular, where passengers are travelling a short distance a change in frequency of service will have a very large impact, because a change of a few minutes can be very significant for a travel time of 10 minutes. A long distance trip is much less sensitive to small changes in service frequency, as a percentage it is much smaller. This is one of the reasons why metro services operate at such small headways, as trip distances are quite short, and the waiting time has more of an impact to the number of passengers.

Transport planners should use the elasticises of demand for travel time that are mandated for use in that country, if that has occurred. A large number of studies have been produced in the past 40 years that have analysed elasticises of demand for transport, mostly in reference to the price charged, but also concerned with the travel time. Whichever country is planning a new rail system should take account of the most relevant study with the most relevant elasticity figures. Elasticity values can vary through an enormous range, and most likely the best way to obtain any elasticity figures is to use the study conducted in the most similar transport environment.

An excellent resource is the website of the Australian Government Department of Infrastructure and Regional Development, who maintain a database of different studies conducted into transport elasticises. Their database is impressive, but seems to contain information that is a little dated, much of it being from the 1970's and 80's. It contains hundred of entries on different transport modes. The link, at the time of printing of this book, is:

http://www.bitre.gov.au/tedb/index.aspx

Some typical values for η are shown below, for both trains and buses:

Different Travel Mode – Time Passenger Demand Elasticities (η)	
Mode	**Elasticity**
Bus, urban	-0.60
Rail, urban	-0.60
Bus, intercity	-2.11
Rail, intercity	-1.58
Air, intercity	-0.43

The elasticises are negative because an increase in travel time will result in a reduction in the number of passengers. Only rail cruises and tourist railways have a positive elasticity.

Interestingly elasticises for rail and bus is very negative for intercity trips, presumably because the travelling public dislikes this mode of travel for intercity trips, and will only choose it when the trip is very efficient and quick.

The graph below shows how passenger demand changes with travel time. This scenario has used the base case where the number of passengers per day is 10,000, and the travel time is 30 minutes. As the travel time gets shorter the number of passengers gets larger, and the increase in number of passengers using the system gets large. As can be seen clearly from this graph, there are significant increases in passenger demand for reductions in travel time.

Passenger Demand P = 10,000, travel time = 30 min, η = -0.6

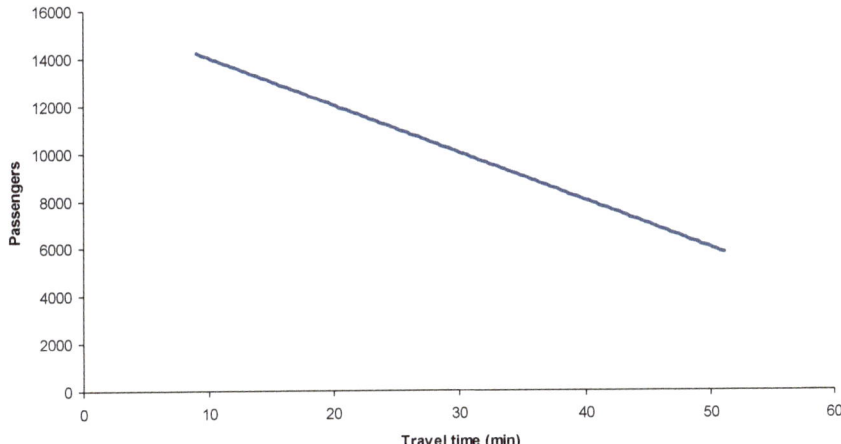

This equation for passenger demand can be used in transport models, where new rail lines or changes to a rail system are modelled.

Chapter 13 Financing Large Projects

Introduction

Large rail projects require large sums of money. Most governments are severely constrained by the amount of money that can be provided to invest in any project, including rail, and finding a source of funding is always difficult. Most governments would prefer that large scale funding is sourced from other places than the government, and in many cases this is possible. How should this be done? What strategies can governments employ to encourage any other party to pay for the costs of any large rail infrastructure?

Seeking alternative sources of funds for a rail project is difficult. They are often provide very poor returns, and so very few private sector organisations would want to pay for a rail line or project. In some limited circumstances there may be situations where a very specific project met their need they may be willing to pay, but in general things are quite difficult. Nonetheless governments have been searching for a way to find someone to help them pay for the enormous cost of building rail lines.

Broadly, there seem to be a small number of ways that governments can obtain funds:
- Pay for the project themselves out of consolidated revenue
- Seek contributions from local government and other organisations, such as shopping centre owners for any rail project
- Raise taxes and direct the money to the rail project
- A private sector corporation may wish to pay for the entire project if it is very lucrative, or organised to be so
- Provide incentives to a private sector corporation to build the project, such as the right to build property around the railway line

Small projects may be funded through the actions of local government, or local business people. Local government may be able to provide funds for some projects, but the larger project they will be unable to contribute any significant amount of money. The larger the project, the more difficult things become.

Many governments consider that the involvement of the private sector in a construction project will bring major benefits, and so is something that should be encouraged if at all possible. This includes obtaining funding, and there are a number of mechanisms that can be deployed to involve the private sector more.

Apart from the cost saving from involving the private sector in a large infrastructure project, involving them is seen to produce other monetary or economic benefits as well. There include:
- The private sector is seen as more efficient and goal orientated that large government bureaucracies, and able to deliver projects with lower costs
- The private sector will take the risk associated with any large rail project, and any project overruns and cost blowouts will be absorbed by the private sector rather than the government
- The financing costs of the project, as well as the loans for the project, not the responsibility of government, and so the government accounts for the country will not show the debt, and the budget position of the government will be better

It is a commonly held view that the private sector is more efficient than government in operating businesses. It is definitely true that private sector companies are more profit driven, and do not have the nebulous goals that make operating a government department difficult. Government departments often have many competing goals based on the politics of the government in power, and these can be very diverse, from procurement, equal opportunity, supporting regional areas, environmental, etc, whereas private companies are often not bound by the same government policies.

The differences between government and private companies and they way they operate is beyond the scope of this book, but nonetheless a very interesting topic. The way these two types of business operate is vastly different, and both systems have strengths and weaknesses. In many countries it is the strong preference of government that as many businesses as possible are operated by the private sector. Alternatively, in many countries, rail systems and operators are still very much operated by the government.

As a final comment on the different approaches between public and private sector organisations, there always seems to be more risk with private sector organisations. Many of the companies that compete for work from the rail industry seem to be small, or temporary ventures, or something with very little stability. In Australia many of the companies that have bid for and won work often have flashy sounding names, but only have the revenue from one contract, and when that contract expires is often wound up. It always seems risky trusting the lives of the travelling public to companies that existed only for a few weeks before the start of performance of the contract.

As regards sources of funding, there are surprisingly many different strategies that can be employed. A short summary of those would be:

- Selling off the rail system or the operation of the rail system, so that any future investment is carried out by the private sector.
- Encouraging private sector investment by providing "sweeteners", such as paying for part of the investment, or providing generous tax incentives to allow the investment to occur. Sometimes governments will provide generous cash grants to any organisation that will take on any transport project.
- Allowing development of the land around a large rail infrastructure project, which will generate large profits, which can be used to offset the cost of the large rail project. This strategy is commonly used in Hong Kong to provide the funds for investment
- Governments can guarantee the debts of the private sector organisation that is making the investment, which reduces the funding costs. Debt guarantees can be a very effective way of reducing the cost of borrowing, which can substantially help with reducing the costs of building infrastructure. This was done with the High Speed Rail system in Taiwan.
- Applying surcharges to particular parts of the rail network, especially where the patrons of the service have the resources to pay for it. Surcharges on rail tickets are very common for rail lines to airports, as the cost of the rail ticket is normally only a small part of the cost of any trip. Care must be taken to ensure that there is some sort of system to allow for employees of the airport or the facility with the surcharge applied to avoid the charge, otherwise those that need to use the station routinely may be penalised.
- A major rail project may be split into two parts, the unprofitable part that is paid for by government, and a profitable part that can be financed by the private sector, and

revenues from that part being used to generate the financing needed.
- Offering a monopoly on the use of certain lines, in exchange for funding for infrastructure projects. This kind of funding arrangement can cause a lot of friction with the users of the service that becomes a monopoly, as the cost of the service can rise substantially. Users of the monopoly service will have no alternative but to accept the higher charges, causing resentment. Nonetheless, converting a service that was competitive to a monopoly has substantial value to the company that acquires the monopoly, and the buyer may be prepared to invest substantially to acquire the monopoly
- Applying levies to the owners of properties around the new rail lines or projects, which is then used to pay for the new rail project. Care must be taken in applying this kind of levy that the local property owners see the rail project as something they would want, and provides a benefit to them or the residents of their property. A rail line that has no station or is an express line, or moves freight, will not be a suitable candidate for this type of system for raising funds. This system is used for the Vancouver Skytrain.
- A rail line may connect a facility of enormous value or size, such as a Disney theme park or a shopping centre of large size. This facility may be so profitable and wealthy that they may pay for the new infrastructure outright, or make a very substantial contribution to the cost of any rail project. Casinos often have the funds to pay for rail projects, and deals can be struck between government and private companies that provide for the financing of this type of project. Hong Kong Disney land is an excellent example of this type of financing.
- A country or government may apply a levy to a service or business that is unrelated to rail, that is imposed only for paying for the project or infrastructure. This is sometimes done with gambling, a cash business that generates large revenues. Gambling is often seen as something of a shady industry, morally questionable, and the operators of gambling establishments may be required to contribute to some sort of public investment scheme in order to dignify/redeem their business operations. Lotteries are also sometimes used as a source of funds for infrastructure and transport investment.
- Infrastructure bonds are a specific type of borrowing where governments go the debt markets and raise cash for specific

projects. This type of funding is used where the governments approach the public for funds, and bonds are sold to raise cash for the infrastructure project. These bonds may be paid for using government revenue, or revenue from the infrastructure project.
- Superannuation funds, or other wealth fund such as a sovereign wealth fund, may be compelled through government legislation or other means into providing the funding for transport infrastructure projects. Care must be taken with this approach, as these funds are really public money, and large losses may create political problems for any government that compelled the fund to support the project.
- Offering a long term contract that generates an income stream, and then guaranteeing this income stream, so that the private sector can borrow against the income stream. This type of financing is commonly used in public private partnerships, where the income stream is used as collateral for any financing. The income stream may be in the form of a lease, and the private sector leases the infrastructure back to the government, or as a guaranteed stream of income for the provision of services.

Public Private Partnerships

PPP stands for public private partnership, and is a common way of attempting to reduce the cost of major infrastructure projects. The key to a PPP is for the private sector to assume the risk in any major project. Governments often are prepared to accept large costs in transport projects, as long as the benefits are there and there is substantial public support for the project. Risk, on the other hand, is something that governments genuinely dislike, and will generally pay substantially more on a project to reduce any risk as much as possible. Government dislike of risk is one of the reasons why the private sector is able to compete more effectively than government businesses, as the appetite for risk is higher, and governments sometimes avoid risky projects that could potentially return very large benefits to the public.

PPPs have become a very common way for governments to get private sector involvement in the funding of rail infrastructure projects. In Australia PPP's are popular, and a commonly used investment vehicle to attract private sector investment. PPPs can be used for a variety of different purposes, including hospitals, prisons, rail project, and road tollways. PPPs are very versatile, and can be an attractive option.

PPP projects have a very specific structure, which is:
- Governments make partial payments early in the life of a project
- The construction consortium continues to operate and maintain the constructed assets after construction is complete
- The operation period if defined ahead of time
- As the construction consortium continues to operate the assets, the remaining capital is paid from the government to the consortium
- Detailed performance requirements are provided for how the assets should be managed
- The construction consortium also receives a fee for managing the assets

PPP structures allow governments to convert a high up front capital cost into a series of payments over many years. The construction consortium borrows against the stream of payments, and so the construction cost is spread over many years, even decades. This structure is very attractive to government.

We should note that governments can almost always borrow more cheaply than private sector companies. The quality of the infrastructure, and the nature of the project, will also contribute to the final cost of raising capital. High quality projects will be able to raise money cheaply, not so good, more expensive. Even the best projects will struggle to raise money as cheaply as a government. This problem does cause some involved with the creation of PPP's to sometimes question the overall benefits of a PPP structure.

As governments are so reluctant to accept any risk, one of the key advantages of a PPP structure is that a private party can innovate regarding the design and implementation of any transport project. As technology advances, solutions to problems can be found where none existed previously, and private companies may want to adopt these designs or techniques, where government may be reluctant. As private companies are generally more flexible, the employment of foreign consultants is easier, and headhunting of talent from overseas employment markets easier, allowing for more rapid technology transfer.

Gifts and Aid

Rail projects are very expensive to implement in any country. In countries with low labour rates the cost of rail projects will be significantly lower, however there are many engineering systems that are produced in a handful of countries that need to be imported. This equipment is not provided at reduced prices as a charitable act, and so full price needs to be paid. For many third world countries complex rail systems are too expensive to implement.

Organisations exist across the world to provide funding for a variety of different infrastructure projects. Almost all wealthy first world countries have aid programs that direct funds towards poorer countries that are unable to provide for themselves. There are also many departments of the UN that also work to provide the same service. These organisations can be a very useful way for many countries to obtain funding for rail projects.

Major countries such as Japan and China has established investment banks who purpose is to fund major construction projects of all kinds. China has established the Asia Investment Bank to fund all sorts of different projects. Japan also has the Japan bank for International Cooperation. These banks provide funds for a variety of different projects.

The provision of these monies often have strict conditions attached, many of which concern corruption and the theft of the funds provided. Many companies are vary of providing funding to countries with notorious corruption problems, and any money provided may be stolen and used for other purposes.

Investments in third world counties are assessed on an economic basis as they should be. A variety of different measures are used to make the assessment, including most importantly the benefits to the local population. Money will be provided where the economic benefits are very large, and local government cannot raise the funds on their own.

Wealthy countries clearly will not be the recipient of this kind of funding, and even relatively strong third world countries would not often receive funding for these kinds of projects, even where there is a very large economic benefit.

This kind of investment is suited only for a small number of rail transport modes. Flashy sexy rail systems such as high speed rail will not be funded this way. Tourist railways may be, as there could be old rail systems left over from the colonial era that could be converted into a tourist railway. Rail systems funded in this way are low tech, and cheap so that they can be used by the local population. Driverless trains would also not be deployed as this restricts employment opportunities.

The best of these types of rail projects are ones that are cheap, connect impoverished areas to areas of employment, result in large economic benefits, and permanent employment. This often means investing in town and cities, with whatever type of rail system is suitable for that area. Freight lines are also common, which allow access for major countries to raw materials that they require.

Success and Failure

Obtaining funding from different sources comes with a degree of risk. Organisations that provide funding have expectations that the money will be used in an appropriate way, and that the promises made about the project are actually delivered. Projects need to be delivered on time, and on budget.

All manner of problems can occur in a project, and these can affect any future funding that might become available. Where projects in a specific area obtain a bad reputation, seeking more funding in the future may be difficult. Where projects are successful things will be a lot more easy.

There have been instances in Australia where large private sector companies have been almost destroyed by entering into a large contract that provided limited benefits, or did not provide the expected revenues. One of the consequences when this happens is that the private company suffers considerable financial damage, and the CEO of the company is fired. After this any company that thinks about dealing with the government prices in so much risk that the financial benefit is really not there to let the contract, and the contracts for any services have so many escape clauses as to be virtually worthless. Even worse, as companies get more cautious about accepting government contracts more money is needed to entice them into the contract, which defeats the entire purpose of getting the private sector involved in the first place.

The experience in Australia has been mixed. Care must be exercised in getting the private sector involved in any rail project, because getting it to work well is really hard, and things go wrong really easily. Things do seem to be getting better, and some hard lessons have been learned. Some of the problems include:

- Contracts are poorly written, so that the scope of the contract is wrong, or key terms are missing. Often the requirements are incorrect, so key needs are not addressed
- The project price is either too high or too low, and the company either goes bankrupt or they make an enormous amount of money which embarrasses everyone.
- In rail especially, the government attempts to remedy a shortfall of qualified experienced technical staff by creating a PPP contract and company to complete the work, only to find that the PPP company cannot recruit skilled people either, as there are none to be found
- The PPP company puts clauses into the contract so that the government will bailout the company if it makes a loss, so the risk to the government is not reduced at all
- Estimates of revenues from the project are wildly optimistic, and the private company that builds the infrastructure goes bankrupt
- Projects have technical requirements that are difficult to measure and even more difficult to monitor. Rail projects often have requirements in the contract concerning reliability and other rather abstract performance measures, and depending on the project these can be almost impossible to manage effectively. Without clear goals management of the project can be very difficult
- Private companies install equipment for the new infrastructure that is very poor quality, cheap, and that public government companies would never install. This equipment is often so poor that maintenance staff are displeased to even see it in service, and when any infrastructure is handed back to the government, will immediately need to launch a project to remove all the low quality infrastructure and replace it with something more suitable.

For any rail project it is best if projects for revenue and economic benefit are realistic and achievable. High quality analysis up front, especially for demand estimation of the use of the railway can help reduce the impact of any problems.

Chapter 14 Tourism and Rail Systems

Introduction

Most rail systems have regular users that patronise the system very frequently. Price, frequency of service, and reliability are very important for these passengers. Tourist railways are very different, where passengers may use the service only once in their lives, and price is not as important, and experience and look and feel are very important. Tourist railways are the "quiet achiever" of rail systems, and there are many of them that operate at a profit.

Tourists have different travel patterns from business travellers, and other travellers that are visiting family, working, studying or attending a conference. Tourists travel for leisure, and during their travel want to experience new and different things, and to see things that are interesting or have historical value. Tourists are prepared to take trips that are more expensive than normal transport if the experience offered is seen to justify the expense.

Rail systems are very suited for tourists. Any large city or region that has large numbers of tourists should have a good quality rail system. Tourists like rail systems, and their presence and quality can significantly affect the number of tourists that come to a region. Tourism brings valuable money into an economy, generates jobs, and earns foreign exchange. Tourism, when done sustain ably, is a good thing that should be encouraged.

Tourist railways are railways that are specifically designed and marketed to tourists. They are not typically used by passengers to move around an area, but are designed to provide an experience that is far beyond what is normally obtained from a "normal" railway. Tourist railways can be quite effective in bringing tourists to a region, and there are many famous examples. The street cars of San Francisco are a very known example, and there are many others. Tourist railways fall into a number of small categories:
- Train journeys that are very scenic, and may take between 1 to 2 hours. The train often travels over and through mountains, and this type of rail service is designed for day trips, rather than trips that take days. Examples of this type of tourist

railway is the Kuranda railway in northern Queensland in Australia.
- Rail cruises, where the trip is meant to resemble that of an ocean cruiser liner in splendour and quality of travel, where the trip can take several days or even longer. The tickets for this type of travel are very expensive, and the quality of service very high. Sleeper compartments are common on this type of rail system, and the trip length can be over 30 days. Perhaps the best known of this style of rail system is Orient Express, which used to travel from Paris to Istanbul. Another example would be a long distance train trip through the Canadian Rockies.
- Short train trips that allow tourists to access difficult to reach places. One very good example of this is the Peak Tram in Hong Kong, which allows tourists to reach the top of Hong Kong Island. Another example is the monorail that connects Harbourside in Singapore with the resort island of Sentosa, where one of the casinos is located in Singapore.
- Historical tramways, which meander through the centre of cities on old tram routes. In addition to San Francisco, there are some of these in Melbourne and Adelaide in Australia. This type of tram is often free, and offers a quite poor service for getting people from one destination to another, but provides a nice scenic ride through the city.
- Rail systems so exotic that people will travel on them for the experience, such as the Maglev in Shanghai. This train is a very interesting experience as it is, at the time of writing, the fastest commercial train in operation. Another example is the very short rail line in the Blue Mountains near Sydney that operates at an incline of 55° to the horizontal. To a lesser extent HSR systems are also an experience, and tourists will use them just for the experience.

Tourist railways can attract significant numbers of tourists, in the order of tens of thousands each year for very good quality systems. The economic benefit of this should not be discounted.

Other than the special case of tourist railways, in general tourists also greatly like using efficient and cost effective rail systems in areas where they want to visit. Tourists often do not bring their cars with them when travelling, especially when travelling large distances, or to countries over seas. The further tourists want to travel, the less likely it is they will want to bring their car. This leaves tourists at the mercy of the local transport systems, which can include car rental, taxis, buses, rail, and other forms of public transportation. Some tourists will rent cars, but this is not always possible, and many tourists will be travelling on a budget.

Tourists often want to use rail systems to get around at their destination, but only where a good quality service if offered. The amenity of a good quality rail system is hard to understate, and there are many examples of cities with well developed rail systems that allow tourist to move around with ease. Rail systems suit tourists, for a variety of reasons listed below, and these include:

- Rail systems are normally immovable, unlike bus lines which change frequently. Rail systems require very heavy investments, and so are normally permanent. For tourists who have only been to a city or region a small number of times, this can be very helpful, as the stability of the system allows tourists to use it more effectively.
- Rail systems are more spacious than buses, and cheaper than taxis. They are often very cheap to use, especially metro systems in large cities.
- It's not necessary to be able to speak the local language when using a metro system, as there are signs in the Latin alphabet which can be easily read (in most rail networks), and the need to explain to a taxi driver where the passenger wants to go can be avoided
- In some countries taxi drivers participate in scams to extract money out of passengers, and can be violent. One unfortunate example of this is the island of Phuket in Thailand.
- Information for rail systems can be obtained from the internet easily, as rail systems are permanent, a map can be downloaded before going to the new city or country.
- Bus stops can be very poorly signposted, and tourists can be overcarried very easily. Bus stops in some countries are clearly signposted, which makes things easier for tourists, but this is often not the case. In Australia it is common to rely on the driver to tell passengers what stop the bus is approaching.
- Ferry services on large rivers or harbours can have an extremely large number of stopping patterns. With a large number or piers/jetties, a very large number of different routes can be generated, which can be extremely confusing. Rail

systems have very consistent stopping patterns which are almost always advertised well in advance of the trip.
- Rail services are often faster than buses and ferries
- Bus services stop on edge of the road, on opposite sides of the road, so any passenger that is overcarried may have terrible trouble crossing a highway to get to the bus service in the other direction
- Rail systems can move large numbers of people for large events, such as the Olympics, or a football match, that would be impossible in any reasonable numbers on any other form of public transportation.
- Rail systems such as HSR systems offer ticket sales through internet sites, which means tourists can buy tickets well in advance. Bus or ferry tickets are commonly only available in the city once the tourist arrives there. This is of course not the case where the bus or ferry system is integrated into the region's ticketing system.

So rail systems generate more tourist income for a city or region, which is due to the larger numbers of tourists that are attracted to a city or region. Some of the disadvantages of rail systems, and there are not many, but some drawbacks for tourists are:
- Rail metro services are slower than taxis, unless the traffic is very bad
- Rail systems can be dangerous, with thefts and petty crime common. This of course depends on the country where the rail system is located
- Very large rail systems can be very confusing to use. Some of the stations in Tokyo are enormous and interchanging can be very difficult
- Rail systems are not suited to get people to remote areas, or mountains or swamps. Areas of great natural beauty frequently do not have any rail system at all, and the cost of constructing it would be far greater than the economic benefit
- Most rail systems do no operate past midnight, and so tourists "hitting the town" may not be able to use a rail system when returning back to their hotel room
- Some rail systems are too crowded for luggage, and may even ban passengers bringing luggage onto the rail system.

So what makes a good tourist rail system? What makes the rail system attractive to use for a tourist? Is it any different to what a commuter passenger would want? Below is a list of some of the things that attracts tourists to a rail system:
- It has a simple ticketing that provides tickets that cover where tourists want to go
- There are direct connections to and from the airport, or major transport interchange
- The rail system is simple and easy to use
- The rail system connects to tourists attractions
- The crime rate is low
- Plenty of space for luggage
- Lifts and escalators for passengers with baggage
- Reasonable pricing
- Good quality signage, in languages that many of the tourists would read, often English, or at least Latin characters. This is particularly important for metro stations with large numbers of exits.
- Interchanges are small or convenient, and do not involve walking kilometres to another station to change trains. This is often difficult to avoid, and even a well planned system such as Hong Kong has large interchanges that involve a lot of walking.

Tourism can represent a large part of the GDP of modern economies. In Australia tourism represents about 4% of GDP, which is a large amount for one industry. It also provides about 5% of the total employment in Australia (in 2013). Likewise tourism accounts for 4.5% of the GDP of Hong Kong, and employs about 6.5% (in 2013). Tourism is also a good way for countries to earn foreign currency, and in many ways tourism is like an export.

Much of the focus of tourism and the related economic studies is related to the construction of places to visit, and theme parks and gardens seem to be a common thing to build. Also countries can build exhibition halls, which can be used to cater for large exhibitions, such as car shows or gift expositions. This too can bring in a large amount of income to a country. One consideration is of course the construction of the infrastructure to support tourism, which normally means airports and hotels, but includes rail systems.

So a good quality rail system can have a profound effect on the tourism in an area. That's a nice statement to make in any cost benefit study for the construction of a new rail line, or a large new project, but how is this assessed?

Economic Benefits of Tourist Railways

Assessing tourist railways is conducted on a different basis to almost all other types of rail system. The purpose of a tourist railway is to provide an experience to tourists, and the economic benefit of a tourist railway is assessed similar to any other government project, such as cost to build, economic benefits, money brought into the economy, jobs provided, etc. For a more general rail project, such as building a metro line in a city, the rail system supports the tourist industry in general, and is often not linked to one specific project. In a small number of cases, the construction of a rail line is directly linked and part of the construction of a larger tourist attraction, and so the cost of the rail line is included in the cost benefit study of the larger project. This was the case for Hong Kong Disneyland, where the rail line was constructed specifically for the theme part.

Many rail projects will clearly have no impact to tourism in the city or region. This is particularly so for:
- Commuter rail lines, where trains operate between city centres and the suburbs. Tourists will rarely be interested in the suburbs of large cities, unless there is some sort of tourist attraction there or are visiting friends or family
- Rail lines that operate between cities and small regional centres that do not attract tourists
- Freight lines of all types
- Rail lines that are designed to take workers to specific worksites, such as large industrial area, where tourists are unlikely to want to go. This can include light rail as well as heavy
- Feeder light rail lines that connect the suburbs to heavy rail lines.

These rail lines will have almost no impact to tourism, and changes in tourist numbers should not be included in any cost benefit economic appraisal.

Some rail lines clearly will have a benefit to tourism, although an indirect one. Changes to rail lines with these characteristics, or the construction of new ones, will increase tourism when:
- The rail line connects to the airport or other major transport interchange such as a cruise liner terminal
- The rail line connects to an exhibition centre
- The rail line passes through the centre of any major city
- The rail line is an HSR line. This is particularly the case the faster the system operates.
- The rail line connects areas with many hotels to other locations where tourists may want to go
- The rail line offers a good view of an important tourist attraction, or natural area
- The rail line connects to major tourist attractions such as theme parks or museums
- A tram line that passes through the centre of a city and offers a convenient way to see different parts of the city

For these projects it is much more likely that the tourism benefits will be high, or at least worth considering.

So, where appropriate, the benefits to tourism of any infrastructure may be assessed through an economic tourism impact study. This type of study is very common, and falls within an area of economics called tourism economics. The benefits of tourism can be broadly characterised as:
- Direct benefits, which is the money spent by tourist when in the region or city. This is normally calculated as a total dollar figure per day per person.
- Indirect benefits, which refers to the money spent by businesses that sell products to tourists. These businesses need to buy supplies to provide their services, which is an indirect benefit.
- Induced benefits, which means the spending and income effect of the employees and owners of businesses supplying goods to the tourist industry. For example, airport employees spend money on renting properties near the airport, and this raises rentals in the area, which is an induced benefit.

It is important for any economic appraisal of tourism to include all the benefits, not just the direct ones. A lot of economic activity is generated by tourism, and this extends to the infrastructure needed to provide the services that tourists want. A restaurant will need to buy chairs, tables, cooking equipment, uniforms, and the business that supply these goods will also benefit. A large tourist industry can support the employment of a lot of people.

A description of the benefits of tourism for a rail project would be described in the following terms:
- The number of additional people that will visit an area or region as a result of a rail project.
- The amount of money they will spend, and inject into the local economy.
- The economic activity that will be generated as a result of the increase in tourism.

In tourism economic benefit studies a common concept is an economic multiplier. The multiplier effect refers to the economic activity that is generated by tourism that is beyond the direct spending by tourists. The multiplier effect is:

$$Multiplier = \frac{(direct\ benefit + indirect\ benefit + induced\ benefit)}{direct\ benefit}$$

Major industrialised counties will normally have a government statistics department that collects this type of information, and should publish the economic multiplier of the benefits of tourism. They will also publish information on the number of arrivals, time spent in the country, and where they went. This information is extremely useful in compiling a tourism economics benefits study.

The Australian Bureau of Statistics has published a number of studies examining the economic benefit of tourism and reported in July 2013 that the multiplier for tourism in Australia is 1.9. The economic multiplier for tourism seems to be commonly somewhere around 1.5 to 2, but this varies significantly based on the country and many other factors.

A related concept is what is called the "leakage effect", where money generated from tourism leaves the country where the money is spent. Leakage of money from an economy for tourism is common, especially in developed countries, where services provided are by foreigners that take the profits offshore. Many of the products provided in countries that have undeveloped infrastructure and industry are imported, which means that the people where the tourism is do not benefit.

Modelling for a tourism impact study seems to be quite complex, but similar to that of modelling changes to demand for rail services. Demand elasticises are commonly used, as well as more complex models using utilities. Recall that utility is the benefit that consumers derive from buying a good, and is not necessarily the same as price.

Complex models for tourist behaviour have been developed. Once created, it is possible to introduce changes to this model, and from this an estimate of the changes to tourism from large scale rail projects. Tourism is driven by major factors such as the sights and places to visit, cost of accommodation and food, as well as the convenience of the travel required to get to the destination, and often this is air travel. Rail services play more of a role in getting people around in their tourist destination, rather than bringing people into the region for tourism.

Of course HSR is the exception to this, and an HSR service may bring in large numbers of tourists. Domestic tourists are much more likely to travel to a location when HSR services are cheap, comfortable and frequent, and the increase in tourism from an HSR system can be significant. This is especially so for places where access before the introduction of the HSR system was difficult or time consuming.

Unfortunately demand elasticises, so useful for estimating the increase in passengers or freight for new rail projects is not really useful for tourism. Rail transport mostly plays only a small role in the cost of any travel, especially where all the long distance travel is by air.

REFERENCES

1. Tourism Research Australia, *Tourism's Contribution to the Australian Economy, 1997-98 to 2011 – 12*, July 2013

2. Ang-Olson, J. & Mahendra, A. *Cost Benefit Analysis of Converting a Lane for Bus Rapid Transit – Phase II Evaluation and Methodology*, National Cooperative Highway Research Program, Research Results Digest 352.

3. Kenworthy, J. *Transport Energy Use and Greenhouse Gases in Urban Passenger Transport Systems: A Study of 84 Global Cities, Institute for Sustainability and Technology Policy*, Murdoch University

4. Kemp, R. *T618 – Traction Energy Metrics*, Rail Safety and Standards Board, Interfleet Technology, Dec 2007

5. Brons, M & Givoni, M., Rietveld, P. *Access to Railway Stations and its potential in increasing rail use*, Transport Research Part A 43(2009) 136 – 149, The Department of Spatial Economics, The Free University

6. CFL, *Rapport Annuel*, 2011 (In French)

7. Koppenjan, J. & Leijten, M. *How to Sell Railways: Lessons on the privatisation of Three Dutch Railway Projects*, European Journal of Transport and Infrastructure Research, Sept 2007

8. Andersonn, M. *Marginal cost of railway infrastructure wear and tear for freight and passenger trains in Sweden*, Swedish National Road and Transport Research Institute (VTI), Department of Transport Economics, 2011

9. Bradbury, N, *Face the Facts on Transport Safety*, Railwatch Nov 2002

10. Bureau of Transport and Regional Economics [BTRE], 2007, *Estimating urban traffic and congestion cost trends for Australian cities*, Working paper 71, BTRE, Canberra ACT.

11. Damart, S. & Roy, B. *The uses of cost-benefit analysis in public transportation decision-making in France*, Transport Policy 16 (2009) 200-212

12. Centre for International Economics, *Business Costs of Traffic Congestion*, August 2006

13. Department of Infrastructure, Transport, Regional Development and Local Government, *Road Deaths Australia 2008 Statistical Summary*, May 2009

14. Paulley, N. et al The Demand for Public Transport: The Effects of Fares, Quality of Service, Income, and Car Ownership, White Rose Research Online, http://eprints.whiterose.ac.uk/2034/

15. Litman, T. *Understanding Transport Demands and Elasticities*, Victoria Transport Policy Institute, www.vti.org, March 2013

16. IBI Group, E&N Railway Corridor Study: Analysis of Tourist Train Potential, (Date Unknown)

17. Daniel J Stynes, Economic Impact of Tourism, Michigan State University

18. Kockelman, K. et al *The Economics of Transportation Systems: A Reference for Practitioners*, Center for Transportation Research, University of Austin, January 2013

19. Baldry, C. Off the rails: factors affecting track worker safety in the rail industry, Employee Relations; 2006;

20. Joint Transport Research Centre of the OECD *Survey on price and demand elasticity in terms of reliability in freight railway services*, International Transport Forum, May 2008

21. West, R. et al *Identification and Evaluation of Freight Demand Factors*, National Cooperative Freight Research Program, Sept 2011

22. Beuthe, M. *Freight transportation demand elasticities: a geographical multimodal transportation network analysis*, Transportation Research Part E 37 (2001) 253 - 266

23. De Rus, Gines *The Economic Effects of High Speed Rail Investment*, OECD International Transport Forum, Discussion Paper No 2008-16, May 2012

24. Cervero, R. & Murakami, J. *Rail and Property Development in Hong Kong: Experiences and Extensions*, Urban Studies, 2009 46:2019 Aug 2009

25. Chun-Hwan, K. *Transportation Revolution: The Korean High-speed Railway*, Japan Railway & Transport Review 40, March 2005

26. Agostini, C & Palmucci *The Anticipated Capitalisation Effect of a New Metro Line on Housing Prices*, Fiscal Studies, vol 29, no 2, pp 233 – 256 (2008) 0143-5671

27. Scarsi, G.C. & Smith, G. *Different Approaches and Responsibilities for Investment Sustainability in EU Railway Infrastructure: Four Case Studies*, EUI Working Papers, RSCAS 2010/88

28. Bureau of Infrastructure, Transport and Regional Economics (BITRE), 2010, *International road safety comparisons 2009*, Canberra ACT.

29. Shughart, L. *Trends and Issues in Container Transport*, TRF Annual Meeting, March 2012

30. Arnott, R. & Small, K. *The Economics of Traffic Congestion*, American Scientist, Volume 82, Sept 1994

31. Victoria Transport Policy Institute Transportation Cost and Benefit Analysis II – Air Pollution Costs, www.vtpi.org/tca/tca0510.pdf, **March 2011**

32. Australian Government Department of Climate Change and Energy Efficiency *National Greenhouse Accounts (NGA) Factors*, July 2010

33. Fouquet, R. *Trends in Income and Price Elasticities of Transport Demand (1850 – 2000)*, Basque Centre for Climate Change, BC3 Working Paper Series, Feb 2012

34. Hess, D.B. & Almeida, T.M. *Impact of Proximity to Light Rail Rapid Transit on Station-area Property Values in Buffalo*, New York, Urban Studies, Vol 44, Nos 5/6, 1041 – 1068, May 2007

35. Burge, P. et al Modelling Demand for Long-Distance Travel in Great Britain, www.rand.org, 2011

36. Australian Transport Safety Bureau Cross Modal Safety Comparisons, https://www.atsb.gov.au/media/36229/cross_modal_safety_comparisons.pdf

37. Li, K & Tiong, R. *Financing and Operating of Singapore's Urban Rail Transit Infrastructure*, 4th International Conference on Wireless Communications, Networking and Mobile Computing, 2008

38. Torija, A.J. *Relationship between road and railway noise annoyance and overall sound exposure*, Transportation Research Part D 16 (2011) 15-22

39. Nijkamp, P. & Pepping, G. *Meta-Analysis for Explaining the Variance in Public Transport Demand Elasticities in Europe*, Journal of Transportation and Statistics Jan 1998

40. Haworth, N. & Vulcan, P. & Sweatman, P. *Truck Safety Benchmarking Study*, National Road Transport Commission, March 2002

41. Flyvbjerg, B et al *Comparison of Capital Costs per Route-Kilometre in Urban Rail*, European Journal of Transport and Infrastructure Research, Feb 2008

42. Queensland Co-ordinator General Northern Link Road Tunnel, April 2010, http://www.statedevelopment.qld.gov.au/resources/project/legacy-way-project/northern-link-road-tunnel-cg-report.pdf

43. BSL Management Consultants GmbH & Co. KG *Survey on price and demand elasticity in terms of reliability in freight railway services*, Hamburg May 2008

44. Nilsson, J-E. *Restructuring Sweden's railways: The unintentional deregulation*, Swedish Economic Policy Review 9 (2002) 229 – 254

Chapter 15 Government Regulation

Introduction

Government plays a very large role in the financial viability of any rail system. Only a small number of rail systems can exist without any form of government support. Most rail systems either have direct support from government, or a form of support that makes the rail system viable.

Rail freight, which is typically seen as a good example of private sector management of businesses, in many cases is dependent on government for subsidies or for the provision of infrastructure. Rarely does a rail company pay entirely for its infrastructure, although there are several coal companies in Australia that are able to run their own infrastructure without any government support.

Given that government needs to provide so much support, their actions have a large impact to any rail operation. The decision they make can have a profound impact to any rail system. Many of the decisions government makes are economic in nature, such as setting access charges or prices for rail tickets.

Governments need to exercise care in making any decision, as the impact can be very large. Many of the questions involving government regulation are economic. This means that the best decision is one where economic outcomes are maximised.

Pricing Rail Tickets

Pricing rail tickets is an intriguing area. Setting the price low will often result in that rail service being very heavily used, alternatively setting them high will mean that more revenue is earned, and but fewer people use the service. This issue is particularly important as most rail systems operate at a loss, and generally it is not possible to charge the full price of providing the service. This makes the decision about the level of fares particularly important.

Rail services are provided as a benefit to society, and for many railways the economic benefit will far outweigh the cost of providing the service. Most rail systems seem to struggle to recoup their costs in either fares or other charges such as freight charges, and so need to be supported by the government. Whilst this is not always the case, it does seem to be a very common scenario, and something that needs to be managed. Where taxpayer money is used to support a financially unviable rail system, there needs to be a clear case that this should be done. The scale of the subsidy is also important, as some governments will not have the resources to support a large rail system, and some level of cost reduction may be needed.

In some cases the economic benefit of the rail service may be quite small, or alternatively no benefit at all. This has been known to happen with some regional services, where the service is provided as a policy decision, and not for an economic benefit. In these instances, prices may be charged on the basis of managing passenger levels, rather than an economic benefit. This is discussed below.

Notwithstanding a special number of cases where a rail system operates at a profit or on a commercial basis, or where the service is provided for policy reasons and so ticket prices are almost irrelevant, or for special passengers with special needs, economics plays an important part in the decision on ticket prices. A rail system is established to provide an economic benefit to society, and so ticket prices are a way of influencing this, and so ticket prices should be set at a price that maximises the economic benefit. Ticket prices too low will mean that government will carry too much of the burden and passengers are willing to pay more, or too high will mean that the very expensive infrastructure built for the rail system will be underutilised. There is a happy balance somewhere in the middle.

Rail ticket pricing is a key issue because of the inflexibility of rail prices. Once the ticket prices are set then it is unusual to change them frequently or in a large way, and when a change is made it is normally small. There might be a yearly review of the prices paid, or at certain times the price structure may be reviewed. Frequent changes in price are to be avoided with rail transport.

Rail ticket prices are not normally priced the same was as air tickets. Air tickets are sold under many different classes of ticket, and as the cheapest class of ticket is sold, people who want to fly on that airline for that flight are forced to pay for a more expensive ticket class. Ticket classes are related to, but often different to seating classes, such as economy, business class and first class. Economy class may be divided up into several ticket classes, and some of these classes may be prioritised over others for seating, etc, and some ticket classes may allow changes to flight schedule, or holders may be able to sit further forward in the aircraft. Rail tickets, even for seated passenger services, are almost never priced like this, although some HSR services in Europe are priced this way. For this type of system, as demand increases for any air service, there is a self adjusting mechanism as the increase in price stops people from buying too many tickets, or when demand is low, encouraging them to buy more. Ordinarily, rail operators need to set rail ticket prices at a flat level, so that everyone gets the same price that buys the same type of ticket. The choice of ticket price is then quite important as it is difficult to change, and the self-adjusting mechanism available for air travel is not available. For HSR systems, it is possible to implement a system where the ticket prices increases as the number of passengers increases, but it would be a very strange and bizarre metro system that implemented such a policy!

For tourist trains the pricing of tickets is easy, and done of the basis of maximising profit. This is especially true for rail cruises and other rail systems that are privately owned and operated. This type of railway often operates without much government interference, and is largely free to do almost anything as regards ticketing. Tourist railways are not considered to be services that are consumed by those with disabilities, or on government pensions, and so a discount for these groups of people is uncommon. This makes the ticketing system rather simple.

Some regional and commuter rail systems also operate on a commercial basis. This is sometimes achieved by the government providing some services at a low rate, such as access charges. As rail systems are normally not viable, the government may pay for the infrastructure, but allow commercial operators to run trains on its system for a reasonable fee. Private operators can then make a profit, and sell tickets at prices they decide, and this results in a business that government does not need to operate, something considered desirable in many countries. Ticket prices may be controlled through a contract with the private company, exchanging access to track for guarantees that ticket prices will remain within certain levels.

Most rail pricing systems offer large discounts to older citizens, and children for whom parents will need to pay. Reducing the price for tickets for needy groups is common, and there may be some restrictions on the times that these groups can travel. Commonly access to the highest speed trains, or rail services during peak periods will be denied to those on pensions and buying cheaper tickets.

Prices are often reduced for army and military staff, war veterans, those with disabilities, and police officers. In some countries monks and others from religious orders can also travel for free. Also those who make a serious contribution to society may be rewarded with free public travel, such as mothers who have a certain number of children. Another variation is that those involved in volunteer organisations can also travel for free, such as members of the Salvation Army, or St Johns Ambulance. The list of people and professions that are allowed to travel for free can be quite long.

So, to summarise the pricing of ticket for groups with either some entitlement to pay less, or reduced capacity to pay:
- Tickets are normally offered at dramatically reduced prices
- Often some sort of proof is required for obtaining cheaper tickets
- Only services that are considered necessities have confessional pricing, tourist railways and premium services may not offer confessional prices (but sometimes do)
- Cheaper tickets only allow travel on the lowest class of rail travel, at non-busy times. These tickets are sometimes not available to be used during peak periods

So for passengers who don't fit into any of the special categories above, a decision will need to be made on the price level. Rail tickets can be priced on a number of different bases. The system used to price tickets will depend on many local factors, and systems used to price tickets includes:

- Ticket prices should be equal to the marginal cost of providing the service
- Tickets priced on a full commercial basis
- Monopoly pricing of tickets for speciality services/maximising revenue (similar to monopoly pricing)
- Maximising the economic benefit to society
- Pricing at a level where the rail system operates at 100% capacity or other predetermined capacity level

- Based on getting as many people as possible onto the rail system
- Free
- The capacity to pay of passengers
- Relative to other competitors

So let's discuss each of these different pricing systems in turn.

Marginal costs are the costs associated with providing extra services, and do not include fixed costs. Marginal costs for a rail system are commonly lower, much lower than the fixed costs. For a rail system the marginal costs include the cost of wear and tear to trains, driver salaries, electricity or fuel for operating a train. Indirect or fixed costs include the cost of infrastructure, maintenance facilities, and head office costs.

One view is that the marginal cost of providing services is the cost that should be charged to passengers and consumers. The marginal cost is lower, which permits the offer of lower prices. Services can be operated at times when the number of passengers is quite low, as the marginal costs are low. Another argument for this approach is that the infrastructure can be fully exploited, and expensive infrastructure fully utilised.

One of the central concepts of economics is that the pricing mechanism for goods is a way of rationing, so that scare goods are allocated to those who need them the most. This can also be done with rail tickets, setting the pricing at a level so that the rail service is not too crowded. This relatively uncommon situation does sometimes arise, especially with smaller rail services that are too crowded, such as monorails, intermediate capacity metros, or trams. These smaller services, where they are very busy, can become extremely crowded, and the only way to manage the situation is to increase prices so that the system can operate without severe overcrowding. Where a rail system has classes, ie a first and a second class, the higher classes may be priced at this level, and economy class priced so that anyone can use it.

Some rail systems are built to get people away from road vehicles and into trains. This is considered desirable for many reasons and it is a common goal in rail transport planning. To encourage people into the rail system the price may be set low. One way of setting the price is to review the capacity to pay of the local population, and then set prices at a level that is clearly affordable. This should result in a system that is very heavily used, and examples from Asia suggest that this is so (and from Melbourne). Another way to approach this problem is to model consumer preferences, and then estimate how many people will switch from road to rail at what price. Coupled with modelling of road traffic, this can be an effective way to get more people out of cars and into trains.

Some rail systems become very unpleasant where the rail service is overcrowded. In Sydney there are targets on minimising the level of overcrowding on certain services, and it is considered undesirable to have too many people on one train. This is not a commonly held view, and it is common for railways to want to increase passenger numbers as much as possible. Some metro services also get very crowded, and in some cases people cannot board trains due to huge passenger numbers. The solution in these cases can be to raise ticket prices, so that the number of passengers is reduced, and moved to a preferred level.

It should be remembered that changes to ticket prices may take some time to influence passenger behaviour. In the short run, if passenger prices are increased or decreased, there may only be a small impact to passenger numbers, but over the long term this affect may be much larger. Typically the long term is years, and the short term is either weeks or months, as a rough guide.

Monopoly pricing is a situation where one business has such complete control over the market that it is free to set whatever price it wants. Monopoly pricing of goods is a topic commonly studied in economics, and it is considered an undesirable situation to have arise, and to be avoided if at all possible. Monopolists can raise prices to a level where profits are very large, and the number of people consuming the good is quite small. The profit maximising situation for monopolists, as any economist knows, is where marginal cost is equal to marginal revenue. The price for a firm that controls a monopoly can be 2 or 3 times that of a perfectly competitive market.

The risk that monopoly pricing will be applied to a rail service is relatively low. For rail systems that operate on a commercial basis, with little or no competition, monopoly pricing can occur. Rail cruises can have monopoly pricing, but the extremely high cost of rail cruises may preclude the rail cruise provider from setting prices too high. Monopolist pricing also sometimes occurs with rail services to a critical facility, such as an airport or exhibition centre, where fares can be set at a very high level. Monopoly pricing, where it is implemented, can create enormous resentment, and some of this may be directed at governments. Note that governments may be tempted to implement monopoly pricing on some rail services to make it more attractive to a company wanting to bid on the contract to provide the service.

A small number of railways operate where the service is entirely free. This is common within airports, where the cost of operating the airport includes the operation of the rail system. Whilst the reader many consider that most rail systems in airports are quite small, some are surprisingly large, and the rail system in Hong Kong airport is several kilometres long (at least), and contains several lines. All rail services in this airport are free, and paid for by the airport. Alternatively, some rail lines may operate free, such as tram lines within the central business district (downtown).

Other than airports, it seems unusual to provide rail services for free. In Victoria, trams were effectively free for many years due to lax enforcement of possession of tickets, and so many trams routes operated full. This decision seemed to be a quiet one of behalf of the government and the people of Melbourne, and visitors from out of town were often shocked by the lack of interest in passengers buying anything resembling a ticket. The author's own experience of this very unusual situation is that the number of people using the system was far beyond what would normally be expected. It did however create some real problems for the operators of the tram system, who were under a lot of financial pressure!

Probably the most complicated, and theoretically correct way to price tickets is through demand based modelling. This has already been discussed earlier in the chapter on demand modelling, and there is no reason this type of modelling cannot be applied to ticket prices. Activity based modelling attempts to estimate the travel patterns of tens of thousands of people, and then aggregate them. An attempt is then made to maximise the utility, and this can also be done of the basis of ticket prices. As mentioned above, this type of modelling is expensive and requires the construction of very data heavy models, and a well funded research organisation or company to maintain it.

HSR systems often compete with air travel, and so pricing of tickets would need to be compared with the comparable flight. Where the rail service is faster, and more convenient than the comparable flight, a premium can be charged for tickets, and prices may be substantially higher for rail than for air travel. Where the rail service is slower and less comfortable, the system may need to be priced at a discount to attract any passengers at all, and where air tickets prices are low the price for rail travel may be very cheap.

It is common to set tickets to a base price, and then modify it for a number of special situations. The price modified is normally quite small, but enough to encourage behaviour that a government may consider desirable, such as travelling outside of peak periods. Some of these are:
- Reducing prices for those that possess "Smart Cards"
- Reducing prices for those that buy long period tickets, such as a monthly ticket in advance
- Offering reduced prices for those that travel outside of peak periods
- Offering reduced prices for students, both for high school and for university/college
- Reduced tickets for tourists on special days or special trains

Another consideration is how to price tickets for busy times. Most railways experience a peak period, where the number of passengers on the rail system is much higher than normal. Tickets for peak periods may be much higher for these time periods than for others, and railways may offer discounts for those who travel outside of peak times. The discount for those who travel outside of peak times may be substantial.

Many railways have a "Smart card" where the cost of the ticket is deducted from money loaded onto the card. Cards can be purchased from vending machines at stations and are "swiped" in front of an electronic reader when passengers enter and leave a station. Most railways charge for the purchase of this card, and may charge a deposit as well for the card, which can be returned to the purchaser when the card is surrendered when no longer needed. Smart cards are not normally the only system to pay with, and many railways with smart cards also offer point to point tickets (or other style tickets in some cases) that can be paid for with cash. Smart cards usually offer small discounts to those that own and use them.

Another consideration is what price to provide for tourists. Tourists bring a lot of money into an economy, and tickets may be provided to tourists at a cheap price to encourage them to come into the country. This is done in Japan, where rail passes are sold that permit tourists to travel all over the country at a reasonable price. This again is a policy decision, to encourage a high level of tourist spending by reducing the prices of some key services.

Special tickets may be offered to families on special days. For example, on days where there is a large fete or circus, or some other event that is family related, railways may offer tickets to families as a group. This ticket will often cost about the same amount as 1 to 2 adults, and will include as part of the price an unlimited number of children. The ticket will cover the different transport modes from a large number of origins to a specific event or location for a particular day. In NSW tickets to zoos often have family passes on Sundays, where a large family can travel cheaply.

Rail Freight Curfews

Rail freight often has restrictions placed on it when operating through cities. This is done to allow the maximum number of passenger trains to move throughout the system, and one way of achieving this is to limit the number of freight movements. A curfew is normally time based, and certain locations are off limits to freight trains until the curfew time has passed.

One of the consequences of a curfew is that when a curfew is lifted, there is a flood of freight trains moving through the rail system. Another consequence is that there may be many more freight trains operating at night, such as at midnight, and this may be a problem for local residents trying to sleep. The experience in Sydney has been that bulk material trains can largely operate any time, and midnight is fine for a coal trains making its way to a fully automated port. For intermodal trains, it seems that it best to operate during business hours, especially where the train has only a short trip distance, such as 30 to 40 kilometres. Curfews seem to impact intermodal trains more than bulk material trains.

Freight curfews often result in the construction of dedicated freight lines. Freight lines, or corridors, are rail lines restricted only to freight traffic. Freight corridors across the world seem to be quite uncommon, and there are only a small number in Australia. Freight providers love them, as they give them access to ports and terminals that otherwise would require running on mixed rail lines to get to.

Setting Access Charges

Access charges are the costs imposed on rail freight operators, and operators of passenger trains, for being allowed to drive their trains through a rail network. As has been mentioned in other parts of this chapter, the setting of the price for access is very important for freight, as freight as an industry is very price sensitive, and small changes in price can have a large impact on the amount of freight moved.

A pricing regime for access charges may be quite complicated. A large number of different variables may be involved in determining what price should be paid. Access charges are normally set per tonne kilometre moved, and so a heavier train will need to pay more. In addition to a cost per tonne kilometre, there can also be a flat fee for entry to the network. Some of the factors that need to be taken into consideration for setting access charges include:
- The type of train
- The type of freight (if there is any)
- The part of the network that will be accessed
- Is the train empty or loaded
- The maximum speed of the train
- The length of the train
- The type of brakes installed on the train
- Will the train draw power from the overhead, if there is any?
- The level of priority given to the train
- Dangerous goods on the train
- Maximum axle loads of any wagons on a train

Access changes will normally be available publicly, and often be presented in the form of tables.

A rail infrastructure company (typically government operated) will want to recover at least the cost of damage to their infrastructure as a minimum from a rail freight operator. As freight trains are heavy, there is often some damage to rails and ballast from freight trains. Bulk materials being transported may spill as freight operators load their trains as much as possible, and spillage at tight curves and bridges is common. This spillage needs to be removed, and the cost of removal can be significant.

Again, the role of the economist and economics is important here. For a publicly funded infrastructure company, which many of them are, the level of access charges should be set to maximise the economic benefit of society, and not necessarily recover the cost of damage to infrastructure. This can be a very frustrating situation for an infrastructure company, as they lose money every time a freight train passes through their system.

Access charges in Australia are not high. For example, the cost of access for an intermodal freight train to move from Sydney to Melbourne, a distance of over 900 kilometres, may only be around $4000 (Australian dollars) in 2012, which is not much considering the damage that can be caused by a heavily loaded freight train to rail freight infrastructure.

Standardising the Regulation of Rail Freight

There are government rules and regulations for any rail freight company. Rail freight can potentially be dangerous, and some materials can be moved that are poisonous, flammable, or toxic. Rail freight may collide with passenger trains, and cause fatalities, and there are definitely real risks to moving freight with rail. These risks, and the need to manage access to any rail system, means that rail freight operators in almost every country need to seek permission to operate their trains.

In addition, rail freight companies need to prove that their trains and drivers can pass through rail systems and urban areas without causing damage. There are numerous ways that a freight train can damage a rail system, with trains that are too heavy, hitting structures along the track, or just simply not stopping when required to stop and running into things. Drivers need to get some sort of license, and a license to drive a freight train is something that is granted only after years of experience on either smaller less dangerous trains, or with extensive training. The licensing regime is a very important way of maintaining the safety of any rail system.

Both the drivers of any freight train and the company that operates freight trains need to be accredited. For drivers this will involve a period of training, and assessment that their competencies are sufficient to drive a train safety. For a freight company, there needs to be a quality system in that company that can assure that trains can be driven safely without excessive risk to anyone. This process of accreditation for a freight company can be expensive, there will need to be process documentation collected, business systems built, and audits done to check compliance of business processes to standard. This is not a cheap process.

Each country will normally have its own accreditation process for freight operators, and often a freight company will need to apply for accreditation in each country. Different infrastructure operators may have their own licensing regime, and may require freight companies to comply with their own rules and regulations in addition to that applied by government. This level of regulation can prevent very serious barriers to the operation of freight trains between different countries or even different tracks owned by different infrastructure companies.

In the European Union there has been a serious effort to harmonise the different rules to make things easier for freight trains to move between areas. Most of the changes to European freight have come through the European Union, rather than individual governments or bilateral agreements, where rules, decisions and laws have been promulgated which are binding on the citizens, governments, and corporations of member states. Some of the rules that have been implemented include:
- The end of monopolies for the rail based movement of freight
- Open access arrangements for any rail freight company
- Harmonisation of the rules for accreditation for any rail freight company
- Creation and implementation of ERTMS, which is a signalling system that enforces maximum speeds across different networks. ERTMS is a European version of ATP (Automatic Train Protection).
- Creation of the European Rail Agency, run by the European Union, the intent of which is to promote the ease of movement of passenger and freight rail trains from one member country to another.
- Splitting infrastructure companies and train operators into two separate companies in all member countries (something that has only partially been complied with)

These efforts, in place now for over a decade, have had the effect of transforming the rail freight market in Europe. Rail freight moves far more easily now between member countries than before, but there are still many barriers to a free flow of freight.

As a final comment on harmonisation, a programme of standardising rules for the movement of freight is critically important between different countries and rail infrastructure companies. Without it the movement of rail freight can be severely hampered.

Rail Freight and Government Policy

Government policy is very important for any rail freight network. Rail freight as a industry is heavily dependent on government support to survive, and a hostile government will quickly reduce the amount of rail freight moved to almost nothing. Government policy is normally favourable to rail freight, as it is seen as a positive and beneficial thing, but where this is not the case rail freight will struggle to survive. There are many ways that a government can influence the amount of rail freight moved, and this support is critical to the continued survival of any rail freight industry.

The target of much government action is to increase the modal share of rail. Governments will often have policy launches where rail freight is discussed, and options for increasing it are laid out. In the European Union the European Commission produces policies and reports into rail freight and how to encourage it. Governments often have strategy documents that address how to increase the rail model share, and which seem to have mixed success, but nonetheless have a lot of useful information in them on the rail industry. Where sensible and useful policies are chosen and implemented, the amount of rail freight moved can increase dramatically.

Rail operators are commonly split from maintainers of infrastructure. The cost of maintaining infrastructure is very high, and often borne by the government, whereas the rail operators may be privately owned. An alternative to this structure is to have a large government organisation that owns and operates everything, so it operates the trains and freight as well. Rail infrastructure is extremely expensive to maintain, and is often the largest group of costs for any rail company. To encourage some private ownership and participation in any rail industry, it is possible, and commonly done, for government to pay for the infrastructure only, and not the cost of operating trains.

Rail freight companies are often privately operated. In Australia, even till recently, there were some freight companies that were government owned, but now all freight companies in Australia have been privatised, and owned by the private sector. The private sector seems able to manage their freight trains and rosters more efficiently, and seem to be able to move freight more cheaply than the public sector. Employee conditions in the public sector are often quite good, and inflexible, which does not help things. It is not clear at to the author why rail freight seems to operate so much better when privatised, and the experience in Australia for privatising freight rail operators has been almost uniformly positive.

So this leaves many governments in the difficult position of needing to provide constant support to an industry that is often completely privatised. In some countries the support of private organisations by government is commonly accepted, but in many others, and Australia included, government support to a private organisation is seen as a negative. This perception is particularly strong where the freight operator is owned by a foreign company, and providing support for this company may be perceived very negatively. Nonetheless government support for rail freight is still critical to its survival.

"Modal share" is a term that refers to the percentage of freight that is moved on different forms of transportation. Road transportation of freight is a "mode", and the mode share refers to how much of the freight travels on this form of transportation compared to any other mode. Other modes are rail, water, and air transportation. Rail and road transportation are often the most direct competitors; water transportation requires rivers or seas, and ports, which are not easy to move or change. Regardless of the mode of transportation for freight, it will need to be moved somehow, and what is not moved by rail will need to be moved through another transport mode. A lack of government support will mostly result in rail freight being moved on roads, and in an area with lots of people there will be a large number of trucks moving around the road system.

Governments control access to most infrastructure, including roads. Even where rail freight operators are privatised, governments can exercise substantial control over freight of all types through taxation, and regulation. Governments may want to encourage any type of freight transport mode, and there are a large number of mechanisms to achieve this. Government support is quite critical to any rail freight operation, and without support it will shrink to almost nothing.

So why is government support for rail freight so important? What can governments do to help rail freight along? The list is quite long, and below are some of the areas and facets of a rail freight business that governments can influence or control:

- Curfews on access to rail systems used by passenger systems
- Investment in infrastructure
- Setting access charges for freight trains to pass over rail infrastructure
- Allowing rail freight lines to operate through suburban areas
- Regulations on what products can be moved
- Standardising the safety and regulation regime for rail freight
- Setting aside land, and resuming land when needed
- Supporting the construction of efficient port infrastructure, that has good quality rail sidings next to it.
- Installing technology that is "freight friendly"
- Financial support when appropriate
- Participating in international efforts to allow freight to operate through many countries more efficiently
- Building rail systems where freight is not excluded

Curfews are sometimes placed on rail networks to stop rail freight from using the network during certain hours. Rail freight, because of its low speed and long length, can seriously interfere and impede faster moving passenger trains, and one solution to this problem can be to prohibit the entry of freight trains into the rail network, or parts of the network during certain times. This is called a curfew. Curfews are a real problem for freight operators, as they limit the number of usable hours per day for freight movements, and generally increase the expense of moving freight. Curfews will often also damage the punctuality of rail freight, as a freight train that reaches an area with a curfew as the curfew is imposed will need to wait until it is lifted. Freight trains often sit outside curfew areas waiting to enter, which is expensive and makes predicting the arrival time of the freight train difficult.

As the government will often control the infrastructure company, which is heavily subsidised, and freight trains do so much damage to the rail infrastructure because of their weight, the pricing of access charges is a key question. A low access charge will encourage large numbers of freight movements, and there will be little recovery of the cost of the damage to the infrastructure. Alternatively, a high access cost will result in very few freight movements, and types of rail freight that generates only a small profit, often intermodal traffic, will shift onto roads.

Many modern rail signalling systems are an additional cost burden for rail freight. Automatic Train Protection (ATP) is a safety system that checks that trains are braking correctly then they need to, and is becoming more common. This system can only be applied with difficulty to freight trains, and only with the support of the rail freight industry. ATP is being implemented in Europe as a way of allowing freight and passenger trains to operate in many different countries, for which it is quite suited, but in one jurisdiction ATP maybe a barrier to rail freight, because it is an additional cost to implement.

Transnational rail freight operations are now common in Europe, a continent with many small countries. Government policy in one country may be to encourage one freight operator over another, and having a preference such as this can strongly influence the ability of freight companies to enter the market. Governments may support companies domiciled in their own country, especially where these companies are government owned. Support for these companies may include subsidies, or cheap finance, or outright gifts of money. This is yet another way that governments can influence the rail freight market.

Perhaps the area where governments play the greatest role is in investment. Wealthy freight operators will be able to pay for some or all of investment in freight systems, but there are also many others that generate meagre returns, or no returns at all, and are operated as a benefit to the community. Where this is the case, the rail freight industry will be completely dependent on government to provide funds for investment in infrastructure, and if this is not done rail freight will struggle to compete. Any government that wants to encourage rail freight will need to take a lead role in improving productivity, as the rail freight companies will want to do this, but will often be unable. Rail freight operators may form industry groups to lobby government for support, but will be unable to provide anything more than moral support when the time comes to provide funds.

Many rail infrastructure companies in Europe publish a document called a "network statement". A network statement provides comprehensive information about the conditions and infrastructure in a rail system, and what a rail operator needs to do to run trains in that network. Network statements are very comprehensive, and detail the infrastructure that is present in a rail system. Some of the information contained in a network statement include:
- Typical tops speeds
- Structure and loading gauges
- Gauges, ie, standard/narrow
- Location of freight/intermodal terminals
- The location of refuelling facilities
- The process for applying for a path through the network
- Location of water supplies
- How access charges are calculated
- The maximum length of freight trains
- Other services provided (for a fee)

Network statements are fascinating documents that contain a great deal of information about how a railway operates. Network statements are often produced by government departments, as many infrastructure companies are government controlled, and government policy will play a role in determining the content of the network statement, and many of the access charges.

Where freight companies are privately owned, and the government owns the infrastructure, and the company that maintains it, then the question arises as to how access is given to freight operators to run trains on the network. A rail freight operator does not just arrive at the boundary to the network, contact the signal box and proceed into the rail system. The rail freight operator will need to be licensed or certified to operate on the network, and this license can be quiet difficult to get. The approval process is mostly overseen by a government department, and the rail freight operator will need to submit an application to operate trains on the network. In addition to this license a rail operator may need to obtain separate certification for safety, sometimes called a rail safety certificate. Some of the approvals that are needed to get a freight train onto a network include:

- Certification of rollingstock
- Certification of drivers
- Certification of companies, and with that procedures of work
- Permission to move goods of certain types
- Application for a path through the network

That's a lot of approvals, and these are usually obtained from each infrastructure company, or from the central government. This can be quite a burden where a freight train must move between many infrastructure boundaries.

Studies have shown that freight transport is very sensitive to price. Encouraging freight onto the rail system is best done through price mechanisms, although other factors are also important. One study detailed a market survey where the different factors relevant to freight were assessed for their importance. The study found that order of importance to rail freight was as follows:
- Price
- Punctuality
- Transport speed
- Other factors such as safety, flexibility, and frequency of service.

The other factors are important, but price is really central to how much freight is moved on any rail system. Governments are in a position to substantially effect the prices that are charged.

Some of the goods moved by freight operators can be classified as dangerous. For example, some poisonous chemicals, if released by harm or kill people nearby to the railway. Alternatively, where goods moved on a rail systems are highly flammable, then there is a risk of fire or even explosion. LPG containers can explode under the right conditions. It is even possible to transport weapons by rail, such as tanks or firearms, and their associated ammunition. The carriage of dangerous goods on a railway in most countries is subject to strict rules, and often a separate licensing regime. Some governments may not permit some types of dangerous goods to be moved on their rail network.

Last but not least in our list of parameters over which governments have control is taxation. In many countries the level of taxation is very high, and there are taxes on almost everything. Governments are in a position to strongly influence which mode of transport is chosen for freight through transportation. Taxes can be imposed on road use, or on road vehicle licensing, or on the carriage of freight. A government can always make rail freight more competitive with the right taxation, but as a lever through which to control people's actions care must be exercised other serious damage can be done to an economy.

Index

Access charges, 282
Activity based modelling, 235
Articulation, 13
at grade. *See* Grade separation
Automatic Train Protection, 282
Ballast, 60, 61
   Fines, 65
Bangkok Skytrain, 29
bi-level. *See* Double decker
Boardings, 2
Broad gauge, 8
Bulk material freight, 145
Bulk materials, 145
Bus Rapid Transit, 3
Cape gauge, 8
Capping layer, 61
Cascading, 171
Codeshare, 43
Community service obligations, 228
Commuter rail, 36
Consumer surplus, 105
Contact band. *See* wear band
Control system, 97
Cost benefit, 103
Curfew, 138, 281
Dangerous goods, 284
Demand
   Elasticity. *See*
Demand elasticity, 110
Demand estimation, 233
Demand inelasticity, 112
Demand supply curve, 104
Derailment, 144
Derived demand, 237
Diesel multiple units, 42
Dispatcher. *See* Signaller
Double decker, 15
Dwell time, 32, 36
Dynamic braking, 212
Economic multiplier, 260
Elasticity of demand, 111
Electric multiple units, 42
EMUs, 137
Equilibrium point, 105
ERTMS, 278
Externalities, 106
Externality, 119
Fixed costs, 113
Flat car, 150
Flat cars, 142
Flying junction, 13
Formation, 61
Freight
   Access charges, 276
   Axle load, 143
   Curfew, 220
   Gross Tonne Kilometres, 143
   Million Gross Tonnes, 143
   Tank wagons, 142
   Weighbridges, 139
Freight corridor, 143
Freight corridors, 275
Grade separation, 12
Halts, 5
Heavy haul, 12
Heavy rail, 135
Horse crossing, 97
Hot box detector, 139
In-cab signalling, 71
Indirect benefits, 259
Induced benefits, 259
Intermodal terminal, 155
Leakage effect, 260
Light metro, 28
Marginal cost, 225
Marginal costs, 271
Market equilibrium, 104

Marshalling yards, 139
Mega Joule, 179
Metro, 31
   Rubber tyred, 60
Mix of power generation, 177
Mixed system, 6
Modal share, 280
Movement authority, 71
Narrow gauge, 8
Network statement, 283
Overhead wiring, 81
Pantograph, 7
Passenger information systems, 38
Peak period, 220
Pedestrian crossing, 97
Portal, 87
Power
   Electrical power, 180
Price elasticity, 163
Producer surplus, 105
Public private partnership, 247
Public private partnerships, 247
Rail
   Tram, 64
Rail cruise, 48
Rail lubricator,, 214
Refuge, 140
Regenerative braking, 212
Regional rail, 40
Road congestion, 123
Road train, 134
Rollingstock
   Pantograph, 81
Route length, 3
Russian gauge, 8
Sensitivity analysis, 237
Shipping container, 147
Shoulder period, 220
Signaller, 73
Signalling

Route signalling, 74
Speed signalling, 74
Sketch planning, 233
Sleeper carriage, 48
Sleepers, 61
Smart card, 274
Social surplus, 106
Stabling, 3
Standard gauge, 8
Stopping pattern, 38
sunk costs. *See* Fixed costs
Supply and demand, 104
Supply demand model, 104
Tank wagon, 146
Tonnage signal, 140
Tourism economics, 259
Tourist railway, 253
Track
   Dual gauge, 69
Track length, 3
Traction power, 80
   AC, 7
   DC, 7
   Third rail, 81
Tragedy of the commons, 125
Trams
   Powerhouse, 6
Tram-train system, 14
Transport orientated development, 108
Tunnels
   Ventilation, 88
Twenty foot Equivalent Units, 149
Twistlock, 147, 149
Unit elasticity, 112
Unwired. *See* Traction Power
Utility, 237
Wear band, 62
Willingness to Pay, 103
Working timetable, 222

www.ingramcontent.com/pod-product-compliance
Lightning Source LLC
Chambersburg PA
CBHW051543010526
44118CB00022B/2566